What Everyone Is Saying About Quicken WillMaker...

"By far the most comprehensive program we reviewed, offering guidance on everything..."

—USA Today

"The most complete of the five products we tried."

—The Wall Street Journal

"From a group of tough critics, Nolo's WillMaker *got the most praise ... superior on every front."*

—Kiplinger's Personal Finance Magazine

*"*WillMaker *is such an easy-to-use program that users may never need to look at the manual—refreshingly painless."*

—Fortune

"The most ... comprehensive and widely praised of the will writing programs."

—Chicago Tribune

"You can complete the documents fairly quickly, or you can spend a great deal of time exploring all the clearly written definitions and explanations ..."

—PC World

"Even if you know you should see a lawyer ... Quicken's question-and-answer technique can help you sort through the options."

—BusinessWeek

"The most sophisticated legal software on the market."

—Worth

"The level of detail and complexity anticipated by the program makes WillMaker *one of the leading legal-advice programs on the market."*

—Inc.

An Important Message to Our Readers

Quicken®
WillMaker®
BOOK & SOFTWARE KIT *Plus*
2012

SEVENTH EDITION	OCTOBER 2011
Editor	BETSY SIMMONS HANNIBAL
Users' Manual	ELLEN BITTER
Proofreading	ROBERT WELLS
	SUSAN CARLSON GREENE
Index	BAYSIDE INDEXING
Printing	BANG PRINTING

International Standard Serial Number (ISSN): 2151-5808
ISBN: 978-1-4133-1635-3

Contributors

Steve Elias received his law degree from Hastings College of the Law in 1969. He worked in California, New York and Vermont as a legal aid lawyer and in Vermont as a public defender. Steve has written and edited Nolo books on a wide range of topics, including wills, special-needs trusts, criminal law, legal research, patents, trademarks, bankruptcy and, most recently, foreclosures. Steve lives in Lakeport, California, where he provides legal advice to people doing their own bankruptcies and cohosts several radio programs with his wife on community radio station KPFZ 88.1 FM.

Shae Irving has been a Nolo author and editor since 1994, specializing in estate planning and family law issues. She has written or cowritten books and software, including *Prenuptial Agreements: How to Write a Fair and Lasting Contract; Living Wills & Powers of Attorney for California* and *Get It Together: Organize Your Records So Your Family Won't Have To.* Shae was for many years the managing editor of Quicken WillMaker Plus and is now a consulting editor for the program. Shae graduated from Berkeley Law (Boalt Hall School of Law) at the University of California, Berkeley.

Mary Randolph is Nolo VP for editorial and production. She earned her law degree from Berkeley Law (Boalt Hall School of Law) at the University of California, Berkeley. In addition working on much of the material in Quicken WillMaker Plus, she has written several books for Nolo, including *The Executor's Guide: Settling Your Loved One's Estate or Trust; 8 Ways to Avoid Probate; Every Dog's Legal Guide: A Must-Have Book for Your Owner* and *Deeds for California Real Estate.* She lives in the San Francisco Bay Area with her family.

Betsy Simmons Hannibal received her law degree from Golden Gate University School of Law and is now a legal editor at Nolo specializing in estate planning. She is the editor of Quicken WillMaker Plus and also edits many popular Nolo titles, including *Plan Your Estate, Make Your Own Living Trust* and *How to Probate an Estate in California.*

Ralph "Jake" Warner founded Nolo with Ed Sherman in 1972. When personal computers came along, he became a pioneer of self-help legal software, cocreating the first version of WillMaker in the early 1980s. In addition to running Nolo for much of the past three decades, Warner has been an active editor and author. He has written many books, including

Get a Life: You Don't Need a Million to Retire Well and *How to Run a Thriving Business*. Today, he serves as the chairman of Nolo's board of directors. Warner holds a law degree from Berkeley Law (Boalt Hall School of Law) at the University of California, Berkeley, and an undergraduate degree from Princeton.

Table of Contents

17 If You Need More Help

Users' Manual Table of Contents

Part 1 Getting the Most Out of Quicken WillMaker Plus

Part 2 Getting Started

Part 3 Creating Documents

Appendixes

B Keyboard Shortcuts

C Error Messages

Your Legal Companion for Estate Planning

If you're like a lot of people, you have a nagging feeling that you need to make a will—but you haven't gotten around to it because it sounds hard or expensive or just unpleasant. (Or maybe you picked up this software because you are the rare individual who loves to plan and get organized. We encourage those tendencies.) We're here to help. With Quicken WillMaker Plus, making a legal will doesn't have to be difficult. In fact, you can probably get it done in under an hour.

You're smart to pay attention to that nagging feeling: Almost everyone needs a will. It lets you leave your property, name a guardian for young children and eliminate uncertainty about your wishes—all of which will spare your family headaches later.

And a will isn't the only thing to think about. In addition, you may want to take steps to help your family avoid probate court proceedings after your death. And everyone should consider preparing a living will and durable powers of attorney—important documents that can help you stay in control of your own health care and financial choices while saving your family lots of hassles and heartaches, too. You can use Quicken WillMaker Plus to prepare these legal tools, and more.

Our carefully designed question-and-answer format makes the process as easy as it can be. Our goal is to help you over any hurdles by providing clear guidance and encouragement at every step. We'll get you started by helping you figure out exactly which estate planning documents you need. Just select the options that best describe your life situation—for example, whether you have young children, are financially comfortable or are elderly or ill—and we'll tell you whether it's most important to consider a simple will, powers of attorney, a health care directive or something more complex. (Or if you know which document you want to make first, you can skip this part and get right to it.)

When you select the document you want to start with, we'll tell you a little more about it and then ask you a series of straightforward questions. The software uses your answers to make a legal document that's valid in your state.

If you're not sure how to answer a particular question, you'll find lots of practical and legal information within easy reach. Our onscreen help is there to guide you through questions large and small. (You'll probably be able to use Quicken WillMaker Plus to handle your own basic estate planning, without hiring a lawyer. But we'll always alert you to situations where you might benefit from help from a lawyer or another expert.) When you're done making a document, we'll tell you everything you need to know about how to finalize it and make it legal.

Keep in mind that you can plan your estate a little bit at a time. Start by making just one document, such as your will. When you're ready, come back to the program to make more. You can think of Quicken WillMaker Plus as your estate planning companion, providing trustworthy legal and practical advice along the path that's best for you.

Congratulations on starting your estate planning—it's a wonderful thing to do for your loved ones. We know from long experience that putting a sound estate plan into place can bring peace and satisfaction to those who take the time to do it.

1

Planning Your Estate With Quicken WillMaker Plus

state planning is the process of arranging for what will happen to your property when you die. (Whatever you own at your death is called your estate.) It can also include:

- making arrangements for the care of your young children in the event of your death
- planning for your own care in case someday you can't make decisions on your own
- taking steps so that your inheritors can avoid probate court proceedings after your death, and
- if you own a large amount of property, planning to avoid federal or state estate tax.

We can help you with all of these issues, and a few others as well. What follows is a discussion of the legal documents you can create with Quicken WillMaker Plus, so you can see what they accomplish and decide whether or not they fit your situation.

Your Will

Perhaps the most essential reason to make an estate plan is to have a say about who gets your property when you die. A will is the easiest way to do this.

If you don't use a will or some other legal method to transfer your property when you die, state law determines what happens to your possessions. (See "Dying Without a Will" in Chapter 2.)

In addition to specifying who will inherit your property, you can also use your will to:

- name alternates, in case your first choices die before you do
- choose an executor—someone you trust to oversee the distribution of your property after your death,
- name a guardian to raise your young children if you can't, and
- name a trusted adult to manage the property that a child or young adult inherits from you. (We give you several ways to handle this; they're explained in Chapter 7.)

Property That Doesn't Pass Through a Will

Usually, you cannot use a will to leave certain kinds of assets, including:

- property you leave through a living trust
- bank accounts for which you have named a pay-on-death beneficiary
- stocks and bonds or vehicles for which you have named a transfer-on-death beneficiary
- real estate left through a transfer-on-death deed
- property owned as "community property with right of survivorship," which automatically goes to the survivor when one co-owner dies
- property owned in joint tenancy or tenancy by the entirety, which automatically goes to the surviving owners at your death, and
- retirement accounts (IRAs and 401(k) plans) and some pension funds that go to the beneficiary you named in forms provided by the account custodian.

Other Ways to Leave Property

A will is not the only way—and, in some cases, not the best way—to transfer ownership of your property when you die. Especially if you are older and own a fair amount of property, you should consider whether it makes sense to plan now to help your inheritors avoid time-consuming and expensive probate court proceedings after your death. If you have a very large estate, you may also have to think about avoiding federal or state estate tax. To learn more about using a will as part of a larger estate plan, see Chapter 13.

Durable Power of Attorney for Finances

It's a good idea for almost everyone with property or an income to make a durable power of attorney for finances. It's particularly important, however, if you fear that health problems may make it impossible for you to handle your financial matters.

Making a durable power of attorney ensures that someone you trust will be on hand to manage the many practical, financial tasks that will arise if you become incapacitated. For example, bills must be paid, bank deposits must be made and someone must handle insurance and benefits paperwork. Many other matters may need attention as well, from property repairs to managing investments or a small business. In most cases, a durable power of attorney for finances is the best way to take care of tasks like these. See Chapter 14 for more information.

Health Care Directives
(Living Will and Power of Attorney)

It's vitally important that those close to you understand the kind of medical treatment you would—or would not—want if you were unable to speak for yourself. You can use a Quicken WillMaker Plus health care directive to describe your health care wishes and name a trusted person to oversee them. The person you name can also make other necessary health care decisions for you if you are too ill or injured to direct your own care.

The program helps you prepare documents that are legal in your state. Depending on where you live, you may get a single document (often called an advance health care directive) or two separate documents (typically called a living will and a durable power of attorney for health care).

For more information about health care directives, see Chapter 15.

Final Arrangements Document

As you go through the process of creating a will or another estate planning document, your thoughts may turn to how you want your body to be handled after your death.

With our final arrangements document, you can let your loved ones know whether you wish to be buried or cremated, what kind of memorial ceremonies you have in mind and other details related to the final disposition of your body. During a difficult time, this document can provide much needed guidance for your survivors.

To learn more about the final arrangements document, see Chapter 16.

Information for Caregivers and Survivors

With our Information for Caregivers and Survivors form, you can create a comprehensive guide to the details of your life, from information about your bank accounts to people you'd like contacted in the event of your illness or death.

When you prepare this form, the program will walk you through the particulars of your life, asking you to provide details on many topics, including things your loved ones may not know—such as the names of your doctors or whether you have life insurance. The result of this interview will be a document that will greatly aid those who need to care for you or manage your estate.

Documents for Executors

Quicken WillMaker Plus offers a number of documents that you can use if you are named as someone's executor—and you can help your own executor by letting him or her know that these forms are available on your computer when they're needed.

An executor, called a personal representative in some states, is the person you name in your will to safeguard and handle your property after you die. Your executor makes sure that debts and taxes are paid and distributes what's left to your beneficiaries, as your will directs. If someone dies without naming an executor, a court will appoint someone to take the job. This person is most often called an administrator.

Here is a brief description of each of the documents for executors that you can make with Quicken WillMaker Plus.

Executor's Checklist

If you have been named the executor of an estate, you'll want to know what kind of tasks you are expected to perform. The Executor's Checklist is a good introduction.

Of course, every estate (and state) is different. An executor's tasks depend on the size of the estate, the kinds of property the deceased person owned and other factors, such as the needs and expectations of the family. State laws governing the administration of estates also vary.

RESOURCE

Help with the executor's job. For a more thorough guide to an executor's duties, see *The Executor's Guide: Settling a Loved One's Estate or Trust*, by Mary Randolph (Nolo).

Executor's Letter to Financial Institution

As the executor or administrator of someone's estate, your tasks include locating and making an inventory of all of the deceased person's property. One category of property you must investigate is bank and other financial accounts held by the deceased. You can use this form to write to financial institutions to find out what accounts or loans the deceased had with that institution, as well as to learn what those accounts were worth at the time of death.

Affidavit of Domicile

An Affidavit of Domicile (sometimes called an Affidavit of Residence) is one of the documents used by an executor to transfer ownership of stock or other securities from the name of the deceased person to the new owner. The purpose of the Affidavit of Domicile is to establish the state of residence of the stockholder (in this case, the deceased person).

Employee Death Benefits Letter

An executor must contact each of the deceased person's former employers to find out whether the estate or survivors are entitled to any death benefits. You can use the Employee Death Benefits Letter to request the information you need.

Requesting Birth or Death Certificates

As you fulfill your duties as executor, you may need to obtain copies of a death or birth certificate. The most convenient way to get copies of a death certificate is to request them from the funeral home or mortuary at the time of the death. Otherwise, you can find forms and instructions on the Internet. Many county websites offer birth and death certificate request forms that you can print out and send; others allow you to submit your request online and pay by credit card.

To find out your options, go to the official website of the county where the birth or death occurred. You can usually find it by using this formula, substituting the state postal abbreviation for "XX": www.co.[COUNTY_NAME].[XX].us. For example, you can find the website for King County, Washington, at www.co.king.wa.us.

You may also be able to order death certificates through your state's department of health or through a private online service such www.vitalchek.com.

Notice to Creditor of Death

Use this form to notify each of the deceased person's creditors of the death and to close the deceased person's credit accounts.

General Notice of Death

An executor may want to notify businesses and organizations of the death. For example, you might want to notify charities to which the deceased person made regular donations. You can use this letter to inform anyone who might need to know of the death.

Forms for Home and Family

We provide a range of forms you can use to take care of your loved ones, pets and property. For example, there are authorizations you can use to give someone else permission to take care of your child and agreements you can complete to arrange for pet care. Here's some information about each of the forms for your home and family.

Child Care Agreement

If you want to hire someone to care for your children in your home, you should prepare a child care agreement.

The Quicken WillMaker Plus child care agreement allows you to spell out the exact responsibilities of the position and to specify the child care provider's hours, amount and schedule of payment, benefits and other important aspects of the job.

Child Care Instructions

Use this form to provide important information for babysitters and child care providers, such as names and phone numbers of doctors and emergency contacts and instructions about meals, naps and other details of your child's care.

Authorization for Minor's Medical Treatment

Creating a medical care authorization allows another adult to authorize necessary medical or dental treatment for your child if he or she is injured or becomes ill while under the care of another adult—for example, while playing on a sports team or staying with a babysitter.

Authorization for Foreign Travel With Minor

If your young child will be traveling outside the United States with another adult, you should prepare an authorization for foreign travel. The form provides necessary proof that you have consented to the travel.

Temporary Guardianship Authorization

If you leave your child in the care of another adult for a few days, weeks or months, you should authorize the caretaker to make any necessary decisions about your child's medical, educational and other care. You can do this by preparing a temporary guardianship authorization.

Elder Care Agreement

The Quicken WillMaker Plus elder care agreement is for people who wish to sign an agreement with an elder care provider who will take care of an older parent or other elderly relative at home. The agreement allows you to spell out the exact responsibilities of the position and to specify the worker's hours, amount and schedule of payment, benefits and other important aspects of the job.

Pet Care Agreement

If you're going on a trip or will otherwise be unable to care for your pet for a period of time, you might leave your animal in the care of a friend, relative or neighbor. If you do, it's a good idea to prepare this written agreement that sets out clear instructions for your pet's care and clarifies each party's responsibilities and expectations.

Housekeeping Services Agreement

If you hire someone to clean or take care of your house on a regular basis, you can use our housekeeping services agreement. It allows you to spell out the exact responsibilities of the position and to specify the housekeeper's hours, benefits and other details.

Housesitting Instructions

Use this form to provide detailed housesitting instructions for a person who will care for your home while you are away. You can specify your wishes about your plants and garden, newspapers and mail, telephone calls, appliances and equipment, lights and security, tools and supplies, vehicles and other matters. You can also include important information, such as how you can be reached while you are away and whom the housesitter can contact for help in your absence.

Authorization to Drive a Motor Vehicle

Lending your vehicle to someone isn't always as simple as handing over the keys. If the person who borrows your car is pulled over by the police or is involved in an accident, he or she will want to quickly prove that you agreed to the use. Otherwise, the driver may be detained while police investigate whether the car is stolen.

This simple authorization takes just a few minutes to complete, and it provides important legal proof that you've given someone else permission to drive your vehicle. The form is designed for a car, but it will work fine for a motorcycle, truck or other motor vehicle, such as a motorboat.

Notice to Put Name on Do Not Call List

The best way to stop telemarketers from calling you is to enter your telephone number in the National Do Not Call Registry, available at www.donotcall.gov. Telemarketers are prohibited from calling numbers listed in the registry. Those who violate the law are subject to stiff fines—up to $16,000 for each offending phone call. A number of states have do not call lists as well. You may want to add your number to your state's registry, if it offers one.

Some companies are exempt from the federal registry's rules. These include long-distance telephone companies, airlines, banks and credit unions. Organizations soliciting money for political organizations or charities are also exempt. But even these businesses and organizations are required to keep their own lists of consumers who say that they do not want to be called again. If you ask a company not to call you, but you get another call within 12 months, you can sue for up to $500 for each violation.

To stop unwanted calls, first put your number in the National Do Not Call Registry, described above. Keep a log to keep track of the date and time of each unwanted call, as well as the name of the company and product or service it was selling. Every time you receive an unwanted call, end the conversation by saying "Put me on your 'do not call' list." Then follow up with that company by sending it our form "Notice to Put Name on Do Not Call List," which states the date of the phone call and the fact that you asked to be put on the do not call list. If the company calls again, you'll can use your log and this form to show that the company violated the law

Cancel Membership or Subscription

Use this form to cancel a magazine subscription or your membership in an organization. The form allows you to state the reason for the cancellation—perhaps you have moved or are no longer interested in the subject—although you do not have to provide a reason. You can also use this form to request a refund of your membership or subscription fee, if you believe it is warranted.

Personal Finance Forms

Finally, we offer some forms to help you with basic financial matters. There are forms to use if you need to borrow or lend money, plus a few other useful documents—such as a power of attorney you can use to have someone take care of a specific financial transaction if you're unavailable. Here's a little more information about each form.

General Bill of Sale

Use this form to record the terms of the sale of an item of personal property, such as a car, computer or guitar. When you sell an item with a written bill of sale, you reduce the chance of a dispute arising after the sale.

Limited Power of Attorney for Finances

A limited power of attorney for finances lets you appoint someone (called your "attorney-in-fact") to help you with one or more clearly defined tasks involving your finances or property. For example, you may want to name someone to monitor certain investments for you while you are on vacation—and sell them if necessary. Or you may need someone to sign business or legal papers for you while you are unavailable. This form lets you temporarily delegate authority to someone you trust.

Revocation of Power of Attorney

If you've made a power of attorney, you can change your mind and cancel it at any time. Use this notice of revocation to put an end to any power of attorney, including a durable power (one that is designed to remain in effect even after you become incapacitated).

Promissory Notes

If you are borrowing or lending money, you should create a promissory note. Like an IOU, a promissory note records the terms of the loan, including the period of repayment and the interest rate (if interest will be charged), as well as the borrower's promise to pay back the loan. We provide four different kinds of promissory notes.

Installment payments. This type of promissory note requires the borrower to make the same monthly payment for a specified number of months. You can choose whether or not the borrower will pay interest on the loan.

Balloon payment. This promissory note requires the borrower to pay the same amount of money each month for a specified number of months, followed by a large balloon payment at the end of the repayment period. The borrower must pay interest on the loan.

Payments of interest only. With this type of note, the borrower pays only the interest on the loan each month for a specified number of months, with a balloon payment of the principal and any remaining interest at the end of the loan term.

One lump-sum payment. As the name indicates, this note requires the borrower to make just one payment on a specified date. You can choose whether the borrower will pay interest on the loan.

Security Agreement for Borrowing Money

Use this form if you are borrowing or lending money and the borrower agrees to provide the lender with a security interest as collateral for the loan. This security agreement allows the borrower to offer tangible personal property as collateral—that is, physical items of property other than real estate, such as a car, jewelry or furniture.

About Wills

Making a will is an excellent way to ensure that your plans for leaving property to family, friends and organizations of your choice are carried out after you die. You can efficiently and safely write your own legal will using Quicken WillMaker Plus. But before you start, it is a good idea to read this chapter and Chapter 3, which explain generally how wills work and how you can use Quicken WillMaker Plus to meet your needs.

Legal Requirements

For a will to be legally valid, both you—the person making the will—and the will itself must meet some technical requirements.

Who Can Make a Will

Before you start your will, make sure you qualify to make one in the eyes of the law.

Age

To make a will, you must either be:
- at least 18 years old, or
- living in a state that permits people under 18 to make a will if they are married, in the military or otherwise considered legally emancipated.

Mental Competence

You must be of sound mind to prepare a valid will. The laws generally require that you must:
- know what a will is, what it does and that you are making one
- understand the relationship between you and the people who would normally be provided for in your will, such as a spouse or children
- understand the kind and quantity of property you own, and
- be able to decide how to distribute your belongings.

This threshold of mental competence is not hard to meet. Very few wills are successfully challenged based on the charge that the person making the will was mentally incompetent. It is not enough to show that the person was forgetful or absentminded.

To have a probate court declare a will invalid usually requires proving that the testator was totally overtaken by the fraud or undue influence of another person—and that person then benefited from the wrongdoing by becoming entitled to a large amount of money or property under the will.

Interestingly, the great majority of undue influence contests are filed against attorneys who draw up wills in which they are named to take clients' property. If the person making the will was very old, ill or suffering from dementia when he or she made the will, it is obviously easier to convince a judge that undue influence occurred.

> **SEE AN EXPERT**
>
> **If a contest seems possible.** If you have any serious doubts about your ability to meet the legal requirements for making a will, or if you believe your will is likely to be contested by another person for any reason, consult an experienced lawyer. (See Chapter 17.)

Will Requirements

State law determines whether a will made by a resident of the state is valid. And a will that is valid in the state where it is made is valid in all other states.

Contrary to what many people believe, a will need not be notarized to be legally valid. But adding a notarized document to the will verifying that the will was signed and witnessed can be helpful when it comes time to file the will in probate court. This option is available in all but a handful of states. (See "The Self-Proving Option" in Chapter 10.)

There are surprisingly few legal restrictions and requirements in the will-making process. In most states, a will must:

- include at least one substantive provision—either giving away some property or naming a guardian to care for minor children who are left without parents
- be signed and dated by the person making it
- be witnessed by at least two other people who are not named to take property under the will, and
- be clear enough so that others can understand what the testator intended. Nonsensical, legalistic language such as: "I hereby give, bequeath and devise" is both unwise and unnecessary.

Handwritten and Oral Wills

In about half the states, unwitnessed, handwritten wills—called holographic wills—are legally valid. And a few states accept oral wills under very limited circumstances, such as when a mortally wounded soldier utters last wishes.

But handwritten wills are fraught with possible legal problems. Most obviously, after your death, it may be difficult to prove that your unwitnessed, handwritten document was actually written by you and that you intended it to be your will. And it may be almost impossible to prove the authenticity of an oral will.

A properly signed, witnessed will is much less vulnerable to challenge by anyone claiming it was forged or fabricated. If need be, witnesses can later testify in court that the person whose name is on the will is the same person who signed it and that making the will was a voluntary and knowing act.

Dying Without a Will

If you die without a valid will, money and other property you own at death will be divided and distributed to others according to your state's intestate succession laws. These laws divide all property among the relatives who are considered closest to you according to a set formula—and completely exclude friends and charities.

These legal formulas often do not mirror people's wishes. For example, dividing property according to intestate succession laws is often unsatisfactory if you are married and have no children, because most state laws require your spouse to share your property with your parents. The situation is even worse for unmarried couples. Except in a few states, unmarried partners receive nothing. And even in the states that offer exceptions, benefits aren't automatic—eligible couples must register their partnerships with the state.

Also, if you have minor children, another important reason to make a will is to name a personal guardian to care for them. This is an important concern of most parents, who worry that their children will be left without a caretaker if both parents die. Intestate succession laws do not deal with the issue of who will take care of your children. When you don't name a guardian in your will, it is left up to the courts and social service agencies to find and appoint a personal guardian.

Making Basic Decisions About Your Will

Making a will is not difficult, but it is undeniably a serious and sobering process. Before you begin, get organized and focus on these important questions:

- What do you own? (See Chapter 5.)
- Who should get your property? (See Chapter 6.)
- If you have minor children, who is the best person to care for them, and who is best suited to manage property you leave them? (See Chapter 4 and Chapter 7.)
- Who will see that your property is distributed according to your wishes after your death? (See Chapter 8.)

This manual offers guidance on how to use Quicken WillMaker Plus to give legal effect to your decisions in all of these areas. The ultimate choices, however, are up to you.

Making Your Own Will

As a way to decide who gets your property, the will has been around in substantially the same form for about 500 years. For the first 450 years, self-help was the rule and lawyer assistance the exception. When this country was founded, and even during the Civil War, it was highly unusual for a person to hire a lawyer to formally set out what should be done with his or her property. However, in the past 50 years, the legal profession has scored a public relations coup by convincing many people that writing a will without a lawyer is like doing your own brain surgery.

In truth, the hardest part of making a will is figuring out what property you own and who will get it when you die—questions you can answer best. Our will-making program, which has been in wide and successful use for two decades, prompts you to answer the right questions—and produces a will that fits your circumstances and is legal in your state.

But you may have a question about your particular situation that Quicken WillMaker Plus does not answer. Or perhaps you have a very large estate and want to engage in some sophisticated tax planning. Or you may simply be comforted by having a lawyer give your Quicken WillMaker Plus will a once-over. Whenever you have concerns such as these or simply feel that you are in over your head, it may be wise to consult an attorney with knowledge and experience in wills and estate planning. (See Chapter 17.)

Helping Someone Else Make a Will

You can use Quicken WillMaker Plus to help a loved one or friend make a will. But you must be sure that your role is only to type in the will maker's wishes. In other words, the will maker, not you, must decide on the terms of the will. If your role exceeds these limits, a court could declare the will invalid—and you may even face legal charges.

If you decide to help someone else prepare a will, you may want to take an extra step to document your role: Make an audio or video recording of the process or ask someone else to be present as a witness while you follow the will maker's directions.

> **EXAMPLE:** Betty asks her neighbor, James, to help her make her will because her hands shake too badly to type her responses into the program. She dictates her answers to James and he types them in at her direction. She also tells James to print out the document for her to sign. For extra security, Betty's friend Wendy watches as a witness so she can later testify to James's role, if necessary.

If the person you want to help cannot clearly direct the will-making process, or if you have any concern that the person may not fully understand what it means to make a will, see an experienced estate planning attorney for help.

About Quicken WillMaker Plus Wills

Because wills reflect how people want to leave their property, they can be as complex and intricate as life. While state laws broadly regulate the procedures for valid will making, you are generally free to write a will to meet your needs. This freedom may seem overwhelming if you are not used to wading through legal documents.

Quicken WillMaker Plus offers considerable help. The program works by asking you to systematically answer questions. As you will soon see, you either already have enough information to answer them easily, or you can quickly get it.

> **CAUTION**
>
> **Keeping track of important information.** As you prepare to make your will, you may wish to make a list of financial and estate planning advisers you have consulted in the past. It may also be a good time to organize other estate planning documents—such as your living trust documents or life insurance policy—and to record their locations so that others will know where to find them.
>
> With Quicken WillMaker Plus you can make an Information for Caregivers and Survivors form to help with this task. With this document, you can provide a comprehensive guide to the details of your life—ranging from information about your property and your financial accounts to the names and addresses of people you want contacted in the event of your death—for people who will care for you if you ever become incapacitated and those who will wind up your affairs after death. To begin in this document, click on the My Documents button at the top of the screen and select Information for Caregivers and Survivors from the list.

What You Can Do With a Quicken WillMaker Plus Will

This chapter gives you a quick survey of what you can and cannot do with the Quicken WillMaker Plus will. Each topic is discussed in greater detail in the on-screen help that runs with the program and in other chapters in this manual.

Tailor Your Will to Your Needs

Quicken WillMaker Plus provides you with unique guidance and options based on the state in which you live, your marital status, whether you have children, whether your children are minors and how you want to leave your property. Recognizing that some people have very simple wishes for leaving their property while those of others are more complex, Quicken WillMaker Plus lets you choose from among several approaches designed to meet your needs. For instance, if you are married, you may choose to:

- leave all property to your spouse
- leave most property to your spouse, with several specific property items going to people you name, or
- divide property among many different people and organizations. (See Chapter 6.)

Name Beneficiaries to Get Specific Property

Quicken WillMaker Plus lets you make an unlimited number of separate gifts—called specific bequests—of cash, personal property or real estate. You may choose to leave these bequests to your spouse, children, grandchildren or anyone else—including friends, business associates, charities or other organizations. You can also use your will to leave property to a living trust, if you've established one. (See Chapter 6.)

> EXAMPLE 1: Using the Quicken WillMaker Plus will, Marcia leaves her interest in the family home to her spouse Duane, her valuable coin collection to one of her children, her boat to another child, her computer to a charity and $5,000 to her two aunts, in equal shares.

> EXAMPLE 2: Raymond, a lifelong bachelor, follows the Quicken WillMaker Plus directions and leaves his house to his favorite charity. He divides his personal possessions among 15 different relatives and friends.

EXAMPLE 3: Darryl and Floyd have lived together for several years. Darryl uses the Quicken WillMaker Plus will to leave Floyd all of his property, which includes his car, time-share ownership in a condominium, a savings account and miscellaneous personal belongings.

Name Someone to Take All Remaining Property

Quicken WillMaker Plus also allows you to name people or organizations to take whatever property is left over after you have made the specific bequests. This property is called your residuary estate. (See "Naming Residuary Beneficiaries" in Chapter 6.)

EXAMPLE: Annie wants to make a number of small bequests to friends and charities but to leave the bulk of her property to her friend Maureen. She accomplishes this by using specific bequests to make the small gifts, and then names Maureen as residuary beneficiary. There is no need for her to list the property that goes to Maureen. The very nature of the residuary estate is that the residuary beneficiary—in this case, Maureen—gets everything that is left over after the specific bequests are distributed.

If you leave your entire estate to one person or to a group of people without making any specific bequests, then your estate will have no residuary beneficiary.

Name Alternate Beneficiaries

Using Quicken WillMaker Plus, all beneficiaries you name take the property you leave them under your will only if they survive you by 45 days. Quicken WillMaker Plus imposes this 45-day rule because you do not want to leave your property to a beneficiary who dies very shortly after you do. When that happens, the property you left to that beneficiary would then be passed along to that person's inheritors who are not likely to be the ones you would have chosen to receive your property.

To account for the possibility that your first choices of beneficiaries will not meet the survivorship requirement, Quicken WillMaker Plus allows you to name alternate beneficiaries for each of your bequests. (See Chapter 6.)

Name a Guardian to Care for Your Children

You may use Quicken WillMaker Plus to name a personal guardian— either an individual or a couple—to care for your minor children until they reach age 18, in case there is no other legal parent to handle these duties. You may name the same guardian for all your children, or different guardians for different children. (It is important, however, that both parents name the same person or couple as guardian for any particular child; see the example below.) You will also have the opportunity to explain your choices in your will.

If your children need a guardian after your death, a court will formally review your choice. Your choice will normally be approved unless the person or couple you name refuses to assume the responsibility or the court becomes convinced that your children would be better off in the care of someone else. (See "Your Children" in Chapter 4.)

> **EXAMPLE:** Millicent names her friend Vera to serve as personal guardian in the event that her husband, Frank, dies at the same time she does or is otherwise unavailable to care for their three children. Millicent and Frank die together in an accident. No one questions Vera's ability to care for them, so the court appoints her to be the personal guardian for all three children.
>
> If Frank had written a will naming another person to serve as guardian, however, the court would have to choose between those nominated. For this reason, parents should choose the same people as personal guardians, if possible.

Avoiding Legalese: Per Stirpes and Per Capita

"Per stirpes" and "per capita" are legal jargon for the way children inherit property in place of a deceased parent—for example, one of these terms might govern how a granddaughter would inherit property left to her mother under a will, if her mother died before the will maker. It's not necessary for your will to include these terms. In fact, it's better to avoid them, because they can be interpreted in different ways. Instead, your Quicken WillMaker Plus will lets you set out exactly whom you want to inherit your property, who will take the property if your first choice beneficiary doesn't survive you and the shares that they will inherit.

Name a Manager for Children's Property

Property left to minors—especially cash or other liquid assets—will usually have to be managed by an adult until the minors turn 18. In many cases, it may be most prudent to have an adult manage property left to minors until they are even older.

Property management involves safeguarding and spending the property for the young person's education, health care and basic living needs; keeping good records of these expenditures; and seeing that income taxes are paid.

Quicken WillMaker Plus allows you to name a trusted person to manage property you leave to young beneficiaries through your will. The management methods available are different from state to state.

Quicken WillMaker Plus also allows you to name a property guardian to manage property that other people leave to your children or property that you leave to them outside of your will.

Setting up property management for children is discussed in detail in Chapter 7.

RESOURCE

Providing for beneficiaries with special needs. It is common to set up management for property that will pass to a beneficiary who has a mental or physical disability. The management provided under Quicken WillMaker Plus is not sufficiently detailed to provide for people with disabilities. If you need this type of management, you can turn to Nolo's book, *Special Needs Trusts*, by Stephen Elias and Kevin Urbatsch, or consult an attorney who specializes in dealing with the needs of people with disabilities. (See Chapter 17.)

Name a Caretaker for Your Pet

While many of us consider our pets to be members of the family, in the eyes of the law, pets are property. That means you can't leave money or other items directly to your pet—but you can use your will to leave your pet to a trusted caretaker. Doing so is a good way to ensure that your pet has a loving home when you die.

With Quicken WillMaker Plus, you can name a caretaker for your pet and leave money to that person for your pet's care. If you choose to leave money to the caretaker, your document will state that you leave it "with the hope that the money will be used for the care and maintenance" of your pet. It will be up to the honor of the caretaker to use the gift as you intend. This shouldn't be a problem if you choose someone you trust to care for your pet.

You can also name an alternate in case your first-choice caretaker is not available when you die. (See "Pets" in Chapter 4.)

Cancel Debts Others Owe You

You can use Quicken WillMaker Plus to relieve any debtors who owe you money at your death from the responsibility of paying your survivors. All you need to do is specify the debts and the people who owe them. Quicken WillMaker Plus will then include a statement in your will canceling the debts. If a debt is canceled in this way, Quicken WillMaker Plus also automatically wipes out any interest that has accrued on it as of your death. (See "Forgiving Debts Others Owe You" in Chapter 9.)

EXAMPLE: Cynthia lent $25,000 at 10% annual interest to her son George as a down payment on a house. She uses Quicken WillMaker Plus to cancel this debt. At Cynthia's death, George need not pay her estate the remaining balance of the loan or the interest accrued on it.

Designate How Debts, Expenses and Taxes Are Paid

Quicken WillMaker Plus allows you to designate a particular source of money or other specific assets from which your executor should pay your debts, final expenses, such as funeral and probate costs, and any estate and inheritance taxes. (See Chapter 9.)

EXAMPLE 1: Brent owns a savings account, a portfolio of stocks and bonds, an RV and two cars. He uses Quicken WillMaker Plus to make a will—leaving his RV and stocks and bonds to his nephew, his cars to his niece and his savings account to his favorite charity, River Friends. He also designates the savings account as the source of payment of his debts and expenses of probate. Under this arrangement, River Friends will receive whatever is left in the savings account after debts and expenses of probate have been paid.

EXAMPLE 2: Calvin's estate is valued at over $6 million. It is likely that his estate will owe some federal estate taxes when he dies. He uses Quicken WillMaker Plus to specify that any estate tax he owes should be paid proportionately from all the property subject to the tax. If there is estate tax liability, his executor will require that each of Calvin's beneficiaries pay part of the tax in the same proportion their bequest bears to the value of Calvin's estate as a whole.

Name an Executor

With Quicken WillMaker Plus, you can name an executor for your estate. This person or institution, called a personal representative in some states, will be responsible for making sure the provisions in your will are carried out and your property distributed as your will directs. Quicken WillMaker Plus also produces a letter to your executor that generally explains what the job requires.

The executor can be any competent adult. Commonly, people name a spouse or another close relative or friend or—for large estates or where no trusted person is able to serve—a financial institution, such as a bank or savings and loan. You are free to name two people or institutions to share the job, but doing so is often unwise. (See Chapter 8.)

It is also a good idea to use Quicken WillMaker Plus to name an alternate executor in case your first choice becomes unable or unwilling to serve.

EXAMPLE 1: Rick and Phyllis both use Quicken WillMaker Plus to complete wills naming each other as executor in case the other dies first. They both name Rick's father as an alternate executor to distribute their property in the event they die at the same time.

EXAMPLE 2: Pat and Babs do not wish to burden their relatives with having to take care of their fairly considerable estate. Each names the Third National Bank as executor after checking that their estate is large enough so that this bank will be willing to take the job.

What You Cannot Do With a Quicken WillMaker Plus Will

Quicken WillMaker Plus allows you to produce a valid and effective will designed to meet most needs. But there are some restrictions built into the program. Some of the restrictions are designed to prevent you from writing in conditions that may not be legally valid. Others are intended to keep the program simple and easy to use.

Make Bequests With Conditions

You cannot make a bequest that will take effect only if a certain condition occurs—an "if, and or but," such as "$5,000 to John if he stops smoking."

Such conditional bequests are confusing and usually require someone to oversee and supervise the beneficiaries to be sure they satisfy the conditions in the will. Consider that someone would have to constantly check up on John to make sure he never took a puff—and someone would have to wrench away his property if he ever got caught in the act.

So, to use Quicken WillMaker Plus, you must be willing to leave property to people outright; you cannot make them jump through hoops or change their behavior to get it.

> ! CAUTION
>
> **Takers must survive by 45 days.** To ensure that property goes to people you want to have it, Quicken WillMaker Plus automatically imposes the condition that each of your beneficiaries must survive you by 45 days. If they do not survive you by that amount of time, the property you had slated for them will pass instead to the person or institution you have named as an alternate beneficiary, or it will go to the one you have named to take your residuary estate.

Write Joint Wills

In the past, it was common for a married couple who had an agreed-upon scheme for how to distribute all their property to write one document together: a joint will. But time has shown that setup to be crawling with problems.

Quicken WillMaker Plus requires that each spouse make his or her own will, even if both agree about how their property is to be distributed. This limitation is not imposed to annoy people or defeat their intentions; there is solid legal reasoning behind it.

Joint wills are intended to prevent the surviving spouse from changing his or her mind about what to do with the property after the first spouse dies. The practical effect is to tie up the property for years in title and probate determinations—often until long after the second spouse dies. Also, many court battles are fought over whether the surviving spouse is legally entitled to revoke any part of the joint will.

There are still some lawyers who will agree to write joint wills for clients, but they take the risk that such wills may become cumbersome or may even be found invalid in later court challenges. For these reasons, it is best for both spouses to write separate wills—a bit more time-consuming, perhaps, but a lot safer from a legal standpoint.

Creating Identical Wills

While you can't create a joint will using Quicken WillMaker Plus, you can create identical wills—that is, two separate wills in which all the provisions (such as beneficiaries and children's guardians) are the same. If you want to do this, the program provides an easy shortcut. See "Creating an Identical Will for a Spouse or Partner," in the program's Users' Manual.

Explain the Reasons for Leaving Your Property

Most of the time, the act of leaving property to people—or choosing not to leave them anything—speaks for itself. Occasionally, however, people making wills want to explain to survivors the reasons they left property as they did. This might be the case, for example, if you opt to leave one of your two children more property than the other to compensate for the loan you made during your lifetime to help one of them buy a house. Although the desire to make such explanations is understandable, Quicken WillMaker Plus does not allow you to do it in your will because doing so could add legally confusing language to the document.

However, there is an easy and legally safe way to provide your heirs with explanations for your bequests. You can draft a letter that you can attach to your will, explaining your reasons for leaving property to some people—or not leaving it to others. (See Chapter 12.)

Name Coguardians for Children's Property

You may name only one guardian to care for the property left to your young children. While you may choose different property guardians for different children, you may not name two people to share the responsibility. (See Chapter 7.)

At first glance, it may seem to be a good idea to divide up the job—after all, sometimes two heads are better than one. But naming more than one property guardian often presents more problems than it solves because those two people will have to make every decision together. A difference of opinion could require court intervention, which will cost both time and money. It is better to name just one trustworthy person to make decisions about your children's property, and then name a second equally trustworthy person to take over the job if the first one becomes unavailable.

In contrast, the program does allow you to name a couple to serve as your children's *personal* guardians. A personal guardian makes decisions about the well-being of the children, rather than the children's property. When those types of decisions will be made in a family setting with two adults, the ability to name a couple is important—so that either adult may take the child to the doctor or to school, for example.

> CAUTION
> **Review wills to avoid conflicts.** People who jointly own property or have children together should review their wills together to be sure they do not provide conflicting information—such as each naming two different guardians for any one child.

Control Property After Death

Property given to others in a Quicken WillMaker Plus will must go to them as soon as you die. You cannot make a bequest by will that gives property to one person for life and then gives the same property to a second person when the first person dies. Such an arrangement involves too many variables for both will makers and beneficiaries to handle. You will need to use more complex estate planning strategies to carry out this type of plan. (See Chapter 13.)

EXAMPLE: Emory wants his grandchildren to get his house when he dies but wants his wife to have the right to live in the house until her death. Emory cannot use Quicken WillMaker Plus to accomplish this. Emory would have to use a trust to leave his house to his spouse for her life and then to his grandchildren upon his spouse's death.

Require a Bond for Executors or Property Managers

A bond is like an insurance policy that protects the beneficiaries in the unlikely event that the executor wrongfully spends or distributes estate property. Because the premium or fee that must be paid for a bond comes out of the estate—leaving less money for the beneficiaries—most wills for small or moderate estates do not require one.

Following this general practice, the will produced by the Quicken WillMaker Plus program does not require a bond. Instead, take care to appoint someone you know to be trustworthy.

Leave Property to Your Pet

Animals aren't legally permitted to own property, so you can't use your will to make gifts to your pet. If you name your pet to receive property through your will, that gift will be void and the intended gift and the pet will become part of your residuary estate.

That said, you can use your will to name a caretaker for your pet and to leave money to that person requesting that they use it for the care of your pet. (See "Pets" in Chapter 4.)

Customize a No-Contest Clause

The Quicken WillMaker Plus will contains a standard no-contest clause. This clause states that a beneficiary who challenges your will after your death forfeits any gifts you have made to that beneficiary under your will. The property you left to the beneficiary would be distributed as if they died before you.

EXAMPLE: Marah's will leaves $15,000 to her sister, Karen. Marah's nephew, Nathaniel, is the alternate beneficiary for the gift. Marah leaves the rest of her property to her partner of five years, Luke. After Marah's death, Karen challenges the will, believing that Marah intended to leave her more property and that Luke unfairly influenced Marah. Under the terms of the no-contest clause, the $15,000 gift to Karen is immediately revoked and the money passes to Nathaniel.

In reality, most states will not uphold a no-contest clause if the challenger has a good reason to object to the will—for example, if the challenger shows that the will is not valid because the signer's name was forged. Other states go further and do not uphold no-contest clauses for any reason.

Although states vary in their willingness to uphold no-contest clauses, all Quicken WillMaker Plus wills include a standard no-contest clause for an important purpose: to discourage challenges to your will by those who do not like what you leave them. If a beneficiary challenges your will anyway, and a court decides not to enforce the no-contest clause, the rest of your will is effective as written.

If you do not want to include a no-contest clause, if you do not like the way the clause would affect the distribution of your estate following a challenge, or if you think that there is a good chance that someone will challenge your will, see an experienced estate planning lawyer for help. If you need it, a good lawyer should be able to craft a no-contest clause that creates maximum protection for your specific situation. And in some states, a lawyer may be able to help you "pre-validate" your will, which would greatly reduce the possibility of a challenge.

A Look at a Quicken WillMaker Plus Will

You may find it helpful to take a look at a Quicken WillMaker Plus will, but do not be alarmed if the sample will does not match the one you produce. Your Quicken WillMaker Plus will is tailored to your property, circumstances and state laws. Nearly every paragraph, or clause, of the sample will is followed by an explanation.

Will of Natalie DeJarlais

Part 1. Personal Information

I, Natalie DeJarlais, a resident of the State of California, Alameda County, declare that this is my will.

Part 2. Revocation of Previous Wills

I revoke all wills and codicils that I have previously made.

This provision makes clear that this is the will to be used—not any other wills or amendments to those wills, called codicils, that were made earlier. To prevent possible confusion, all earlier wills and codicils should also be physically destroyed.

Part 3. Marital Status

I am married to Michael Sexton.

Here you identify your spouse if you are married—or your partner, if you are in a registered domestic partnership, civil union or other marriage-like relationship recognized by your state. If you are not married or in a registered partnership, this provision will not appear in your will.

Part 4. Children

I have the following children now living: Sammie DeJarlais and Chester DeJarlais.

This part of your will should list all of your biological and adopted children; your stepchildren should not be included here. By naming all your children, you will prevent a child from claiming that he or she was accidentally overlooked in your will. It will also ward off later claims that any child is entitled to take a share of your property against your wishes.

Part 5. Pets

I leave my Boston terrier, Clementine, and $1,500, to Ann Heron, with the hope that the money will be used for Clementine's care and maintenance. If Ann Heron does not survive me, I leave Clementine and $2,000 to Michael Sexton, with the hope that the money will be used for Clementine's care and maintenance.

> *Here you can leave your pet to a trusted caretaker. You can also leave money to the caretaker with a request that the caretaker use the money for your pet's care.*

Part 6. Disposition of Property

A beneficiary must survive me for 45 days to receive property under this will. As used in this will, the phrase "survive me" means to be alive or in existence as an organization on the 45th day after my death.

> *This language means that to receive property under your will, a person must be alive for at least 45 days after your death. Otherwise, the property will go to whomever you named as an alternate. This language permits you to choose another way to leave your property if your first choice dies within a short time after you do.*
>
> *This will clause also prevents the confusion associated with the simultaneous death of two spouses, when it is hard to tell who gets the property they have left to each other. Property left to a spouse who dies within 45 days of the first spouse, including a spouse who dies simultaneously, will go to the person or organization named as alternate.*

If I leave property to be shared by two or more beneficiaries, and any of them does not survive me, I leave his or her share to the others equally unless this will provides otherwise.

> *This clause states that if you leave a gift to two or more beneficiaries without stating the percentage each should receive, the beneficiaries will share the gift equally. This clause is included as a catchall; you can determine the shares for almost every shared gift.*

My residuary estate is all property I own at my death that is subject to this will that does not pass under a general or specific bequest, including all failed or lapsed bequests.

> *This definition is included so that you and your survivors are clear on the meaning of "residuary estate."*

I leave $10,000 to Justin Disney. If Justin Disney does not survive me, I leave this property to Bhamita Ranchod.

> *This language leaves a specific item of property—$10,000—to a named beneficiary, Justin Disney. If Justin Disney does not survive the testator, then Bhamita Ranchod will get the money.*

I leave my rare stamp collection to Ann Heron, Eric K. Workman and André Zivkovich in the following shares: Ann Heron shall receive a 1/4 share. Eric K. Workman shall receive a 1/4 share. André Zivkovich shall receive a 1/2 share.

> *This language leaves a specific item of property—a stamp collection—to three people in unequal shares.*

I leave my collection of Nash cars to The Big Sky Auto Museum and Richard Jenkins in equal shares. If Richard Jenkins does not survive me, I leave his share of this property to Patricia Jenkins.

> *This will leaves specific property to an organization and a person equally. Since the testator here was concerned about providing for the possibility that the person would not survive to take the property, she named an alternate for him.*

I leave my residuary estate to my spouse, Michael Sexton.

> *This clause gives the residuary estate—all property that does not pass under this will in specific bequests—to the testator's spouse. Your residuary estate may be defined differently depending on your plans for leaving your property.*

If Michael Sexton does not survive me, I leave my residuary estate to Sammie DeJarlais and Chester DeJarlais in a children's pot trust to be administered under the children's pot trust provisions.

> *If the person named here to take the residuary estate does not survive the testator, the residuary estate will pass to the two people named: the testator's children. The property will be put in one pot for both of the children to use as they mature. Specifics of how this pot trust operates are explained later in the will. Keep in mind that, in this example, the pot trust will come into being only if the testator's spouse does not survive the testator by at least 45 days.*

If both of these children are age 18 or older at my death, my residuary estate shall be distributed to them directly in equal shares.

> *This clause makes clear what should happen if the children are older than the age at which the testator specified the pot trust should end. In this case, no pot trust will be created; the children will get the property directly and divide it evenly.*

If either of these children does not survive me, I leave his or her share to the other child.

> *This clause explains that if either child here does not survive, the other will get the property directly.*

If Michael Sexton, Sammie DeJarlais and Chester DeJarlais all do not survive me, I leave my residuary estate to Delia Holt.

All personal and real property that I leave in this will shall pass subject to any encumbrances or liens placed on the property as security for the repayment of a loan or debt.

> *This language explains that whoever gets any property under this will also gets the mortgage and other legal claims against the property, such as liens. And anyone who takes property that is subject to a loan, such as a car loan, gets the debt as well as the property.*

Part 7. Custodianship Under the Uniform Transfers to Minors Act

All property left in this will to Delia Holt shall be given to James Leung as custodian under the California Uniform Transfers to Minors Act, to be held until Delia Holt reaches age 21. If James Leung is unwilling or unable to serve as custodian of property left to Delia Holt under this will, Michael Eisenberg shall serve instead.

> *This clause provides that all property left to the child named in the clause will be managed by the person named as the custodian until the child turns the age indicated. An alternate custodian is also named in case the first-choice custodian is unable or unwilling to serve when the time comes.*

Part 8. Children's Pot Trust

A. Beneficiaries of Children's Pot Trust

Sammie DeJarlais and Chester DeJarlais shall be the beneficiaries of the children's pot trust provided for in this will. If a beneficiary survives me but dies before the children's pot trust terminates, that beneficiary's interest in the trust shall pass to the surviving beneficiaries of the children's pot trust.

B. Trustee of Children's Pot Trust

Dave Jenkins shall serve as the trustee of the children's pot trust. If Dave Jenkins is unable or unwilling to serve, Keely Jenkins shall serve instead.

C. Administration of the Children's Pot Trust

The trustee shall manage and distribute the assets in the children's pot trust in the following manner.

The trustee may distribute trust assets as he or she deems necessary for a beneficiary's health, support, maintenance and education. Education includes, but is not limited to, college, graduate, postgraduate and vocational studies and reasonably related living expenses.

In deciding whether or not to make distributions, the trustee shall consider the value of the trust assets, the relative current and future needs of each beneficiary and each beneficiary's other income, resources and sources of support. In doing so, the trustee has the discretion to make distributions that benefit some beneficiaries more than others or that completely exclude others.

Any trust income that is not distributed by the trustee shall be accumulated and added to the principal.

D. Termination of the Children's Pot Trust

When the youngest surviving beneficiary of this children's pot trust reaches 18, the trustee shall distribute the remaining trust assets to the surviving beneficiaries in equal shares.

If none of the trust beneficiaries survives to the age of 18, the trustee shall, at the death of the last surviving beneficiary, distribute the remaining trust assets to that beneficiary's estate.

Part 9. Individual Child's Trust

A. Beneficiaries and Trustees

All property left in this will to Bhamita Ranchod shall be held in a separate trust for Bhamita Ranchod until she reaches age 25. The trustee of the Bhamita Ranchod trust shall be Connor Jenkins.

> *This clause provides that all property given to the child named in the clause shall be held in trust—that is, managed strictly for the benefit of the child— by the person named as the trustee until the child turns the age indicated. An alternate trustee may also be named in case the first-choice trustee is unable or unwilling to serve when the time comes.*

B. Administration of an Individual Child's Trust

The trustee of an individual child's trust shall manage and distribute the assets in the trust in the following manner.

Until the trust beneficiary reaches the age specified for final distribution of the principal, the trustee may distribute some or all of the principal or net income of the trust as the trustee deems necessary for the child's health, support, maintenance and education. Education includes, but is not limited to, college, graduate, postgraduate and vocational studies and reasonable living expenses.

> *This clause lets the trustee spend the trust principal and income for the child's general living, health and educational needs. The clause gives the trustee great latitude in how this is done and what amount is spent.*

In deciding whether or not to make a distribution to a beneficiary, the trustee may take into account the beneficiary's other income, resources and sources of support.

> *This clause lets the trustee withhold the trust principal or income from the trust beneficiary if, in the trustee's opinion, the beneficiary has sufficient income from other sources.*

Any trust income that is not distributed by the trustee shall be accumulated and added to the principal.

> *Every trust involves two types of property: the property in the trust—called the trust principal—and the income that is earned by investing the principal. This clause ensures that the trustee must add to the trust principal any income that is earned on the principal, unless the income is distributed to the trust beneficiary.*

C. Termination of an Individual Child's Trust

An individual child's trust shall terminate as soon as one of the following events occurs:

- the beneficiary reaches the age stated above, in which case the trustee shall distribute the remaining principal and accumulated net income of the trust to the beneficiary
- the beneficiary dies, in which case the principal and accumulated net income of the trust shall pass under the beneficiary's will, or if there is no will, to his or her heirs, or
- the trust principal is exhausted through distributions allowed under these provisions.

> *This clause sets out three events that may cause the trust to end. The first is when the minor or young adult reaches the age specified for the trust to end. If the trust ends for this reason, the minor or young adult gets whatever trust principal and accumulated income is left. The trust will also end if the minor or young adult dies before the age set for the trust to end. If the trust ends for this reason, the principal and income accumulated in*

the trust goes to whomever the young adult named in his or her will to get it or, if there is no will, to the minor or young adult's legal heirs—such as parents, brothers and sisters. A third occurrence that will cause the trust to end is when there is no trust principal left—or so little left that it's no longer financially feasible to maintain it.

Part 10. General Trust Administration Provisions

All trusts established in this will shall be managed subject to the following provisions.

A. Transferability of Interests

The interests of any beneficiary of all trusts established by this will shall not be transferable by voluntary or involuntary assignment or by operation of law and shall be free from the claims of creditors and from attachment, execution, bankruptcy or other legal process to the fullest extent permitted by law.

This important clause removes the trust principal and accumulated income from the reach of the minor or young adult's creditors—while it is being held in the trust. Also, this clause prevents the minor or young adult from transferring ownership of the principal or accumulated interest to others— again, while it is in the trust. Once property is distributed to the minor or young adult, however, there are no restrictions on what he or she can do with it.

B. Powers of the Trustee

In addition to other powers granted a trustee in this will, a trustee shall have the powers to:

1. Invest and reinvest trust funds in every kind of property and every kind of investment, provided that the trustee acts with the care, skill, prudence and diligence under the prevailing circumstances that a prudent person acting in a similar capacity and familiar with such matters would use.

2. Receive additional property from any source and acquire or hold properties jointly or in undivided interests or in partnership or joint venture with other people or entities.

3. Enter, continue or participate in the operation of any business, and incorporate, liquidate, reorganize or otherwise change the form or terminate the operation of the business and contribute capital or loan money to the business.

4. Exercise all the rights, powers and privileges of an owner of any securities held in the trust.

5. Borrow funds, guarantee or indemnify in the name of the trust and secure any obligation, mortgage, pledge or other security interest, and renew, extend or modify any such obligations.

6. Lease trust property for terms within or beyond the term of the trust.

7. Prosecute, defend, contest or otherwise litigate legal actions or other proceedings for the protection or benefit of the trust; pay, compromise, release, adjust or submit to arbitration any debt, claim or controversy; and insure the trust against any risk and the trustee against liability with respect to other people.

8. Pay himself or herself reasonable compensation out of trust assets for ordinary and extraordinary services, and for all services in connection with the complete or partial termination of this trust.

9. Employ and discharge professionals to aid or assist in managing the trust and compensate them from the trust assets.

10. Make distributions to the beneficiaries directly or to other people or organizations on behalf of the beneficiaries.

> *This list of powers should cover the gamut of activities that trustees might be called upon to exercise in administering any trust set up in this will.*

C. Severability

The invalidity of any trust provision of this will shall not affect the validity of the remaining trust provisions.

> *This language ensures that in the unlikely event that a court finds any individual part of this trust to be invalid, the rest of the document will remain in effect.*

Part 11. Personal Guardian

If at my death a guardian is needed to care for my children, I name Ann Heron as personal guardian. If this person is unable or unwilling to serve as personal guardian, I name Michael Eisenberg to serve instead.

Reasons for my choice for guardian for all my children: Ann Heron has established a close relationship with all of the children. She frequently takes care of them when my husband and I must work on weekends—and her training as a doctor makes her especially knowledgeable about handling their health care needs. Best of all, she is a loving and trustworthy friend who has unerring judgment and common sense—an excellent choice to raise the children if Mikey and I cannot.

No personal guardian shall be required to post bond.

This clause names someone to provide parental-type care for a minor child if there is no legal (biological or adoptive) parent able to provide it. The clause also provides for an alternate to step in if the first choice is not able or willing to act when the moment comes. When making your own will, be aware that if there is another legal parent on the scene, that parent will usually be awarded custody of the children, unless a court concludes that the children would be at risk of harm. The explanation provided for the choice helps ensure that a court will follow your reasoning and approve your choice of guardian. The clause also provides that the personal guardian need not provide a bond—a kind of insurance of good performance—to guarantee faithful performance of his or her duties.

Part 12. Property Guardian

If at my death, a guardian is needed to care for any property belonging to Sammie DeJarlais or Chester DeJarlais, I name Eric K. Workman as property guardian. If Eric K. Workman is unwilling or unable to serve as property guardian, I name Justin Disney to serve instead.

No property guardian shall be required to post bond.

This clause appoints someone to manage property that passes to your children outside of your will. For example, if your children receive an inheritance from another relative, proceeds from a life insurance policy or

*income from a trust, and those instruments do not provide a property
guardian, you can name an adult to manage those funds until the children
become adults. You may also appoint an alternate property guardian in
case your first choice is not able or willing to serve when the time comes. The
clause also provides that the personal guardian need not provide a bond to
guarantee that he or she will act faithfully.*

Part 13. Forgiveness of Debts

I wish to forgive all debts specified below, plus accrued interest as of the
date of my death: Sheila Jenkins, April 6, 2011, $10,000.

*Forgiving a debt is equivalent to making a bequest of money. It is a
common way to equalize what you leave to all your children when you
have loaned one of them some money—that is, the amount that you would
otherwise leave that child can be reduced by the amount of the debt being
forgiven.*

Part 14. Executor

I name Michael Sexton to serve as my executor. If Michael Sexton is
unwilling or unable to serve as executor, I name Ann Heron to serve as my
executor.

No executor shall be required to post bond.

*This clause identifies the choices for executor and an alternate executor
who will take over if the first choice is unable or unwilling to serve when the
time comes.*

Part 15. Executor's Powers

I direct my executor to take all actions legally permissible to have
the probate of my will done as simply and as free of court supervision
as possible under the laws of the state having jurisdiction over this will,
including filing a petition in the appropriate court for the independent
administration of my estate.

This clause sets out the specific authority that the executor will need to competently manage the estate until it has been distributed under the terms of the will. The will language expresses your desire that your executor work as free from court supervision as possible. This will cut down on delays and expense.

When you print out your will, a second paragraph will list a number of specific powers that your executor will have, if necessary. It also makes clear that the listing of these specific powers does not deprive your executor of any other powers that he or she has under the law of your state. The general idea is to give your executor as much power as possible, so that he or she will not have to go to court and get permission to take a particular action.

Part 16. Payment of Debts

Except for liens and encumbrances placed on property as security for the repayment of a loan or debt, I direct all debts and expenses owed by my estate to be paid using the following assets: Account #666777 at Cudahy Savings Bank.

This clause states how debts will be paid. Depending on the choice you make when using Quicken WillMaker Plus, your debts may be paid either from specific assets you designate or from your residuary estate—all the property covered by your will that does not pass through a specific bequest.

Part 17. Payment of Taxes

I direct that all estate and inheritance taxes assessed against property in my estate or against my beneficiaries to be paid using the following assets: Account #939494050 at the Independence Bank, Central Branch.

This clause states how any estate or inheritance taxes owed by the estate or beneficiaries should be paid. Depending on the choice you make when operating Quicken WillMaker Plus, your taxes may be paid from all of your property, from specific assets you designate or by your executor according to the law of your state.

Part 18. No-Contest Provision

If any beneficiary under this will contests this will or any of its provisions, any share or interest in my estate given to the contesting beneficiary under this will is revoked and shall be disposed of as if that contesting beneficiary had not survived me.

> *This harsh-sounding clause is intended to discourage anyone who receives anything under the will from challenging its legality for the purpose of receiving a larger share. Many states will not enforce a no-contest clause if the challenger has a good reason for the contest. Other states have passed laws specifically stating that a no-contest clause will not be enforced. If a court decides not to carry out the no-contest clause in your will, the rest of the document will be enforced as written.*

/////
//////
//////
//////
//////
/////
//////
//////
//////
//////
//////
//////
//////
//////
//////

> *These hashmarks will automatically appear to fill up the rest of the page so that your signature appears with some text of the will—one way to help guard against an unethical survivor tampering with the document.*

Part 19. Severability

If any provision of this will is held invalid, that shall not affect other provisions that can be given effect without the invalid provision.

> *This is standard language that ensures that in the unlikely event that a court finds any individual part of your will to be invalid, the rest of the document will remain in effect.*

SIGNATURE

I, Natalie DeJarlais, the testator, sign my name to this instrument, this _____ day of _____ , _____ , at _____ . I declare that I sign and execute this instrument as my last will, that I sign it willingly, and that I execute it as my free and voluntary act. I declare that I am of the age of majority or otherwise legally empowered to make a will, and under no constraint or undue influence.

Signature: _____

WITNESSES

We, the witnesses, sign our names to this document, and declare that the testator willingly signed and executed this document as the testator's last will.

In the presence of the testator, and in the presence of each other, we sign this will as witnesses to the testator's signing.

To the best of our knowledge, the testator is of the age of majority or otherwise legally empowered to make a will, is mentally competent and under no constraint or undue influence. We declare under penalty of perjury that the foregoing is true and correct, this _____ day of _____ , _____ , at _____ _____ .

First Witness

Sign your name: _____

Print your name: _____

Address: _____

City, State: _____

Second Witness

Sign your name: _____

Print your name: _____

Address: _____

City, State: _____

About You and Yours

A s you go through the Quicken WillMaker Plus will, the program first asks you to answer a number of questions about yourself and your family. This chapter discusses those questions in the order in which they appear in the program.

Your Name

Enter your name—first, middle, if you choose, then last—in the same form that you use on other formal documents, such as your driver's license or bank accounts. This may or may not be the name that appears on your birth certificate.

If you customarily use more than one name for business purposes, enter all of them, separated by aka, which stands for "also known as."

Your name is needed here to identify you and all the property you own. Be sure to include all names in which you have held bank accounts, stocks, bonds, real estate or other property. There is room for you to list several names. But use your common sense—you need not list every nickname, or names you use for nonbusiness purposes.

Your Gender

The program also asks you to state whether you are male or female. This is not to be nosy, but to avoid the awkward "he or she" in your final document.

Your Social Security Number

At the end of the interview, Quicken WillMaker Plus will give you the option to enter your nine-digit Social Security number. If you choose to enter it, the number will *not* be included in your will, where it could become part of the public record. Instead, the program will print your Social Security number in a letter for your executor that prints with your will.

Your State

You are asked to specify the state of your legal residence, sometimes called a domicile. This is the state where you make your home now and for the indefinite future. This information is vital for a number of will-making reasons, so it is important to check your answer for accuracy.

Your state's laws affect:

- marital property ownership
- property management options for young beneficiaries
- how your will can be admitted into probate, and
- whether your property will be subject to state inheritance tax.

If you live in two or more states during the year and have business relationships in both, you may not be sure which state is your legal residence. Choose the state where you are the most rooted—that is, the state in which you:

- are registered to vote
- register your motor vehicles
- own valuable property—especially property with a title document, such as a house or car
- have checking, savings and other investment accounts, and
- maintain a business.

To avoid confusion, it is best to keep all or at least most of your roots in one state, if possible. For people with larger estates, ideally this should be in a state that does not levy estate or inheritance taxes. (See "Estate and Inheritance Taxes" in Chapter 9.)

> **CAUTION**
>
> **Wills valid in the United States only.** Quicken WillMaker Plus produces valid wills in all of the United States except for Louisiana—and the program guides you by showing you screens geared specifically to the state of residence you indicate when using it.
>
> Because the property and probate laws in Puerto Rico and Guam, for example, may differ from a state you have selected to use in making your will, we do not guarantee that a Quicken WillMaker Plus will is valid there. However,

some users who reside outside the United States do use Quicken WillMaker Plus to help draft their wills and then have them looked over by an experienced local professional.

SEE AN EXPERT

If your choice is not clear. If you do not maintain continuous ties with a particular state, or if you have homes in both the United States and another country, consult a lawyer to find out which state to list as your legal domicile when using Quicken WillMaker Plus.

Living Overseas

If you live overseas temporarily because you are in the armed services, your residence will be the home of record you declared to the military authorities.

Normally, your home of record is the state you lived in before you received your assignment, where your parents or spouse live or where you now have a permanent home. If there is a close call between two states, consider the factors listed above for determining a legal residence or get advice from the military legal authorities.

If you live overseas for business or education, you probably still have ties with a particular state that would make it your legal residence. For example, if you were born in Wisconsin, lived there for many years, registered to vote there and receive mail there in care of your parents who still live in Milwaukee, then Wisconsin is your legal residence for purposes of making a will.

Your County

Including your county in your will is optional but recommended. Including it will help others identify you and track down your property after your death.

Also, a county name may provide those handling your estate with important direction, because wills go through probate in the court system of the county where you last resided, no matter where you died. The one exception is real estate: That property is probated in the court of the county in which it is located.

If you live in Alaska, which is divided into boroughs and judicial districts instead of counties, you may enter the name of your borough. The correct term will appear in your will.

The Importance of Your Marital Status

You should make a new will whenever you marry or divorce. (See Chapter 11.)

If your marital status changes but your will does not, your new spouse or ex-spouse may get more or less of your property than you intend. For example, if you remarry after making a will and do not provide for the new spouse—either in the will or through transfers outside the will—your spouse, in many states, may be entitled to claim a big share of your property at your death.

Also, if you name a spouse in a will, then divorce or have the marriage annulled and die before making a new will, state laws will produce different, often unexpected, results. In most states, the former spouse will automatically get nothing. In other states, the former spouse is entitled to take the property as set out in the will.

In a few states, registered domestic partnerships provide the same rights and responsibilities as marriage. In those states, changes in your partnership status may affect the distribution of your property. Therefore, like married folks, you should make a new will whenever your domestic partnership status changes.

Marital or Domestic Partnership Status

Quicken WillMaker Plus asks you to indicate your marital or domestic partnership status. (When we say "domestic partnership," we mean any marriage-like partnership registered with a state government, including civil unions and reciprocal beneficiary relationships.) The law treats married people and registered domestic partners differently than other will makers, so your answer to this question is important. Rest assured, however, that you will be able to leave your property in almost any way you please, regardless of your relationship status.

It will probably be easy to select your relationship status. However, if you are separated, have filed for divorce or have a same-sex partner, the answer may not be clear. Read the following sections to help you make the best choice.

If you are married or in a registered domestic partnership, you should also review the property ownership laws affecting married and partnered people. (See "Property Ownership Rules for Married People" in Chapter 5.)

Divorce

If you're not sure whether or not you are legally divorced, make sure you see a copy of the final order signed by a judge. To track down a divorce order, contact the court clerk in the county where you believe the divorce occurred. You will need to give the first and last names of you and your former spouse and make a good guess at what year the divorce became final. If you cannot locate a final decree of divorce, it is safest to assume you are still legally married.

If the divorce was supposed to have taken place outside the United States, it may be difficult to verify. If you have any reason to think that someone you consider to be a former spouse might claim to be married to you at your death because an out-of-country divorce was not legal, consult a lawyer. (See Chapter 17.)

Separation

Many married couples, contemplating divorce or reconciliation, live apart from one another, sometimes for several years. Although this often feels like a murky limbo while you are living it, for will-making purposes, your status is straightforward: You are legally married until a court issues a formal decree of divorce, signed by a judge. This is true even if you and your spouse are legally separated as declared in a legal document. Note that many separation agreements, however, set out rights and restrictions that may affect your ownership of property.

Common Law Marriage

It is uncommon to have a common law marriage. In most states, common law marriage does not exist.

But in the states listed in the chart below, couples can become legally married if they live together and either hold themselves out to the public as being married or actually intend to be married to one another. Once these conditions are met, the couple is legally married. And the marriage will still be valid even if they later move to a state that does not allow couples to form common law marriages there.

States That Recognize Common Law Marriage	
The following states recognize some form of common law marriage.	
Alabama	Montana
Colorado	Nevada (if created before 3/29/43)
District of Columbia	New Hampshire (for inheritance purposes only)
Florida (if created before 1/1/68)	New Jersey (if created before 12/1/39)
Georgia (if created before 1/1/97)	Ohio (if created before 10/10/91)
Idaho (if created before 1/1/96)	Oklahoma
Indiana (if created before 1/1/58)	Pennsylvania (if created before 1/1/2005)
Iowa	Rhode Island
Kansas	South Carolina
Michigan (if created before 1/1/57)	South Dakota (if created before 7/1/59)
Minnesota (if created before 4/26/41)	Texas
Mississippi (if created before 4/5/56)	Utah

No matter what state you live in, if either you or the person you live with is still legally married to some other person, you cannot have a common law marriage.

As you can see, some states recognize common law marriages only if they were created long ago. If you live in one of these states and you entered into what you believe to be a common law marriage, you may want to consult a lawyer to determine the legal status of your relationship.

There is no such thing as a common law divorce; no matter how your marriage begins, you must go through formal divorce proceedings to end it.

Same-Sex Couples

In the last several years, many significant changes have been made to the laws affecting same-sex couples. Most states still don't legally recognize same-sex relationships. But a handful of states permit same-sex couples to marry, while many others offer a variety of rights to lesbian and gay couples who register their relationships. (For details about the laws in your state, see "Same-Sex Relationship Recognition by State" at www. nolo.com/legal-encyclopedia/chart-32259.html.)

> **CAUTION**
> **Federal law does not recognize same-sex partnerships.** The federal government does not currently recognize any same-sex relationships, no matter what state laws say. (This is because of a federal law called the Defense of Marriage Act.) So, same-sex couples who marry or register their partnerships are not entitled to the federal estate and gift tax benefits married couples enjoy—or to Social Security benefits or any of the more than 1,000 other benefits extended to heterosexual married couples.

If you're married. When making your will, you may not be sure whether you should identify yourself as married or single, given that some states recognize your marriage and others don't. But either way, your document will be valid, and you can leave your property as you wish, subject to your spouse's rights.

If you and your partner live in a state that recognizes same-sex marriages, simply state that you are married. Your document will refer to your partner as your spouse.

If you got married and then moved to a state that doesn't recognize same-sex marriages, you can still state that you're married when you make your will. Even if your current state doesn't acknowledge your marriage, your partner will receive everything that your will directs. You may want to attach a signed letter to your will that expresses your wish that your partner be treated in all ways as your legal spouse. You can find a sample in Chapter 12.

SEE AN EXPERT

If you're not sure of your marital status. If you're confused about the legal status of your relationship, you're not alone. A good estate planning lawyer who specializes in issues affecting gay and lesbian couples can provide you with the latest information for your state and answer questions about making the best estate plan for your situation.

If you registered your partnership in the state where you live. If you and your partner registered as partners in a state that offers benefits to same-sex couples and you still live in that state, choose "I have a registered domestic partner," when asked for your relationship status. Although some states use different terms (such as "civil union partners" or "reciprocal beneficiaries"), we generally use "domestic partners" to refer to a registered same-sex couple. If you live in a state that uses another term, your finished document will contain the correct term for your state. (If you live in New Jersey, where you may have a domestic partnership or a civil union, you will be asked to select the appropriate term for your relationship.)

If you have not registered your partnership in the state where you live. If you and your partner have not registered with your state or if you no longer live in the state where you registered, you should make your will as a single person by choosing "I'm not married, nor do I have a registered domestic partner."

Indicating that you are single does not limit your ability to leave property to your partner or to name your partner as executor of your will or guardian of your young children. You can do all of those things in your will.

> **RESOURCE**
>
> **More information for same-sex couples.** For detailed information about the many legal issues faced by same-sex couples, see *A Legal Guide for Lesbian & Gay Couples*, by Emily Doskow, Frederick Hertz and Denis Clifford (Nolo). For a comprehensive discussion about the complex and ever-changing rules of same-sex relationship laws, see *Making It Legal: A Guide to Same-Sex Marriage, Domestic Partnerships & Civil Unions*, by Emily Doskow and Frederick Hertz (Nolo).

Your Spouse or Domestic Partner

Quicken WillMaker Plus prompts you to provide the full name of your spouse or domestic partner. As with your own name, list all names used for business purposes, following the tips suggested for entering your own name, above.

Also indicate whether your spouse or domestic partner is male or female. This way, the program can refer to him or her with the correct pronoun.

Your Children

Becoming a parent is what may have motivated you to buckle down to the task of writing your will in the first place.

If you are the parent of young children, your will is the perfect place to address some driving concerns you are likely to have if you die before they are grown. These concerns include:

- who will care for your children, and
- who will manage their property.

Quicken WillMaker Plus lets you make these decisions separately. This gives you the option of placing the responsibilities in the hands of the same person or, if need be, naming different people. First, you are asked to name someone to care for your children. Later in the program, you'll deal with the issue of providing property management for your own or other people's young children. (See Chapter 7.)

Identifying Your Children

Quicken WillMaker Plus asks you whether or not you have any children and, if you do, it asks you to name each of them. You are not required to leave property to your children, but it is important that you at least state each child's name. If you don't, it may not be clear whether you intentionally left a child out of your will, or whether the child was accidentally overlooked (called "pretermitted," under the law). Children unintentionally omitted from your will—usually because you made your will before they were born—have a right to take a share of your estate.

> **SEE AN EXPERT**
>
> **Children born after a parent dies.** If a child is conceived before your death but is born after you die, he or she will most likely be entitled to part of your estate even if your will doesn't mention the child. But the law is now rushing to answer a new question posed by advancing medical technology: What happens if a child is *conceived* after the death of a parent? If sperm, eggs or embryos are preserved before the parent's death, a child could be born years later. Individual states are taking different approaches to this matter. Some are giving posthumously conceived children the rights to inherit property and receive other benefits from their deceased parents. Others are refusing such rights. If you are curious about this issue or planning for a posthumously conceived child, you should consult a knowledgeable estate planning lawyer.

When naming your children, you should include all children born to you or legally adopted by you.

If you are the parent of a child who has been legally adopted by a person other than your spouse or partner—or you have otherwise given up your legal parental rights—then you need not name that child in your will.

You should not name stepchildren you have not adopted, since they are not entitled by law to a share of your property when you die. The pretermitted heir rule does not apply to them. Also, Quicken WillMaker Plus offers a number of options that include your children as a group, and if you include stepchildren in the list and use one of these options, your will might contain provisions you did not intend.

However, you are free to leave your stepchildren as much property in your will as you wish. If you want to treat your children and stepchildren equally and not differentiate between them, when Quicken WillMaker Plus asks how you wish to leave your property, choose the option labeled "Leave it some other way." (See Chapter 6.)

To list your children, enter their full names in the sequence and format you want the names to appear in your will.

> **CAUTION**
> **Don't use "all my children."** Some people are tempted to skimp on naming their children individually and want to fill in "all my children," "my surviving children," "my lawful heirs" or "my issue." Don't do it. That shorthand language is much more confusing than listing each child by name.

Your Children's Birthdates

Quicken WillMaker Plus also asks you to enter your children's dates of birth—month, day and year. The program will automatically compute their ages in years—an important consideration when you are asked to name a personal guardian and provide management for property you or others leave them.

Personal Guardians for Your Minor Children

Among the most pressing concerns of parents with minor children is who will care for the children if one or both of them die before the children reach adulthood.

Although contemplating the possibility of your early death can be wrenching, it is important to face up to it and adopt the best contingency plan for the care of your young children. If the other parent is available, then he or she can usually handle the task.

However, you and the other parent might die close together in time. Or you may currently be a single parent and need to decide what will happen if you do not survive until your children become adults.

This section discusses using Quicken WillMaker Plus to choose a personal guardian to care for the children's basic health, education and other daily needs. Choosing a person to manage your children's property is discussed in Chapter 7.

Reasons for Naming a Personal Guardian

The general legal rule is that if there are two parents willing and able to care for the children and one dies, the other will take over physical custody and responsibility for caring for the child. In many states, the surviving parent may also be given authority by a court to manage any property the deceased parent left to the children—unless the deceased parent has specified a different property management arrangement in a will.

But there is no ready fallback plan if both parents of a minor child die or, in the case of a single parent, there is not another parent able or willing to do the job. Using Quicken WillMaker Plus, you can deal with these concerns by naming a personal guardian as well as an alternate. The person you name will normally be appointed by the court to act as a surrogate parent for your minor children if both of the following are true:

- There is no surviving biological or adoptive parent able to properly care for the children.
- The court agrees that your choice is in the best interests of the children.

If both parents are making wills, each should name the same person as guardian for each child. This will help avoid the possibility of a dispute and perhaps even a court battle should the parents die simultaneously. But remember, if one parent dies, the other will usually assume custody and will then be free to make a new will naming a different personal guardian if he or she wishes. In short, if both parents are active caretakers, the personal guardian named in a will cares for the children only if both parents die close together in time.

However, if you feel strongly that the other parent is not the best person to care for the children, be sure to explain your reasoning when the Quicken WillMaker Plus program prompts you to do so. (See "Explaining Your Choice," below.)

Naming Different Guardians for Different Children

One obvious concern when choosing a personal guardian for your children is to keep them together if they get along well with one another. This suggests that it is best to name the same personal guardian for all the children.

There are families, however, where the children are not particularly close to one another but have strong attachments with one or more adults outside the immediate family. For instance, one child may spend a lot of time with a grandparent while another child may be close to an aunt and uncle. Also, in a second or third marriage, a child from an earlier marriage may be closer to a different adult than a child from the current marriage.

In these situations and others, logic dictates other advice: Choose the personal guardian you believe would best be able to care for the child. This may mean that you will choose different personal guardians for different children.

Choosing a Personal Guardian

To qualify as a personal guardian, your choice must be an adult—18 in most states—and competent to do the job. For obvious reasons, you should first consider an adult with whom the child already has a close relationship—a stepparent, grandparent, aunt or uncle, older sibling, babysitter, close friend of the family or even neighbor. Whomever you choose, be sure that person is mature, good-hearted and willing and able to assume the responsibility.

Naming More Than One Person as Guardian

In many cases, it's a poor idea to name more than one person to serve as guardian for your children. Naming coguardians raises the possibility that they may disagree about the best way to raise a child, resulting in conflict and perhaps even requiring court intervention. However, there is one situation in which naming two guardians makes good sense: when you want to name a couple to care for your children.

If you know a couple—for example, your sister and her husband— who are willing and able to take good care of your children, it's fine to name them both as coguardians. The couple will act as your children's surrogate parents. Both of them will be allowed to do things for your children that require legal authority, such as picking up your children from school, authorizing field trips or taking them to the doctor.

Keep in mind, however, that if you name a couple as coguardians, they must be able to agree on what's best for your children. Any severe difference of opinion between them could require court intervention— and this would be difficult for the couple and upsetting to your kids. Also, if you name a couple that parts ways while you are still alive, you should revise your will to name one or the other to care for your children or choose a different couple to act as coguardians.

Choose carefully when naming a couple as personal coguardians for your children. Select a couple that can make joint decisions without conflict, has a unified parenting style and is likely to stay together a long time. If you have any reservations about the longevity of the couple's relationship or any concerns about either person's parenting style, you may be better off just naming one of them—for example, name just your sister. If you like, you can explain the reasons for your choice in your will. See "Explaining Your Choice," below.

Choosing an Alternate Personal Guardian

Quicken WillMaker Plus lets you name a backup or alternate personal guardian to serve in case your first choice for each child either changes his or her mind or is unable to do the job at your death. The considerations involved in naming an alternate personal guardian are the same as those you pondered when making your first choice: maturity, a good heart, familiarity with the children and willingness to serve.

If you name a couple as coguardians, the alternate will become the personal guardian only if both coguardians are unable or unwilling to serve.

Explaining Your Choice

Leaving a written explanation of why you made a particular choice for a personal guardian may be especially important if you think a judge may have reason to question your decision.

If you don't want the other parent to have custody. You may have strong ideas about why the child's other parent, or perhaps a grandparent, should not have custody of your minor children. In an age when many parents live separately, the following predicaments are sadly common:

- "I have custody of my three children. I don't want my ex-husband, who I believe is emotionally destructive, to get custody of our children if I die. Can I choose a guardian to serve instead of him?"
- "I have legal custody of my daughter and I've remarried. My present wife is a much better mother to my daughter than my ex-wife, who never cared for her properly. What can I do to make sure my present wife gets custody if I die?"
- "I live with a man who's been a good parent to my children for six years. My father doesn't like the fact that we aren't married and may well try to get custody of the kids if I die. What can I do to see that my partner gets custody?"

There is no definitive answer to these questions. If you die while the child is still a minor and the other parent disputes your choice in court, the judge will likely grant custody to the other parent, unless that parent:

- has legally abandoned the child by not providing for or visiting the child for an extended period, or
- is clearly unfit as a parent.

It is usually difficult to prove that a parent is unfit, absent serious and obvious problems, such as chronic drug or alcohol abuse, mental illness or a history of child abuse. The fact that you do not like or respect the other parent is never enough, by itself, for a court to deny custody to him or her.

> **EXAMPLE:** Susan and Fred, an unmarried couple, have two minor children. Although Susan loves Fred, she does not think he is capable of raising the children on his own. She uses Quicken WillMaker Plus to name her mother, Elinor, as guardian. If Susan dies, Fred, as the children's other parent, will be given first priority as personal guardian over Elinor, despite Susan's will, assuming the court finds he is willing and able to care for the children. However, if the court finds that Fred should not be personal guardian, Elinor would get the nod, assuming she is fit.

If you honestly believe the other parent is incapable of caring for your children properly—or simply will not assume the responsibility—you should reinforce that belief by explaining why you elected to name other people as guardians and alternates.

> **EXAMPLE:** Justine and Paul live together with Justine's minor children from an earlier marriage. The children's biological father has not spent time with the kids for many years and Justine believes he has no interest in parenting them. Justine wants Paul to have custody because he knows the children well and loves them. She can use Quicken WillMaker Plus to name Paul as personal guardian and add a statement making the reasons for this choice clear.

If Justine dies and the biological father does not want custody of the kids, Justine's explanation will give the court good reason to name Paul their personal guardian.

Tips on What to Include

When deciding who should become a child's personal guardian, the courts of all states are required to act in the child's best interests. In making this determination, the courts commonly consider a number of facts, which you might want to mention when explaining your choice for personal guardian. They include:

- whom the parents nominated to become the personal guardian
- whether the proposed personal guardian will provide the greatest stability and continuity of care for the child
- which person will best be able to meet the child's needs, whatever these happen to be
- the quality of the relationship between the child and the adults being considered for guardian
- the child's preferences to the extent these can be gleaned, and
- the moral fitness and conduct of the proposed guardians.

If you name your same-sex partner as guardian. If you coparent your children with a same-sex partner, you probably want to nominate your partner as the personal guardian of your children. Whether or not the court will respect your nomination depends on where you live and on two legal relationships: the relationship between you and your partner and the relationship between your partner and your kids.

If your children have another legal parent, perhaps from a prior relationship, the court will choose that parent over your partner unless you provide a good reason not to.

If you live in any of the states that recognize same-sex marriage or marriage-like relationships (such as registered domestic partnerships or civil unions) and your children were born after you and your partner entered into a legal relationship under the laws of that state, then you and your partner are both legal parents under state law and the court should respect your partner's legal right to continue parenting your children after your death. This is true whether or not you nominate your partner in your will, but you should go ahead and make the nomination and explain your reasons for it, as discussed below.

If you live in a state that doesn't offer any legal relationship for same-sex couples, the court will make the final decision about who will care for your children. The court will consider your choice for personal guardian, but it may not understand or fully respect your relationship with your partner.

For these reasons, take advantage of the opportunity to fully explain to the court why you named your partner to care for your children. You might say, for example, "I name my life partner, Ruth Williams, as the personal guardian for our son Matthew Price because we conceived and raised him together and she is his only other parent." Or, "I name my domestic partner, Richard Bennett, as personal guardian for our daughter Jane Bennett-Hines because he is her other legal parent, as recognized by the state of California."

> **RESOURCE**
>
> **Learn more about same-sex families.** For a detailed discussion of parenting issues for same-sex couples, see *A Legal Guide for Lesbian & Gay Couples*, by Emily Doskow, Frederick Hertz and Denis Clifford (Nolo). For a comprehensive discussion about the complex and ever-changing rules of same-sex relationship laws, see *Making It Legal: A Guide to Same-Sex Marriage, Domestic Partnerships & Civil Unions*, by Emily Doskow and Frederick Hertz (Nolo).

Your Grandchildren

Quicken WillMaker Plus asks you to name your grandchildren. Name all of them—including those to whom you leave no property. Include children adopted by your child and those born while your child was not married.

It is important that you name all grandchildren, because the rule that allows unintentionally omitted children to take a share of your estate also applies to grandchildren you may have overlooked in your will if their parent—that is, your child—dies before you do. (See "Your Children," above.)

As it does for your own children, Quicken WillMaker Plus automatically provides the statement that if you have not left any property to a grandchild, that is intentional—and therefore eliminates the problem. Again, you are free to leave the grandchild property if you choose. Also, if you have additional grandchildren after making your will, it is wise to make a new will that includes them.

Keep Your Will Current

Here are two situations in which you should make a new will:

If a child is born to or legally adopted by you after you make your will. You should draft a new will to list the new child. If you do not, that child may challenge your will and receive a share of what you leave.

If one of your children dies before you do and leaves children of his or her own. The laws of many states require that you name and provide for the children of deceased children. If you do not, they may be considered accidentally overlooked and entitled to part of your property. To protect against this, make a new will, naming these grandchildren so that you can signal that you are aware that these grandchildren exist. You are still free to leave them as little or as much property as you wish in your will.

(See Chapter 11 for information on updating your will.)

SEE AN EXPERT

If you don't know your family. If family estrangement or other circumstances leave you thinking that you might not know the names of all of your grandchildren—or even your children—seek the advice of a good estate planning lawyer. You'll want to be certain that your will is not subject to unexpected claims.

Pets

You can use the Quicken WillMaker Plus will to leave your pet to a caretaker you choose. You can also leave money to that person to help with the costs of caring for your pet, although your will cannot force the caretaker to use the money that way. If you want the caretaker to be legally bound to use the money for the care of your pet, you will need a pet trust. See "Setting up a trust for your pet," below.

Using a will to provide for your pet is a simple and inexpensive way to make sure your pet has a caring home after your death. It is not the only way to provide for your pet, but most folks find that it makes the most sense.

Leaving Details About Your Pet's Care

In addition to naming a caretaker for your pet, you may want to leave information and suggestions about your pet's habits and needs. You can use the Quicken WillMaker Plus Information for Survivors and Caregivers form for this purpose. It allows you to leave specifics about each animal, including health needs, food and exercise requirements and sleeping habits. You can also use the document to describe memorial plans or final arrangements for your pet.

SEE AN EXPERT

Setting up a trust for your pet. In a majority of states, you can leave your pet money in a trust, managed by a trustee you name. You'll need to hire an attorney to be sure the document is properly drafted and valid in your state.

Finding a Loving Home for Your Pet

If you're not able to find someone both willing and able to take care of your pet after you die, you're not without options. More and more programs are springing up across the country to help assure people that their pets will have a loving home when they can no longer care for them.

SPCA programs. The San Francisco SPCA was the first to offer a special service to find good homes for the pets of its deceased members. The pets' new owners are entitled to free lifetime veterinary care for the pets at the SPCA's hospital. Other SPCAs have created similar programs. Contact local SPCAs and similar organizations in your area for more information.

Veterinary school programs. A number of veterinary schools take in pets whose owners leave substantial endowments to the school. These programs typically provide a homelike atmosphere and lifetime veterinary care for the animals. Here is a list of some schools that you can contact:

California
The Tender Loving Care (TLC) for
  Pets Program
Center for Companion Animal Health
UC Davis School of Veterinary Medicine
530-752-7295
www.vetmed.ucdavis.edu/ccah/tlc/
  default.cfm

Indiana
Peace of Mind Program
School of Veterinary Medicine
Purdue University
800-830-0104
www.vet.purdue.edu/giving/
  PeaceOfMind.html

Kansas
Perpetual Pet Care Program
Kansas State University School of
  Veterinary Medicine
785-532-4378
www.vet.k-state.edu/depts/
  development/perpet/index

Oklahoma
Cohn Family Shelter
Oklahoma State University, Center for
  Veterinary Health Sciences
405-744-5630
www.cvhs.okstate.edu

Texas
Stevenson Companion Animal
  Life-Care Center
College of Veterinary Medicine
Texas A&M University
979-845-1188
www.cvm.tamu.edu/petcare

About Your Property

This chapter discusses the grist of will making: what you own, how you own it and what legal rules affect how you can leave it. Once you have considered the information about property in this chapter, you will be ready to use Quicken WillMaker Plus to leave it to others—a task discussed in detail in Chapter 6. If you have children, see Chapter 7 for a discussion of their right to inherit property and your right to disinherit them.

Many readers will not need the information in this chapter. If you plan to leave your property in a lump—that is, without giving specific items of property to specific people—it makes little difference what you own and how you own it. That will be sorted out when you die, and the people you have named to take "all" your property will get whatever you own.

This chapter is important for you to read if either of the following is true:

- You are married or in a registered domestic partnership and you plan to name someone other than your spouse or partner to receive all or most of your property. This includes everyone who has not received a final decree of divorce or dissolution.
- You plan to leave specific items of property to specific people or organizations.

TIP

Keeping track of your property. There are many things your survivors will need to know about your property—and it will help them to have some relevant information about it, including:

- the location of some items
- the location of ownership, warranty and appraisal papers
- the value of some items—especially if they have special significance
- directions for maintaining the property, and
- details about caring for your pets.

You can use the Quicken WillMaker Plus Information for Caregivers and Survivors form for this task.

Inventory Your Valuable Property

The first step is to take inventory—write down the valuable items of property you own. The categories listed below should jog your memory. Even if you plan to leave everything to your spouse or children, you should make a list to keep you from overlooking things.

To help you with this task, Quicken WillMaker Plus provides a property worksheet that you can print out and keep with you as a reference while you make your estate planning documents. You can access the property worksheet from the screen called "Leaving Your Property," which introduces you to the topic of leaving your property to others. Click on the "Property Worksheet" link to start making your list.

Property You Should Not Include in Your Will

In almost all cases, your will does not affect property that you have arranged to leave by another method. (There's an exception in the state of Washington; see below.)

Property with a right of survivorship. If you hold property in joint tenancy, tenancy by the entirety or community property with right of survivorship, your share of that property automatically belongs to the surviving co-owner after you die. A will provision leaving your share would have no effect unless all co-owners die simultaneously.

Property you place in a trust. Property you place in a trust passes automatically to the beneficiary named in the trust document; you cannot pass this property in your will. This includes property placed in a revocable living trust. (To learn more about living trusts, see Chapter 13.)

Property for which you've already named a beneficiary. There are many ways to pass property without a will or trust. You shouldn't include in your will any type of property on this list.

- Money in a pay-on-death bank account. If you want to change the beneficiary, contact the financial institution.
- Property held in beneficiary (transfer-on-death or TOD) form. This may include stocks, bonds and—in a handful of states—real

Valuable Property

Animals

Antiques

Appliances

Art

Books

Business interests

   Sole proprietorship

   Partnership

   Corporation

   LLC

   Limited partnership

Business property*

Cameras and photo equipment

Cash accounts

   Certificates of deposit

   Checking

   Money market funds

   Savings

China, crystal and silver

Coins and stamps

Collectibles

Computers

Copyrights, patents and trademarks

Electronic equipment

Furniture

Furs

Jewelry

Precious metals

Real estate

   Agricultural land

   Boat/marina dock space

   Co-ops

   Condos

   Duplexes

   Houses

   Mobile homes

   Rental property

   Time-shares

   Undeveloped land

   Vacation houses

Retirement accounts

Royalties

Securities

   Bonds

   Commodities

   Mutual funds

   Stocks

   U.S. bills, notes and bonds

Tools

Vehicles

   Bicycles

   Cars

   Motorcycles

   Motor homes/RVs

   Planes

   Boats

---

* If you own a sole proprietorship

estate or vehicles. To change the beneficiary, you'll need to make a new beneficiary form, deed or title document.

- Proceeds of a life insurance or annuity policy for which you've named a beneficiary. To make changes, contact the insurance company.
- Money in a pension plan, individual retirement account (IRA), 401(k) plan or other retirement plan. You name the beneficiary on forms provided by the account administrator.

To learn more about these property ownership methods, most of which are designed to avoid probate court proceedings, see Chapter 13.

Note for Washington Readers

The state of Washington has changed some of the rules discussed above. If you like, you can leave the following types of property in your will:

- your share of joint tenancy bank accounts
- pay-on-death bank accounts
- transfer-on-death securities or security accounts, and
- property in a living trust.

If you set up one of these devices for leaving your property and then later use your will to change the beneficiary, the property goes to the person you name in your will. However, if you designate a new beneficiary after you make your will—for example, by updating the paperwork for a pay-on-death account or changing your living trust—the gift in the will has no effect. (Wash. Rev. Code § 11.11.020.)

Property You Own With Others

If you are not married or in a registered domestic partnership, and you own property with someone else, you probably own it in tenancy in common. This is the most common way for unmarried people to own property together. Each co-owner is free to sell or give away his or her interest during life or leave it to another at death in a will. To tell whether or not you own property as tenancy in common, check the deed or other title document; it should specifically note that the property is held as a tenancy in common.

> **CAUTION**
> **More rules for married or legally partnered people making wills.** If you are married or in a registered domestic partnership, a whole host of legal rules may affect what property you own jointly and separately. (See "Property Ownership Rules for Married People," below.)

Property on Which You Owe Money

Using Quicken WillMaker Plus, if you leave property on which you owe money, the beneficiary who takes it at your death will also take over the debt owed on that property. This means the beneficiary of the property is responsible for paying off the debt. (But your survivors will not inherit your debt, per se. For example, if you die with nothing to your name except credit card debt, your survivors will not be responsible for paying those bills.)

Property Ownership Rules for Married People

Most people who are married or are in registered domestic partnerships leave all or the greatest share of their property to their surviving spouses or partners. For them, the nuances of marital property law are not important, since the survivor gets the property anyway.

But if you plan to leave your property to several people instead of, or in addition to, your spouse or partner, the picture becomes more complicated. Under your state's laws, your spouse or partner may own some property you believe is yours. And if you do not own it, you cannot give it away—either now or at your death. Questions of which spouse or partner owns what property are important if your spouse or partner does not agree to your plan for property disposition.

Your Digital Legacy

When you're thinking about making a plan for your property, don't forget to consider your digital legacy—that is, all of your accounts, blogs, social networking identities and digital files that will be left online when you die. Although you can't leave these items through your will, you may still want to consider their fate. Here are some things to think about:

- Do you want someone to have access to your email accounts?
- What do you want done with your Facebook profile?
- Do you want someone to make final entries on your blog?
- Do you want any of your online communities to be notified of your death?
- Would you like someone to download any photos that you store online?
- What do you want done with your domain names?

If you have ideas about what should happen with your digital legacy after you die, you can leave instructions for your loved ones. For example, you might want to ask someone to archive the data from your blog, transfer your domain names to your children, or close your seller's accounts on websites like Amazon or eBay.

If you want your survivors to be able to log in to your accounts as a user, include log-in names and passwords with your instructions. If you choose not to leave log-in information, your estate representative may still be able to get limited access to your account. However, every company has its own guidelines and limitations about this, so getting access this way is bound to be a hassle.

You can write your instructions and log-in information in an explanatory letter; see Chapter 12. Store the letter with your other estate planning documents. Your wishes won't be legally binding, but your survivors will thank you for helping them wrap up the details of your life.

There are two issues to consider:

- What do you own?
- Will your spouse or partner have the right to claim a share of your property after your death? (See "Your Spouse's Right to Inherit From You," below.)

This section will help you determine what you own and so can leave to others in your will. To figure it out, you need to know a little about the laws in your state. When it comes to property ownership, states are broadly divided into two types: community property states and common law property states.

Community Property States		
Alaska[1]	Louisiana	Texas
Arizona	Nevada	Washington[2]
California[2]	New Mexico	Wisconsin
Idaho	Tennessee[1]	

[1] If the couple makes a written agreement stating that they wish their property to be treated as community property. (See a lawyer if you want to make this kind of agreement.)

[2] Registered domestic partners are also covered by community property laws.

Common Law States
All other states

Community Property States

If you live in a community property state, there are a few key rules to keep in mind while making your will:

- You can leave your separate property to anyone you wish.
- You can leave half of the community property (property you and your spouse or partner own together) to anyone you wish.

- After your death, your spouse or partner automatically keeps his or her half of the community property.
- If you are in a registered domestic partnership in California, all of the community property rules that apply to married couples also apply to you and your partner.

Another Option: Community Property With Right of Survivorship

Alaska, Arizona, California, Nevada, Texas and Wisconsin allow a form of community property that works just like joint tenancy; in other words, the surviving spouse or domestic partner automatically inherits the property when the other spouse or partner dies. To take advantage of this type of ownership, the property's title document must state that the property is owned "as community property with right of survivorship" or something similar.

Your Separate Property

The following property qualifies as separate property in all community property states:

- property that you own before marriage
- property that you receive after marriage by gift or inheritance
- property that you purchase entirely with your separate property, and
- property that you earn or accumulate after permanent separation.

In some states, additional types of property—such as personal injury awards received by one spouse during marriage—may also qualify as separate property. (See "Property That Is Difficult to Categorize," below.)

Community property states differ in how they treat income earned from separate property. Most hold that such income is separate. But a number of states take the opposite approach, treating income from separate property as community property.

Normally, separate property stays separate as long as it is not:

- so mixed with marital property that it is impossible to tell what is separate and what is not, or
- transferred in writing by the separate property owner into a form of shared ownership.

Just as separate property can be transformed into shared property, community property can be turned into separate property by a gift from one spouse to the other. The rules differ somewhat from state to state, but, generally speaking, gifts made to transform one type of property into another must be made with a signed document.

Community Property

The basic rule of community property is simple: During a marriage, all property earned or acquired by either spouse or domestic partner is owned 50-50 by each spouse or partner, except for property received by only one of them through gift or inheritance.

More specifically, community property usually includes:

- All income received by either spouse or partner from employment or any other source (except gifts to or inheritance by just one spouse or partner)—for example, wages, stock options, pensions and other employment compensation and business profits.
  This rule generally applies only to the period when the couple lives together as husband and wife or domestic partners. Most community property states consider income and property acquired after the spouses or partners permanently separate to be the separate property of the spouse or partner who receives it.
- All property acquired with community property income during the marriage.
- All separate property that is transformed into community property under state law. This transformation can occur in several ways, including when one spouse or domestic partner makes a gift of separate property to both of them or when property is so mixed together that it's no longer possible to tell what property is separate (lawyers call this "commingling").
- As mentioned above, in a few community property states, income earned during marriage from separate property—for example, rent,

Classifying Property in Community Property States: Some Examples

Property	Community or Separate	Why
A painting you inherited while married	Separate; you can leave it in your will.	Inherited property belongs only to the person who inherited it.
A car you bought before you got married	Separate; you can leave it in your will.	Property owned before marriage is not community property.
A boat you bought with your income while married and registered in your name	Community; you can leave only your half-interest in your will.	It was purchased with community property income (income earned during the marriage).
The family home you and your spouse own together	Community; you can leave only your half-interest in your will.	It was purchased with community property income (income earned during the marriage).
A loan that your brother owes you	Community; you can leave only your half-interest in your will.	The loan was made from community property funds and belongs half to you and half to your spouse.
A fishing cabin you inherited from your father	Separate; you can leave it in your will.	Inherited property belongs only to the person who inherited it.
Stock you and your spouse bought with savings from your spouse's earnings	Community; you can leave only your half-interest in your will.	It was purchased with one spouse's earnings, which are community property during marriage.

interest or dividends—is community property. Most community property states consider such income to be separate property, however.

EXAMPLE: Beth and Daniel live in Idaho, one of the few community property states where income earned from separate property belongs to the community. Beth inherits 22 head of Angus cattle from her father. Those cattle go on to breed a herd of more than 100 cattle. All the descendants of the original 22 animals are considered income from Beth's separate property and are included in the couple's community property estate.

Property That Is Difficult to Categorize

Normally, classifying property as community or separate property is easy. But in some situations, it can be a close call. There are several potential problem areas.

Businesses. Family businesses can create complications, especially if they were owned before marriage by one spouse or domestic partner and expanded during the marriage or partnership. The key is to figure out whether the increased value of the business is community or separate property. If you and your spouse or partner do not have the same view of how to pass on the business, it may be worthwhile to get help from a lawyer or accountant.

Money from a personal injury lawsuit. Usually, but not always, awards won in a personal injury lawsuit are the separate property of the spouse or partner receiving them. There is no easy way to characterize this type of property. If a significant amount of your property came from a personal injury settlement, research the specifics of your state's law or ask an estate planning expert.

Pensions. Generally, for married people, the part of a pension gained from earnings made during the marriage is considered to be community property. This is also true of military pensions. However, some federal pensions—such as Railroad Retirement benefits and Social Security retirement benefits—are not considered community property, because federal law deems them to be the separate property of the employee earning them. Also, because the federal government does not recognize domestic partnerships, community property rules will not apply to federal benefits acquired by registered domestic partners.

Common Law Property States

Common law property states are all states other than the community property states listed above.

In these states, you own:
- all property you purchased using your property or income, and
- property you own solely in your name if it has a title slip, deed or other legal ownership document.

In common law states, the key to ownership for many types of valuable property is whose name is on the title. If you and your spouse or registered domestic partner take title to a house together—that is, both of your names are on the deed—you both own it. That is true even if you earned or inherited the money you used to buy it. If your spouse or domestic partner earns the money, but you take title in your name alone, you own it.

If the property is valuable but has no title document, such as a computer, then the person whose income or property is used to pay for it owns it. If joint income is used, then you own it together. You can each leave your half in your will, unless you signed an agreement providing for a joint tenancy or a tenancy by the entirety.

EXAMPLE 1: Will and Jane are married and live in Kentucky, a common law property state. They have five children. Shortly after their marriage, Jane wrote an extremely popular computer program that helps doctors diagnose illness. She has received royalties averaging about $200,000 a year over a ten-year period. Jane has used the royalties to buy a car, boat and mountain cabin—all registered in her name alone. The couple also owns a house as joint tenants. In addition, Jane owns a number of family heirlooms which she inherited from her parents. Throughout their marriage, Jane and Will have maintained separate savings accounts. Will works as a computer engineer and has deposited all of his income into his account. Jane put her unspent royalties in her account, which now contains $75,000.

Jane owns:
- the savings account listed in her name alone
- one-half interest in the house (which, because it is held in joint tenancy, will go to Will at Jane's death)
- the car, boat and cabin, since there are title documents listing them in her name (if there were no such documents, she would still own them because they were bought with her income), and
- her family heirlooms.

Will owns:
- the savings account listed in his name alone, and
- one-half interest in the house (which, because it is held in joint tenancy, will go to Jane at Will's death).

EXAMPLE 2: Martha and Scott, who are married, have both worked for 30 years as schoolteachers in Michigan, a common law state. Generally, Scott and Martha pooled their income and jointly purchased a house, worth $200,000 (in both their names as joint tenants); cars (one in Martha's name and one in Scott's); a share in a vacation condominium (in both names as joint tenants); and household furniture. Each maintains a separate savings account, and they also have a joint tenancy checking account containing $2,000. In addition, Scott and his sister own a piece of land as tenants in common.

Martha owns:
- her savings account
- half-interest in the house, the joint checking account and the condo (which, because they are held in joint tenancy, will go to Scott at her death)

- her car, and
- half the furniture.

Scott owns:
- his savings account
- half-interest in the house, the joint checking account and the condo (which, because they are held in joint tenancy, will go to Martha at his death)
- his car
- half the furniture, and
- a half-interest in the land he owns with his sister.

Moving From State to State

Complications may set in when a husband and wife acquire property in a common law property state and then move to a community property state. California, Idaho, Washington and Wisconsin treat the earlier-acquired property as if it had been acquired in the community property state. The legal term for this type of property is "quasi-community property." Wisconsin calls it "deferred marital property."

The other community property states do not recognize the quasi-community property concept for will-making purposes. Instead, they go by the rules of the state where the property was acquired. If you and your spouse move from a non-community-property state into one of the states that recognizes quasi-community property, all of your property is treated according to community property rules. However, if you move to any of the other community property states from a common law state, you must assess your property according to the rules of the state where the property was acquired.

Couples who move from a community property state to a common law state face the opposite problem. Generally, each spouse retains one-half interest in the community property the couple accumulated while living in the community property state. However, if there is a conflict after your death, it can get messy; courts dealing with the issue have not been consistent.

> **SEE AN EXPERT**
>
> **If you move.** If you move from a community property state to a common law one, and you and your spouse have any disagreement as to who owns what, it may be wise to check with a lawyer. (See Chapter 17.)

> **SEE AN EXPERT**
>
> **Same-sex couples.** If you are moving from the state in which you registered your domestic partnership, there is a good chance that the state you are moving to will not recognize the property rights you received through your partnership status. You may want to consult a knowledgeable attorney in your new state to be sure you both fully understand your property rights and have an appropriate plan in place.

Your Spouse's Right to Inherit From You

If you intend to leave your spouse or registered domestic partner very little or no property, you may run into some legal roadblocks. All common law property states (see above) protect a surviving spouse or partner from being completely disinherited—and most assure that a spouse has the right to receive a substantial share of a deceased spouse's property. Community property states offer a different kind of protection.

Spousal Protection in Common Law States

In a common law state, a shortchanged surviving spouse or domestic partner usually has the option of either taking what the will provides, called "taking under the will," or rejecting the gift and instead taking the minimum share allowed by state law, called "taking against the will." In some states, your spouse or partner may have the right to inherit the family residence, or at least use it for his or her life. The Florida constitution, for example, gives a surviving spouse the deceased spouse's residence.

Laws protecting spouses and domestic partners vary among the states. In many common law property states, a spouse is entitled to one-third of the property left in the will. In a few, it is one-half. The exact amount of the spouse's minimum share may also depend on whether there are also minor children and whether the spouse has been provided for outside the will by trusts or other means.

> **EXAMPLE:** Leonard's will leaves $50,000 to his second wife, June, and the rest of his property, totaling $400,000, to May and April, his daughters from his first marriage. June can choose instead to receive her statutory share of Leonard's estate, which will be far more than $50,000. To the probable dismay of May and April, their shares will be substantially reduced; they will share what is left of Leonard's property after June gets her statutory share.

Of course, these are just options; a spouse who is not unhappy with the share he or she receives by will is free to let it stand. And in almost all states, one spouse or partner can give up all rights to inherit any property by completing and signing a waiver. If you want to make that type of arrangement, consult a lawyer. (See Chapter 17.)

Family Allowances

Some states provide additional, relatively minor protections for immediate family members. These vary from state to state in too much detail to discuss here. Generally, however, these devices attempt to ensure that your spouse and children are not left out in the cold after your death, by allowing them temporary protection (such as the right to remain in the family home for a short period) or funds (typically, living expenses while an estate is being probated).

In many common law states, how much the surviving spouse is entitled to receive depends on what that spouse receives both under the will and outside of the will—for example, through joint tenancy or a living trust—as well as what the surviving spouse owns. The total of all of these is called the augmented estate.

While the augmented estate concept is rather complicated, its purpose is easy to grasp. Basically, almost all property of both spouses is taken into account, and the surviving spouse gets a piece of the whole pie.

> **SEE AN EXPERT**
>
> **Leaving little to a spouse.** If you do not plan to leave at least half of your property to your spouse or domestic partner in your will and have not provided for him or her generously outside your will, consult a lawyer.

Spousal Protection in Community Property States

Most community property states do not give surviving spouses or registered domestic partners the right to take a share of the deceased spouse's or partner's estate. Instead, they try to protect spouses and domestic partners while both are still alive, by granting each spouse or partner half ownership of property and earnings either spouse or partner acquires during the marriage. (See "Community Property States," above.)

However, in a few states—under very limited circumstances—a surviving spouse or domestic partner may elect to take a portion of the deceased spouse's community or separate property. These laws are designed to prevent spouses and domestic partners from being either accidentally overlooked—for example, if one spouse or partner makes a will before marriage or partnership and forgets to change it afterward to include the new spouse or partner—or deliberately deprived of their fair share of property. These protections are available in Alaska (Alaska Stat. §§ 13.12.201 and following), California (California Prob. Code §§ 21610 and following), Idaho (Idaho Code §§ 15-2-202 and following), Washington (Wash. Rev. Code §§ 26.16.240 and following) and Wisconsin (Wis. Stat. §§ 861.02 and following). If you want to learn more about them, consult a lawyer. (See Chapter 17.)

How to Leave Your Property

The heart of will making is deciding who gets your property when you die. For many, this is an easy task: You want it all to go to your spouse or partner, your kids or your favorite charity. For others, it's a little more complicated—for example, you want most of your property to go to your spouse, partner, child or charity, but you also want certain items to go to other people. You may even have a fairly complicated scheme in mind that involves dividing your property among a number of people and organizations.

Chapter 5 introduced some basic concepts about your property and whether you can leave it to others in your will. This chapter explains how to put your plan into effect using the Quicken WillMaker Plus program. If you want to leave all or most of your property to a loved one or favorite charity, the program offers you some shortcuts. Quicken WillMaker Plus also accommodates more complex wishes.

After you name those who will get your property, Quicken WillMaker Plus lets you name alternates—that is, who should get property if your first choices do not survive you.

You do not need to read all of this chapter to figure out how to write the will you want. Start with the discussion that is tailored to your situation:

- married or in a registered domestic partnership, with children
- married or in a registered domestic partnership, with no children
- not married or in a registered domestic partnership, with children, or
- not married or in a registered domestic partnership, with no children.

If You Are Married or in a Registered Domestic Partnership and You Have Children

Many married or partnered people have simple will-making needs. They want to leave all or most of their property to their spouses or partners. As alternates, they may want to choose their children or name another person or organization. Quicken WillMaker Plus lets you choose any of those paths easily. And if you do not want to make your spouse or partner the main beneficiary of your will, that option is available, too.

Choosing Beneficiaries

Quicken WillMaker Plus prompts you to choose one of three approaches to leaving your property. You can:

- leave everything to your spouse or domestic partner
- leave most of your property, with some specific exceptions, to your spouse or domestic partner, or
- make a plan that may or may not include your spouse or domestic partner.

The third option offers flexibility. You should choose it if you want to divide up your property more evenly among a number of beneficiaries or if you want to give all or most of your property to someone other than your spouse or domestic partner. But if you do choose this approach to making your will, be sure that you understand the rules governing what you own and the rights of your spouse or partner. (See "Property Ownership Rules for Married People" and "Your Spouse's Right to Inherit From You" in Chapter 5.)

> **EXAMPLE 1:** Anne and Robert are a married couple with one young child. Anne wants a simple will, in which she leaves all of her property to Robert. She chooses the first option—everything to your spouse—to get a will that reflects her wishes.

> **EXAMPLE 2:** Arnie wants his wife to receive most of his property when he dies, but he has a valuable violin that he wants to go to his best friend, Eddie, and a coin collection that he wants his nephew to receive. Arnie chooses the second option—most to your spouse. Then, later in the program, he can name Eddie to receive his violin and his nephew to receive his coin collection.

> **EXAMPLE 3:** Sylvia is married to Fred. She wants to leave him her share of their investment portfolio and family business but also

wants to leave a number of specific property items to different friends, relatives and charities. She chooses the third option when using Quicken WillMaker Plus. The program then prompts her to list specific property items and the person or organization she wants to receive each one. Before she does, Sylvia reviews Chapter 5 to make sure she understands what property is appropriate to leave in her will.

> **SKIP AHEAD**
>
> **When you can skip ahead.** If you do not want to name your spouse or registered domestic partner to receive all or most of your property, skip the rest of this section and go to "Making Specific Bequests," below, for a discussion of what comes next.

Choosing Alternates for Your Spouse or Partner

If you want your spouse or registered domestic partner to receive all or most of your property, your next task will be to choose an alternate for your spouse or partner.

The will you create with Quicken WillMaker Plus provides that all beneficiaries—including your spouse—must survive you by 45 days to receive the property you leave them. This is a standard will provision, called a survivorship requirement. It is based on the assumption that if a beneficiary survives you by only a few days or weeks, you would prefer the property to go to another beneficiary that you choose and name in your will.

The alternate or alternates you choose will receive the property only if your spouse or domestic partner dies less than 45 days after you do.

Depending on your previous choices, Quicken WillMaker Plus offers two or three options for alternates. You can name:

- your child or children, or
- other alternate beneficiaries.

These two approaches to naming alternates are shortcuts. You won't specify which items go to which beneficiaries because these alternates will receive all of the property that would have gone to your spouse or partner.

You also have a third option: You can make a completely new plan for leaving your property which will take effect only if your spouse does not survive you by at least 45 days. If you make this choice, you can divide your property among a number of alternate beneficiaries.

Each of these approaches to naming alternates is discussed below.

Naming Your Children as Alternates

It is common for married or partnered people who have children to simply leave all or most of their property to the surviving spouse or partner and name the children to take the property as alternates. This means if your spouse or partner does not survive you by 45 days, the property your spouse or partner would have received will pass to your child or children.

If you have more than one child, you must decide how the children should share the property.

> **EXAMPLE:** Meg and Charlie have three grown children. When Charlie makes his will, he leaves everything to Meg and names the children as alternates for her. He directs that all three children should receive equal shares of his property if Meg doesn't survive him and they take it, instead.

If any of your children are minors or young adults, you may:
- specify the share each child will receive; later, you may designate how each child's share will be managed and doled out if a child is under 35 when you die, or
- direct that the property be held in one undivided fund, called a pot trust; under this option, the person you select to serve as trustee will use the assets in the trust for all your children as needed, until your youngest child turns an age you choose—up to age 25.

(See Chapter 7 for a discussion of these methods for managing property left to children.)

EXAMPLE 1: Julia and Emanuel have three young children. When Julia makes her will, she names Emanuel to inherit most of her property and leaves a few small items to her sister. As alternates for her husband, she picks her children. But because they are too young to manage money or property, later in the program she names her sister to manage any property the children may take under her will while they are still young.

EXAMPLE 2: Barry and his wife, Marta, have two young daughters close in age. In his will, Barry leaves Marta all his property and chooses the children as alternate beneficiaries. He also picks the pot trust option and names his mother as trustee. If Marta does not survive him by at least 45 days, all of Barry's property will go into a trust for the two girls, administered by Barry's mother.

Quicken WillMaker Plus also lets you name a second level of alternates—that is, alternates who will take the property a child would have received, if that child does not survive you. You can name an alternate for each child or, if you have two or more children, you can designate that the surviving children receive any property that would have gone to the deceased child.

Naming Alternates Who Are Not Your Children

If you decide to specify alternates to receive the property left to your spouse or domestic partner, you may name whomever you want. You are not constrained, as with the first option, to naming only your children as alternates. For instance, you may name a charity, a friend or just one of your children. If your spouse or partner does not survive you by 45 days, the alternates you name will receive the property your spouse or partner would have received. If you name more than one person or organization, you may specify what share each is to receive.

EXAMPLE: Celeste is married with two grown children. The children have both been provided for nicely with money from trusts and are financially secure. In her will, Celeste leaves her husband most of her property, with a few exceptions of some heirlooms for her children. As an alternate for her husband, she names the university where she taught for many years.

You can also name a second level of alternates—that is, alternates to take the property should both your spouse or partner and a first level of alternates you name all die before you do. You can name a backup alternate for each alternate. If you named more than one first-level alternate, you may also designate that the survivors receive any property that would have gone to a deceased alternate.

Making a Different Plan

This option—Plan B—is available only if you choose to leave all your property to your spouse or registered domestic partner.

It lets you create a whole new plan to take effect if, and only if, your spouse or partner doesn't survive you by 45 days. This option is for people who think like this: I want to leave all my property to my spouse, period. But in case my spouse does not survive me, I want to make a whole new plan from the ground up—my Plan B—that does not include my spouse. So, if my spouse survives me, he or she gets all my property. But if not, I'll have been able to divide my property just as if I weren't married.

Your Plan B can include as many specific bequests as you wish. (See "Making Specific Bequests," below.) After you have made all your specific bequests, you can also name someone to take the rest of your property. This is called your residuary beneficiary. (See "Naming Residuary Beneficiaries," below.) Again, all of these Plan B bequests will take effect only if your spouse or domestic partner does not survive you by 45 days.

> **EXAMPLE:** Sean wants to leave all his property to Eva, his wife, if she's alive when he dies. But thinking about what he would want to happen if Eva were not around to take everything, he decides that he would want to divide his property among several friends, relatives and charities.

When he sits down with Quicken WillMaker Plus to make his will, Sean names Eva to get all his property. Then, when it's time to name alternates, he chooses the Plan B option and leaves $10,000 to a local food bank, his piano to his niece and the rest of his property to his brother.

If You Do Not Name Alternates

If you leave your entire estate to one person or a group of people, you do not name alternate beneficiaries and your primary beneficiaries do not survive you, then your estate will be distributed according to the laws of your state. (See "Dying Without a Will" in Chapter 2.)

If You Are Married or in a Registered Domestic Partnership and You Do Not Have Children

Many married or partnered people have simple will-making needs. They want to leave all or most of their property to their spouses or domestic partners. Then, as alternates, they may name one or more other people or organizations. Quicken WillMaker Plus lets you choose this path easily. And if you do not want to make your spouse or partner the main beneficiary of your will, that option is available, too.

Choosing Beneficiaries

Quicken WillMaker Plus prompts you to choose one of three approaches to leaving your property. You can:
- leave everything to your spouse or domestic partner
- leave most of your property, with some specific exceptions, to your spouse or domestic partner
- make a plan that may or may not include your spouse or domestic partner.

The third option offers flexibility. You should choose it if you want to divide up your property more evenly among a number of beneficiaries or if you want to give all or most of your property to someone other than your spouse or partner. If you choose it, be sure that you understand the rules governing what you own and the rights of your spouse or registered domestic partner. (See "Property Ownership Rules for Married People" and "Your Spouse's Right to Inherit From You" in Chapter 5.)

EXAMPLE 1: Mark and Abby are a young married couple with no children. Mark wants simply to leave everything to Abby in his will. He chooses the first option—everything to your spouse—so that his will reflects his intentions.

EXAMPLE 2: Paul wants his wife to receive most of his property when he dies, but he wants his golf clubs to go to his best friend, Eric, and wants his niece to take his photography equipment. Paul chooses the second option—most to your spouse. Then, later in the program, he can name Eric to receive his golf clubs and his niece to receive the photography equipment.

EXAMPLE 3: Eleanor is married to William. She wants to leave William her share of their investment portfolio and family business, but also wants to leave a number of specific items to different friends, relatives and charities. She chooses the third option when using Quicken WillMaker Plus—make a different plan. The program then prompts her to list specific property items and the person or organization she wants to receive each of them. Before she does, Eleanor reviews Chapter 5 to make sure she understands what property is appropriate to leave in her will.

SKIP AHEAD

When you can skip ahead. If you do not want to name your spouse or domestic partner to receive all or most of your property, skip the rest of this section and go to "Making Specific Bequests," below, for a discussion of what comes next.

Choosing Alternates for Your Spouse or Partner

If you want your spouse or domestic partner to receive all or most of your property, your next task will be to choose an alternate or alternates for your spouse or partner.

The will you create with Quicken WillMaker Plus provides that all beneficiaries—including your spouse or domestic partner—must survive you by 45 days to receive the property you leave them. This is a standard will provision, called a survivorship requirement. It is based on the assumption that if a beneficiary survives you by only a few days or weeks, you would prefer the property to go to another beneficiary that you name in your will.

The alternate or alternates you choose will receive the property only if your spouse or partner does not live at least 45 days longer than you do.

The simplest ways to provide for alternates are to name:

- one person or organization to receive everything your spouse or partner would have received, or
- more than one person or organization to share the property.

If you choose either of these options, the alternate or alternates you name will receive all the property that would have gone to your spouse or partner, so you won't specify which items go to which beneficiaries.

Or you can make a different plan for leaving your property—Plan B— which will take effect only if your spouse or partner does not survive you by 45 days. If you choose to make a different plan, you can leave specific items of property among several alternate beneficiaries.

These approaches to naming alternates are discussed below.

Naming Alternates for Your Spouse or Partner

You may name whomever you want as the alternate for your spouse or domestic partner. For instance, you may name a charity, friend or relative. If your spouse or partner does not survive you by 45 days, the alternate you name will receive the property your spouse or partner would have received. If you name more than one person or organization, you may specify what share each is to receive.

> **EXAMPLE:** In her will, Sharon leaves most of her property to her husband, Alex, with a few exceptions of some small items for friends. As an alternate for Alex, she names the charity at which she volunteered for many years.

You can also name a second level of alternates—that is, alternates to take the property should both your spouse and alternate not survive you. You can name a backup alternate for each alternate. Or if you named more than one first-level alternate, you may designate that the surviving alternates receive any property that would have gone to a deceased alternate.

Making a Different Plan

If you choose to leave all of your property to your spouse or domestic partner, you can create a whole new plan to take effect if, and only if, your spouse or partner doesn't survive you by 45 days. This option is for people who think like this: I want to leave all my property to my spouse, period. But in case my spouse does not survive me, I want to make a different plan from the ground up—my Plan B—that does not include my spouse. So, if my spouse survives me, he or she gets all my property. But if not, I'll divide my property just as if I weren't married.

Your alternate plan—Plan B—can include as many specific bequests as you wish. (See "Making Specific Bequests," below.) After you have made all your specific bequests, you can also name someone to take the rest of your property. This is called your residuary beneficiary. (See "Naming Residuary Beneficiaries," below.) Again, all of these Plan B bequests will take effect only if your spouse or domestic partner does not survive you by 45 days.

> **EXAMPLE:** Sean wants to leave all his property to Eva, his wife, if she's alive when he dies. But thinking about what he would want to happen if Eva were not around to take everything, he decides that he would want to divide his property among several friends, relatives and charities.
>
> When he sits down with Quicken WillMaker Plus to make his will, Sean names Eva to take everything. Then, when it's time to

name alternates, he chooses to create a different plan and leaves $10,000 to a local food bank, his piano to his niece and everything else to his brother.

If You Do Not Name Alternates

If you leave your entire estate to one person or a group of people, you do not name alternate beneficiaries and your primary beneficiaries do not survive you, then your estate will be distributed according to the laws of your state. (See "Dying Without a Will" in Chapter 2.)

If You Are Not Married or in a Domestic Partnership and You Have Children

If you are a single parent, your children probably figure prominently in your plans for distributing your property after your death. With that in mind, Quicken WillMaker Plus offers some shortcuts when making your will.

Choosing Beneficiaries

Quicken WillMaker Plus prompts you to choose one of three approaches to leaving your property. You can:

- leave everything to your child or children
- leave most of your property, with some specific exceptions, to your child or children, or
- make a plan that may or may not include your children.

The third option offers flexibility. You should choose it if you want to divide your property more evenly among a number of beneficiaries or if you want to give all or most of your property to someone other than your children. If you choose it, be sure that you understand the rules governing what you own. (See Chapter 5.)

> **EXAMPLE 1:** Raquel is a divorced mother of two young children. She wants to leave all her property to the children, in equal shares. She chooses the first option.

EXAMPLE 2: Carlo, a widower, has one son, who is now 40 years old. Carlo wants to leave most of his property to his son but also make a few small bequests to charities. He chooses the second option. Then, later in the program, he can name the charities and the amounts he wants to leave to each.

EXAMPLE 3: Brenda has three children, all of whom are grown and financially healthy. She wants to leave a number of specific property items to her children but also to many different friends, relatives and charities. She chooses the third option. The program then asks her to list specific property items and the person or organization she wants to receive each one. Before doing this, Brenda reviews Chapter 5 to make sure she understands what property she can leave in her will.

> **SKIP AHEAD**
>
> **When you can skip ahead.** If you do not want to name your child or children to receive all or most of your property, skip the rest of this section and go to "Making Specific Bequests," below, for a discussion of what comes next.

Designating Children's Shares

If you have a number of children, you must decide how you want them to share the property they receive through your will.

EXAMPLE: Charlie has three grown children. When Charlie makes his will, he names the children to receive everything. He directs that all three children should receive equal shares of his property.

If any of your children are minors or young adults, you may:

- specify the share each child will receive; later, you may designate how each child's share will be managed and doled out if a child is under 35 when you die, or

- direct that the property be held in one undivided fund, called a pot trust; under this option, the person you select to serve as trustee will use the assets in the trust for all your children as needed, until your youngest child turns an age you choose, up to age 25.

(See Chapter 7 for an explanation of all of these methods for managing property left to children.)

> **EXAMPLE 1:** Tess has three children, two teenagers and one 26-year-old son. When she makes her will, she leaves the children most of her property and leaves a few small items to her sister. Because her oldest child is self-supporting, she leaves him just a 1/5 share and leaves the two younger children 2/5 each. Later in the program, Tess names her sister to manage any property the two younger children come to own while they are still young.

> **EXAMPLE 2:** Frank has two young sons close in age. In his will, he leaves them all his property. He then picks the pot trust option and names his sister as trustee. That means that if the boys inherit Frank's property while they are still young, all of it will go into a trust for them, administered by Frank's sister.

Choosing Alternates for Your Children

If you choose your child or children to receive all or most of your property, your next task will be to decide who should get that property if a child were to predecease you.

The will you create with Quicken WillMaker Plus provides that a beneficiary must survive you by 45 days to receive property through the will. This is a standard will provision, called a survivorship requirement. It is based on the assumption that if a beneficiary survives you by only a few weeks, you would prefer the property to go to another beneficiary that you name in your will.

The alternate you choose for a child will receive the property only if the child does not survive you by at least 45 days.

> ⓘ **CAUTION**
>
> **No alternates necessary for pot trusts.** If you chose a pot trust, you don't need to name alternates. If one child does not survive you, the other surviving children will still share the property.

If you have one child, you can either:
- name one or more alternates for that child, or
- make a different plan that allows you to divide up specific items of property to several other people or organizations.

If you have more than one child and have designated a share for each child, you can either:
- name one or more alternates for each child, or
- specify that if one child doesn't survive you, the surviving children should take the deceased child's share.

If you chose a pot trust, you need not name alternates. If any child does not survive you, the others will share the property.

Naming Alternates for Your Children

You may name whomever you want—for instance, a charity, friend or relative—as the alternate for a child. If the child does not survive you by 45 days, the alternate will receive the property the child would have received. If you name more than one alternate, you may specify the share each is to receive.

> **EXAMPLE:** In her will, Sharon leaves her daughter most of her property and gives the rest to friends. As an alternate for her daughter, she names her daughter's two young children.

Surviving Children

Rather than name alternates for each of your children, you may want to provide that whatever property you leave them will go to all the children who survive you.

EXAMPLE: In his will, Patrick leaves his daughter and two sons all of his property. He specifies that each should receive an equal share. When the program asks him to name alternates for the children, he specifies that the survivors should take the share of any deceased child.

If You Do Not Name Alternates

If you leave your entire estate to one person or a group of people, you do not name alternate beneficiaries and your primary beneficiaries do not survive you, then your estate will be distributed according to the laws of your state. (See "Dying Without a Will" in Chapter 2.)

If You Are Not Married or in a Domestic Partnership and You Do Not Have Children

As a single person, your beneficiaries will probably be your loved ones, friends, or organizations you value highly. You can divide your property as you see fit, whether that means leaving it all to one beneficiary or giving specific items to specific people. Or, you may prefer to combine these approaches, leaving most of your assets to one or more beneficiaries and a few unique items to others. In any case, you'll have the opportunity to choose alternate beneficiaries as well.

Choosing Beneficiaries

Quicken WillMaker Plus prompts you to choose one of three approaches to leaving your property. You can:

- Leave everything to one or more beneficiaries. For example, you might leave everything you own to your girlfriend or to your sisters.
- Leave almost everything to one or more beneficiaries, but also leave some specific items to particular people. For example, you might want to leave all of your property to your sisters, but you want to leave your antique dining table to your neighbor.

- **Leave your property some other way.** You can leave specific items of property to certain beneficiaries, then choose one or more beneficiaries who will receive everything that's left. For example, you could leave your antique furniture to your sister, your ABC stock to your nephew, your comic book collection to your neighbor and everything else to the American Cancer Society.

If you want to leave specific items of property, be sure that you understand what kinds of property should be left in a will, and what might be passed to your survivors in other ways. (See "Property You Should Not Include in Your Will" in Chapter 5.)

EXAMPLE 1: Fernando and Robert have been together for many years, but they do not live in a state that offers registered domestic partnerships. When Fernando makes his will, he wants all his property to go to Robert. He chooses the first option—leave everything to one person—to make a will that reflects his wishes.

EXAMPLE 2: Theresa, whose husband died several years ago, wants to divide her money and possessions among different friends, relatives and charities. She chooses the third option. Quicken WillMaker Plus then asks her to list specific property items and the person or organization she wants to receive each one. Then she names one person who will receive any other property that she owns at her death.

> **SKIP AHEAD**
>
> **When you can skip ahead.** If you do not want to name one or more beneficiaries to receive all or most of your property, skip the rest of this section and go to "Making Specific Bequests," below, for a discussion of what comes next.

Choosing Alternates

If you specify that one or more beneficiaries should receive all or most of your property, your next task will be to decide who would get that property if any of your first-choice beneficiaries were to die before you do.

The will you create with Quicken WillMaker Plus provides that all beneficiaries must survive you by 45 days to receive the property you leave them. This is a standard will provision, called a survivorship requirement. It is based on the assumption that if a beneficiary survives you by only a few days or weeks, you would prefer the property to go to another beneficiary that you name in your will.

The alternates you choose will receive the property only if your first-choice beneficiaries do not survive for at least 45 days after you die.

Quicken WillMaker Plus offers two options for alternates. You can:

- name alternate beneficiaries for each of your first-choice beneficiaries, or
- make a completely new plan which will take effect only if your first-choice beneficiaries do not survive you by 45 days. This way, you can divide your property among several alternate beneficiaries.

Naming Alternates

You may name whomever you want as alternates for each of your first-choice beneficiaries. For instance, for each of your first-choice beneficiaries, you may name a charity or a group of friends. If you name more than one person or organization, you may specify the share each is to receive.

If a first-choice beneficiary does not survive you by 45 days, the alternates you name will receive the property he or she would have received.

EXAMPLE 1: Christine is not married and has no children. She is very close to her sister Karen and wants to leave all her property to her.

In her will, Christine names Karen as her first-choice beneficiary. As alternates, she names Karen's two children.

EXAMPLE 2: Ari leaves all of his property to his two brothers Seth and David. Because Seth is more financially stable, he indicates that Seth should get one-quarter of his estate and David should get three-quarters. He names his cousin Rachel as an alternate beneficiary for David's share. She will get three-quarters of Ari's estate if David does not survive Ari. Ari names his favorite charity as an alternate for Seth's share. If Seth does not survive Ari, the charity will get one-quarter of the estate.

If you like, you may also name a second level of alternates—that is, alternates to take the property should both your first-choice and alternate beneficiaries not survive you by 45 days or more.

If you name more than one alternate beneficiary but don't name any second alternates for those beneficiaries, the surviving alternate beneficiaries will equally share the property that any deceased beneficiary would have received.

EXAMPLE: In her will, JoEllen leaves all her property to her partner, Katrine. She names her nephews, Jacob and Joseph, as alternates and does not name second alternates. When JoEllen dies, Katrine and Jacob have already passed away. Joseph inherits all of JoEllen's property.

If you name more than one second alternate and one or more of them does not survive you, the surviving second alternates will equally share any property that would have gone to that deceased second alternate.

Making a Different Plan

This option lets you create a whole new plan that takes effect only if your first-choice beneficiary or beneficiaries do not survive you by 45 days. Your alternate plan—Plan B—can include as many specific bequests as you wish. (See "Making Specific Bequests," below.)

After you have made all your specific bequests, you can also name someone to take the rest of your property. This is called your residuary beneficiary. (See "Naming Residuary Beneficiaries," below.)

EXAMPLE: Sven wants to leave all his property to Jeannette, his girlfriend. But thinking about what he would want to happen if Jeannette were to die before him, he decides that he would want to divide his property among relatives and charities.

When he sits down with Quicken WillMaker Plus to make his will, Sven names Jeannette to take all of his property. Then, when it's time to name alternates, he chooses the Plan B option and leaves $10,000 to a local food bank, his piano to his niece and everything else to his brother.

If You Do Not Name Alternates

If you leave your entire estate to one person or a group of people, you do not name alternate beneficiaries and your primary beneficiaries do not survive you, then your estate will be distributed according to the laws of your state. (See "Dying Without a Will" in Chapter 2.)

Making Specific Bequests

This section discusses how to make specific bequests—that is, leave specific property items to specific people or groups. You should read this section if you:

- left most of your property to one or more main beneficiaries but want to leave some items to others
- want to divide your property among several beneficiaries, without leaving most or all of it to one or more main beneficiaries, or
- left everything to one or more beneficiaries, but instead of naming alternates for those beneficiaries, you want to make a Plan B to take effect if your first-choice beneficiaries don't survive you.

Quicken WillMaker Plus lets you make an unlimited number of separate specific bequests. For each one, you must provide this information:

- a description of the item—for example, a house, cash, an heirloom or a car
- the names of the people or organizations you want to get the items, and
- if you wish, the name of an alternate beneficiary, who will receive specific property if your first beneficiary does not survive you by 45 days. You can name more than one alternate beneficiary; if you do, you will also decide what share of the property each will receive.

Describing the Property

The first part of making a specific bequest is to describe the property you want to pass to a certain beneficiary or beneficiaries you have in mind. For example, if you want to leave your guitar to your best friend, you would begin by entering a brief description of the guitar, such as "my 1959 Martin guitar."

When describing an item, be as concise as you can, but use enough detail so that people will be able to identify and find the property. Most often, this will not be difficult: "my baby grand piano," "my collection of blue apothecary jars" or "my llama throw rug" are all the description you will need for tangible items that are easy to locate. If an item is very valuable or could be easily confused with other property, make sure you include identifying characteristics, such as location, serial number, color or some other unique feature.

> **CAUTION**
>
> **Do not include property that will pass by other means.** Before describing the property you wish to leave in a specific bequest, take a moment to reflect on what property you are legally able to pass in your will. If you have already arranged to leave property outside your will by using legal devices, such as life insurance, pay-on-death bank accounts or living trusts, you usually should not include that property in a specific bequest. (See "Property You Should Not Include in Your Will" in Chapter 5.)

Naming Beneficiaries

The second step in making a specific bequest is to name one or more beneficiaries. Beneficiaries' names need not be the names that appear on their birth certificates. Just make sure that the names you use clearly identify the beneficiaries.

Tips on Describing Property in Your Will

Here is how to identify different types of property with enough detail to prevent confusion:

- **Household furnishings.** You normally need not get very specific, unless an object is particularly valuable. It is enough to list the location of the property: "all household furnishings and possessions in the apartment at 55 Drury Lane."

- **Real estate.** You can simply provide the street address or, for unimproved property, the name by which it is commonly known: "my condominium at 123 45th Avenue," "my summer home at 84 Memory Lane in Oakville" or "the vacant lot next to the McHenry Place on Old Farm Road." You do not need to provide the legal description from the deed.

- **Bank, stock and money market accounts.** List financial accounts by their account numbers. Also, include the name and location of the organization holding the property: "$20,000 from savings account #22222 at Independence Bank, Big Mountain, Idaho"; "my money market account #23456 at Beryl Pynch & Company, Chicago, Illinois"; or "100 shares of General Foods common stock."

- **Personal items.** As with household goods, it is usually adequate to briefly describe personal items and group them, unless they have significant monetary or sentimental value. For example, items of extremely valuable jewelry should normally be listed and identified separately, while a drawer full of costume jewelry and baubles could be grouped.

Do Not Place Conditions on Bequests

Don't place conditions on any of your bequests; it risks making a confusing and even unenforceable will.

Here are some examples of *what not to do*:

- "I leave my gold Rolex to Andres, but only if he divorces his current wife, Samantha." Such a bequest would not be considered legally valid, because it encourages the breakup of a family.
- "I leave my dental office equipment to Claude, as long as he sets up a dental practice in San Francisco." The reason this bequest is unwieldy becomes obvious once you think ahead to the need for constant supervision. Who would be responsible for tracking Claude's dentistry career and making sure he ends up in San Francisco? What if Claude initially practices in San Francisco, using the equipment he was willed, then moves to grow grapes in the Napa Valley? Must he give up the equipment? To whom?
- "I leave my vintage Barbie doll collection to Collette, if the dolls are still in good condition." Who is to judge whether the dolls are in good condition? What happens if they aren't?

 SEE AN EXPERT

When to see a lawyer. If you are determined to place conditions on beneficiaries or property, consult a lawyer who is experienced in drafting bequests that will adequately address these potentially complex arrangements.

California Readers: Be Cautious About Gifts to Caregivers

If you live in California and want to leave a substantial gift to any non-relative who helps you with personal or health care, see a lawyer first. You can leave such a gift—but first you may need to have a lawyer sign a statement, verifying that you're acting freely and aren't being unduly influenced.

If you don't, the gift could be void—meaning the intended recipient won't get it. That's because of a California law that aims to thwart caregivers who take advantage of people who depend on them. Because of the law's broad terms, it could invalidate perfectly reasonable gifts that you really want to make. For example, a gift to a new neighbor who brings meals and helps you pay bills could be voided, as could a gift to a paid live-in caregiver who has become a good friend.

The law might come into play if you're 65 or older and you want to leave a gift of more than $5,000 (or less if your entire estate will be worth less than $100,000) to:

- a nonrelative you pay to help you, or
- a nonrelative who helps you without pay, if you've just recently struck up the relationship.

If you think you might be affected, see a lawyer who handles family or elder care matters and get a statement, called a "certificate of independent review," which states that you are freely making the gift.

Minors or Young Adults

If any of the beneficiaries you name is a minor (under 18) or young adult (under 35), you will have a chance, in a later part of Quicken WillMaker Plus, to choose someone to manage the property for them until they are older. (See Chapter 7.)

Multiple Beneficiaries

If you name two or more beneficiaries to share a specific bequest, you will later be asked to specify each person's share. To avoid possible tiffs among your beneficiaries, the property you plan to leave them either should be property that is easily divided or property that you intend to be sold so that the proceeds can be split. For property that requires discretion to divide it may be wiser to leave items separately.

Organizations

You may want to leave property to a charity or a public or private organization—for example, the American Red Cross, the Greenview Battered Women's Shelter or the University of Illinois at Champaign-Urbana.

The organization you name need not be set up as a nonprofit, unless you wish your estate to qualify for a charitable estate tax deduction. (See Chapter 13.) It can be any organization you consider worthy of your bequest. The only limitation is that the organization must not be set up for some illicit or illegal purpose.

The organization you name will receive your gift with no strings attached. You cannot use your will to describe how the property should be used. If you want to do that—for example, if you want a gift to your alma mater to be used as a scholarship for a student who gets above a 3.5 grade point average—see an experienced estate planning attorney for advice.

When naming an organization, be sure to enter its complete name, which may be different from the truncated version by which it is commonly known. Several different organizations may use similar names—and you want to be sure your bequest goes to the one you have in mind. Someone at the organization will be more than happy to help you get it straight.

Specifying Shares

If you name a group of beneficiaries to receive specific property, Quicken WillMaker Plus will ask you whether you want them to receive equal or unequal shares of the property. If you want it shared unequally, the shares must add up to one. Quicken WillMaker Plus will warn you if your computations are off.

EXAMPLE: Fred Wagner wants to leave an undeveloped real estate parcel to his three children, Mary, Sue and Peter. Because he has already paid for Mary's graduate school education, he wants to give Sue and Peter greater percentages of the property in case they want to go back to school, too. He lists his children and the share of his property to which they are entitled this way: Mary Wagner (1/5), Susan Wagner (2/5) and Peter Wagner (2/5).

> **TIP**
>
> **Update your will when you gain or lose property.** If you leave a specific item of property to a beneficiary, and you no longer own that property when you die, that beneficiary will get nothing in its place. For more on this and other reasons to update your will periodically, see Chapter 11.

Naming Alternates

To receive property under your will, a beneficiary must survive you by 45 days. Quicken WillMaker Plus assumes that if a beneficiary survives you by only a few days or weeks, you would prefer the property to pass to an alternate or residuary beneficiary named in your will, rather than have the property pass along with the beneficiary's other property.

With Quicken WillMaker Plus, you can name one or more alternate beneficiaries to take the bequest if your first choices do not survive you by the required period.

EXAMPLE: Joan leaves her horse to her brother Pierre. In case Pierre does not survive her by 45 days and so become eligible to receive this bequest, Joan names her sister Carmen as Pierre's alternate beneficiary.

If you name multiple beneficiaries to receive property, you can name an alternate for each beneficiary.

EXAMPLE: Gideon leaves his house to his three nephews—Aaron, Thomas and Zeke—in equal shares. In case Aaron does not survive him by 45 days, Gideon specifies that the house should then go to the survivors, Thomas and Zeke. In case Thomas does not survive him by 45 days, Gideon names his brother Horace to take Thomas's share. In case Zeke does not survive him by 45 days, Gideon specifies that Aaron and Horace should take Zeke's share.

If you do not name alternates for specific bequests, and the primary beneficiary dies before you do, the property will become part of your residuary estate.

Reviewing Specific Bequests

When you complete a specific bequest—that is, you have identified the property, named the beneficiary and named an alternate beneficiary—Quicken WillMaker Plus will display the beneficiary's name and the text of the bequest. From this screen you can edit or delete this bequest, or you can add a new one.

Naming Residuary Beneficiaries

Quicken WillMaker Plus will ask you to name a beneficiary for your residuary estate only if either of the following is true:

- You chose not to name one main beneficiary to receive most or all of your property.
- After leaving all your property to one beneficiary, you chose to create an alternate plan, or Plan B, in case your first choice does not survive you. In this case, you name a residuary beneficiary as part of your alternate plan.

If you left all or most of your property to one or more beneficiaries, they will receive property that does not pass in a specific bequest or by means other than your will. In effect, they will automatically become your residuary beneficiaries.

EXAMPLE: When Mikki makes her will, she leaves all her property to her husband, Tyler. By the time she dies, 15 years later, she has acquired a new car, stocks and other items. Everything goes to her husband.

What a Residuary Beneficiary Receives

Your residuary beneficiary receives anything that does not go, for one reason or another, to the beneficiaries you named to receive specific bequests.

Specifically, the residuary beneficiary receives property that:

- you overlook when making your will
- you acquire after you make your will, and
- does not go to the person you named to get it in a specific bequest—for example, because that person died before you did and you did not name an alternate beneficiary, or the alternate also failed to survive you.

EXAMPLE: In her will, Sara, a widow, leaves many different items to many different beneficiaries: books to her daughter, jewelry to a friend, a car to her nephew and so on. She doesn't name alternate beneficiaries for these specific bequests, but she names her daughter as residuary beneficiary.

When Sara dies, some years after making the will, the friend to whom she left the jewelry has already died. The jewelry goes to Sara's daughter, as does any other property that Sara acquired since making her will.

There is no need to describe, in your will, the property the residuary beneficiary will receive. By definition, your residuary estate is the rest of your property that does not pass outside of your will or in a specific bequest, so it is impossible to know exactly what it will include. When your executor inventories your entire estate after your death, he or she will identify your residuary estate.

How to Name Residuary Beneficiaries

You can name one or more individuals or organizations, or a combination of both, as residuary beneficiaries. If you name more than one residuary beneficiary, Quicken WillMaker Plus will ask you what shares you want each to receive.

> **EXAMPLE:** After making a large number of specific bequests in his Quicken WillMaker Plus will, Maurice leaves his residuary estate to his four children, Clara, Heinrich, Lise and Wiebke. He wants Lise and Wiebke each to receive 30% (3/10) of the property and the other two children to each receive 20% (2/10) each. So, he indicates that he wants to leave the residuary estate in unequal shares and enters the desired shares on the screen provided for this purpose.

If any of the beneficiaries you name is a minor (under 18) or young adult (under 35), you will have a chance, in a later part of Quicken WillMaker Plus, to choose someone to manage the property for them until they are older. (See Chapter 7.)

Naming Alternates

Quicken WillMaker Plus also asks you to choose an alternate residuary beneficiary, in case your first choice does not survive you by 45 days.

If you do not name alternates for specific bequests, and the primary beneficiary dies before you do, the property will become part of your residuary estate.

> **EXAMPLE 1:** After making many specific bequests, Alfredo leaves his residuary estate to his daughter, Vanessa. He then specifies that if Vanessa does not survive him, her share should go to her two children—Alfredo's grandchildren in equal shares. If Vanessa does not survive Alfredo, and Alfredo does not write a new will, Vanessa's children would each take one-half of Alfredo's residuary estate.

EXAMPLE 2: Jack makes a large number of specific bequests to friends and relatives and then leaves his residuary estate to his friend, Joe. He names another friend, Josette, as alternate residuary beneficiary. Josette will be entitled to take property under Jack's will only if Joe does not survive Jack by 45 days and there is property left over after the specific bequests are distributed.

Naming a Trust as Beneficiary

If you like, you can also name a trust as a beneficiary of your will. When you die, the property you leave will be transferred to the trust, rather than directly to a person or organization. This is generally done for one of two reasons—either you want all of the property that passes through your will to "pour" into your living trust, or you want to leave property to a loved one's "special needs trust."

Leaving property to a living trust with a pour-over will. If you have a living trust, you can use your will to transfer property to the trust after your death. If the primary purpose of your will is to funnel property to a living trust, the will is called a "pour-over" will.

Making a pour-over will means you don't have to transfer every minor asset into your living trust. Also, if you name your trust as the sole beneficiary or the residuary beneficiary of your will, the pour-over will covers any property that you might have neglected to transfer to the trust during your life.

But there's one important thing to keep in mind when you make a pour-over will: The property you leave through the will may have to go through probate when you die. Because living trusts are designed to avoid probate, if you leave too much property through your will, you may end up thwarting your own best intentions.

Most people who make a pour-over will leave most or all of their property through the living trust or through other beneficiary designations (such as life insurance), so that very little property ends up passing through the will. Whatever approach you take, before you make a pour-over will, be sure you know how much property your state allows you to pass through your will without triggering probate proceedings. (For more information about probate and how to avoid it, see Chapter 13.)

To leave property to your living trust using Quicken WillMaker Plus, name your trust as beneficiary for that property, using the trustee's name and the name of the trust (for example: "John Doe as trustee of the John Doe Living Trust, dated January 1, 20xx").

Leaving property to a special needs trust. Special needs trusts allow people with disabilities to receive additional support without risking their eligibility for government benefits. Money or property given directly to people with disabilities is likely to interfere with their ability to receive disability benefits. For this reason, if a loved one has a special needs trust, you may want to name that trust as a beneficiary of your will. To name a special needs trust as a beneficiary of your will using Quicken using WillMaker Plus, enter the name of the trustee and the full legal name of the trust as beneficiary (for example, "James Leung as the trustee of The Eric Workman Special Needs Trust").

Providing Management for Children's Property

E xcept for items of little value, minors are not permitted by law to receive property directly. This legal rule is most important if the property is:

- cash or other liquid assets—for example, a savings account that can easily be spent, or
- property that comes with a title document—for example, real estate.

Instead, that property will have to be distributed to and managed by a responsible adult. It is of vital importance—both to your own children and any other young beneficiaries—that you arrange for this management yourself, in your will. If you don't, a court may need to appoint and supervise someone—an expensive and time-consuming alternative. It's better to make your own choice and state it in your will, instead of leaving the decision to someone else.

> **TIP**
>
> **Keeping track of children's property.** The person you name to take care of your child's property will need access to financial records related to property that the child will own. For help collecting this information, use the Quicken WillMaker Plus Information for Caregivers and Survivors form.

Property management consists of naming a trusted adult to care for a young person's property until the minor turns a specific age. The property being managed must be held, invested or spent in the best interest of the minor. In other words, someone other than the young person will decide if his or her inheritance will be spent on college tuition or a new sports car.

With Quicken WillMaker Plus you can establish management for two types of property:

- property that passes to minors under your will (they do not have to be your own children), and
- property that passes to your minor children outside of your will.

For property received under your will, this management may last until the minor turns an age you choose (up to age 35). For property that your minor children receive outside of your will, the management provided by Quicken WillMaker Plus lasts until the children become adults—18 years old in most states.

Explaining Your Bequests to Your Children

Using Quicken WillMaker Plus, you are free to divide your property among your children as you see fit. If your children are already responsible adults, your prime concern will likely be fairness—given the circumstances and the children's needs. Often, this will mean dividing your property equally among your children. Sometimes, however, the special health or educational needs of one child, the relative affluence and stability of another or the fact that you are estranged from a child will be the impetus for you to divide the property unevenly.

Doing this can sometimes raise serious angst; a child who receives less property may conclude that you cared for him or her less. To clear up confusion, you may wish to explain your choices. Because of the risk of adding illegal or confusing language, Quicken WillMaker Plus does not allow you to make this explanation in your will. Fortunately, there is a sound and sensible way to express your reasons and feelings. Simply prepare a separate letter to accompany your will. (See Chapter 12.)

What Happens If the Minor Does Not Get Property

If you arrange for property management for a minor, but the minor never actually becomes entitled to the property, no harm is done. The management provisions for that minor are ignored. For instance, suppose you identify a favorite niece to take property as an alternate beneficiary and provide management for that property until the niece turns 25. If the niece never gets to take the property because your first-choice beneficiary survives you, no property management will be established for her, since none will be needed.

Property Management for Property That Passes Under Your Will

Quicken WillMaker Plus offers three approaches to property management for property that passes to minors under your will:

- the Uniform Transfers to Minors Act, an option in all states except South Carolina and Vermont
- the Quicken WillMaker Plus child's trust, an alternative to the UTMA and an option for will makers who live in one of the two states that have not adopted the UTMA, and
- the Quicken WillMaker Plus pot trust, an option if you have two or more children and at least one of your children is younger than 25 years old.

The Uniform Transfers to Minors Act

The Uniform Transfers to Minors Act (UTMA) allows you to name a custodian to manage property you leave to a minor. The management ends when the minor reaches age 18 to 25, depending on state law.

States are free to adopt or reject the UTMA, which is a model law proposed by a group of legal scholars. All but two states have adopted the UTMA, many making minor changes to it. It is likely that the UTMA will be universally adopted in a few more years.

If the UTMA has been adopted in your state, you may use it to specify a custodian to manage property you leave to a minor in your will until the age at which the laws of your state require that it be turned over to the minor. Depending on your state, this varies from 18 to 25. Quicken WillMaker Plus keeps track of the state you indicate as your residence and tells you whether the UTMA is available and, if so, the age at which property management under it must end.

Age Limits for Property Management in UTMA States

State	Age at Which Minor Gets Property	State	Age at Which Minor Gets Property
Alabama	21	Missouri	21
Alaska	18 to 25	Montana	21
Arizona	21	Nebraska	21
Arkansas	18 to 21	Nevada	18 to 25
California	18 to 25	New Hampshire	21
Colorado	21	New Jersey	18 to 21
Connecticut	21	New Mexico	21
Delaware	21	New York	21
District of Columbia	18 to 21	North Carolina	18 to 21
Florida	21	North Dakota	21
Georgia	21	Ohio	18 to 21
Hawaii	21	Oklahoma	18 to 21
Idaho	21	Oregon	21 to 25
Illinois	21	Pennsylvania	21 to 25
Indiana	21	Rhode Island	21
Iowa	21	South Dakota	18
Kansas	21	Tennessee	21 to 25
Kentucky	18	Texas	21
Maine	18 to 21	Utah	21
Maryland	21	Virginia	18 to 21
Massachusetts	21	Washington	21 or 25
Michigan	18 to 21	West Virginia	21
Minnesota	21	Wisconsin	21
Mississippi	21	Wyoming	21

States That Have Not Adopted the UTMA

The UTMA has not been adopted in South Carolina or Vermont.

If you are a resident of one of these states, you can set up property management for any minor or young adult beneficiary using the Quicken WillMaker Plus child's trust, discussed below. If you have two or more children and at least one of them is under 25 years old, you may also use the Quicken WillMaker Plus pot trust, discussed below.

Among the powers the UTMA gives the custodian are the rights to collect, hold, manage, invest and reinvest the property and to spend it "for the use and benefit of the minor." All of these actions can be taken without getting approval from a court. The custodian must also keep records so that tax returns can be filed on behalf of the minor and must otherwise act prudently in controlling the property.

Special Rule for Life Insurance

Often the major source of property left to children comes from a life insurance policy naming the children as beneficiaries. If you want the insurance proceeds for a particular child to be managed, and you live in a state that has adopted the UTMA, instruct your insurance agent to provide you with the form necessary to name a custodian to manage the property for the beneficiary under the terms of this act.

The Quicken WillMaker Plus Child's Trust

The Quicken WillMaker Plus child's trust, which can be used in all states, is a legal structure you establish in your will. If you create a trust, any property a minor beneficiary gets will be managed by a person or an institution you choose to serve as trustee until the beneficiary turns an age you choose—through age 35. The trustee's powers are listed in your will. The trustee may use trust assets for the education, medical needs and living expenses of the beneficiary. All property you leave to a beneficiary for whom a trust is established will be managed under the terms of the trust.

Because management under the Quicken WillMaker Plus child's trust can be extended through age 35, it is also suitable to use for property left to young adults. (The pros and cons of management options are discussed in "Choosing Among Management Options," below.)

The Quicken WillMaker Plus Pot Trust

The Quicken WillMaker Plus pot trust is a legal structure you can establish in your will. However, instead of creating a separate child's trust for the property you leave to each child, you create one trust for all the property you leave to your children. You name a single trustee to manage the property for the benefit of the children as a group, without regard to how much is spent on an individual child.

For example, if there are three children and one of them needs an expensive medical procedure, all of the property could be spent on that child, even though the other children would receive nothing. While this potential result may seem unfair, it, in fact, mirrors the reality faced by many families: Some children need more money than others.

The pot trust will last until the youngest child turns an age you specify, up to age 25. A word of caution: if there is a significant age gap between your children, the oldest children may have to wait many years past the time they become adults before they receive their shares of the property. For instance, if one of your children is five and another child is 17—and you specify that the pot trust should end when the youngest turns 18—the 17-year-old will have to wait at least until age 30 to receive a share of the property left in the trust.

> CAUTION
>
> **All or none must go in the pot.** The Quicken WillMaker Plus pot trust option is available only for property you leave to all of your children as a group. If you want to use the pot trust for some but not all of your children, you will need to see a lawyer. (See Chapter 17.)

> ## When Will Property Management End?
>
> The age at which property management ends depends on the type of management you select.
>
> - **UTMA.** State law determines when property management ends. In some states, you may choose from a limited age range. See "The Uniform Transfers to Minors Act," above.
> - **Quicken WillMaker Plus child's trust.** The trust ends when the child turns an age you choose, up to age 35.
> - **Quicken WillMaker Plus pot trust.** The trust ends when your youngest child turns an age you choose, up to age 25.
> - **Other property management.** Property management for property your child receives outside of your will ends when the child becomes a legal adult—age 18 in most states.

Choosing Among Management Options

For each minor or young adult to whom you leave property in your will, you must decide which management approach to use: the UTMA, a child's trust or the pot trust. This section helps you decide which is best.

 SEE AN EXPERT

Needs not covered by Quicken WillMaker Plus. The property management features offered by Quicken WillMaker Plus—the UTMA, child's trust and pot trust—provide the property manager with broad management authority adequate for most minors and young adults. However, they are not designed to:

- provide skilled, long-term management of a business
- provide for management of funds beyond age 35 for a person with spendthrift tendencies or other personal habits that may impede sound financial management beyond young adulthood, or
- meet the special needs of beneficiaries who have disabilities. A physical, mental or developmental disability will likely require management

customized to the beneficiary's circumstances, both to perpetuate the beneficiary's way of life and to preserve the property, while assuring that the beneficiary continues to qualify for government benefits.

To learn more about preparing trusts for people with disabilities, read *Special Needs Trusts* (Nolo), by Stephen Elias and Kevin Urbatsch. For other situations described here, consult an experienced estate planning attorney. (See Chapter 17.)

Using the UTMA

As a general rule, the less valuable the property involved and the more mature the child, the more appropriate the UTMA is, because it is simpler to use than a child's trust or pot trust. There are a couple of reasons for this.

Because the UTMA is built into state law, banks, insurance companies, brokerage firms and other financial institutions know about it, so it should be easy for the custodian to carry out property management duties. To set up a child's trust or pot trust, the financial institution would have to be given a copy of the trust document and may tie up the proceeding in red tape to be sure the trustee is acting under its terms.

Also, a custodian acting under the UTMA need not file a separate income tax return for the property being managed; it can be included in the young beneficiary's return. However, in a child's trust or a pot trust, both the beneficiary and the trust must file returns.

Because the UTMA requires that management end at a relatively young age, if the property you are leaving is worth $100,000 or less—or if the child is likely to be able to handle more than that by age 21 (25 in Alaska, California, Nevada, Oregon, Pennsylvania, Tennessee or Washington)—use the UTMA. After all, $100,000 is likely to be used up before management under the UTMA ends.

Using the Quicken WillMaker Plus Child's Trust

Generally, the more property is worth, and the less mature the young beneficiary, the better it is to use the child's trust, even though doing so creates more work for the property manager than does the UTMA.

For example, in a child's trust, the property manager must keep the beneficiary informed, manage trust assets prudently (meeting the requirements of state law) and file a separate tax return for the trust each year.

However, if a minor or young adult stands to get a fairly large amount of property—such as $100,000 or more—you might not want it all distributed by your state's UTMA cutoff age, which is usually 18, 21 or 25. In such circumstances, you may be better off using the Quicken WillMaker Plus child's trust. Under the child's trust, management can last until an age you choose, to age 35.

Choosing an age for a particular beneficiary to get whatever trust property has not been spent on the beneficiary's needs will depend on:
- the amount of money or other property involved
- how much control you would like to impose over it
- the beneficiary's likely level of maturity as a young adult (for small children, this may be difficult to predict, but by the time youngsters reach their teens, you should have a pretty good indication), and
- whether the property you leave, such as rental property or a small business, needs sophisticated management that a young beneficiary is unlikely to master.

Using the Quicken WillMaker Plus Pot Trust

As a general rule, the pot trust makes sense only when you have two or more children and they are young and fairly close in age. For instance, if your children are ages two and 20, and you specify that the pot trust should end when the younger child turns 18, the 20-year-old would have to wait until age 36 to receive the property. However, the pot trust option is available to you as long as any of your children is under age 25.

Like the trustee of a child's trust, a pot trust trustee must invest trust assets following the rules set out in state law, communicate regularly with the trust beneficiaries to keep them informed and file annual tax returns. The trustee of the pot trust also has the significant added responsibility of weighing competing claims from the children when deciding how to spend trust assets.

Property Management for Property That Does Not Pass Under Your Will

The UTMA, Quicken WillMaker Plus child's trust and pot trust are good management options for property that minor or young adult beneficiaries receive under your will. However, if you have minor children and they receive property of significant value outside of your will, a court will usually have to step in and appoint a guardian to manage the property under court supervision until the children turn 18.

The two most common ways that children receive property outside of a will are from life insurance or through a living trust. (See Chapter 13.) While it is possible to provide for management of this type of property through your life insurance agent under the UTMA or within the living trust itself, often no such management is established and a property guardianship is required.

In addition, property that your children receive from other sources—the lottery, a gift from an aunt or uncle or earnings from playing in a rock band—may also need to be managed by a property guardian.

It is always better to specify who will manage any such property that your minor children come to own. Otherwise, the court will appoint someone who may or may not have your children's best interests in mind.

If you are using the Quicken WillMaker Plus child's trust, a pot trust or the UTMA to provide management for property you are leaving to your children in your will, the person you have named as trustee or custodian would also be a good choice for property guardian. Another possible choice is the person you chose to be personal guardian, if you think he or she will handle the property wisely for the benefit of the minor. You also may wish to choose someone else entirely. Next, we offer some tips to help you pick the right person.

Naming a Property Manager

You may name one person to manage the property of a minor. You can also name one alternate (sometimes called "successor"), who will take over if your first choice is unable to serve.

Choosing a property manager is an important decision. Name someone you trust, who is familiar with property management and who shares your attitudes and values about how the money should be spent.

> ! CAUTION
>
> **Parents do not get the job automatically.** You may be surprised to learn that the child's other parent probably will not be able to automatically step in and handle property you leave your children in your will. Rather, unless you provide for management in your will, that other parent usually will have to petition the court to be appointed as the property manager and then handle the property under court supervision until the children turn 18. So, if you want your children's other parent to manage the property you are leaving your children, name that person to manage your children's property.
>
> Keep in mind that you can only name the other parent as custodian or trustee if there is a chance that the other parent will be alive when the child receives the gift. For example, if you leave a gift to the other parent and you name the child as alternate for that gift, you cannot name the other parent to be trustee or custodian of that gift because the child would only receive the property if the other parent is not alive.

Whomever you choose, it is essential to get his or her consent first. This will also give you a chance to discuss, in general terms, how you would like the property to be managed to be sure the manager you select agrees with your vision and fully understands the beneficiary's needs.

The next sections offer tips on choosing the right property manager. In most situations, a trusted adult will be the best choice, but in some rare cases, you may want to name an institution, such as a bank.

Choosing a Property Manager

As a general rule, name a trusted adult who lives in or near to the state where the property will be managed—or is at least be willing to travel there if needed.

You need not worry about finding a financial wizard to be your property manager because that person will have the power to hire professionals to prepare accountings and tax returns and to give investment advice. Anyone hired for such help may be paid out of the property being managed. The main job is to manage the property honestly, make basic decisions about how to take care of the assets wisely and sensibly mete out the money to the trust beneficiary.

It is usually preferable to combine the personal care and property management functions for a particular minor child in the hands of one person. Think first who is likely to be caring for the children if you die, and then consider whether that person is also a good choice for property manager.

If you believe that the person who will be caring for the minor is not the best person to handle the minor's finances, consider another adult who is capable and is willing to serve. If you must name two different people, try to choose people who get along well because they will have to work together.

For property you leave to young adults who are too old to have a person guardian, select an honest person with business savvy to manage the property.

> **EXAMPLE:** Orenthal and Ariadne agree that Ariadne's sister, Penny, should be guardian of their kids should they both die, but that the $200,000 worth of stock the three kids will inherit might better be handled by someone with more business experience and who will be better able to resist the children's urgings to spend the money frivolously. In each of their wills, they name Penny as personal guardian of the children, but also create trusts for the property they are leaving to their children. They name each other as trustees and Orenthal's mother, Phyllis, who has investment and

business knowledge and lots of experience in handling headstrong adolescents, as the alternate trustee, after obtaining her consent. Orenthal and Ariadne also decide that one of their children, who is somewhat immature, should receive his share of the estate—at least the portion not already disbursed for his benefit by the trustee—upon turning 25, and the other two children should get their shares when they turn 21.

Selecting an Institution as Trustee

If you are using the UTMA, you must name a person as custodian; you cannot name an institution. If you're creating a trust, you can name an institution to serve as trustee, but it is rarely a good idea. Most banks will not accept a trust with less than several hundred thousand dollars' worth of liquid assets.

When banks do agree to take a trust, they charge large management and administrative fees. All trustees are entitled to reasonable compensation for their services—paid from trust assets. But family members or close friends who act as trustees often waive payments or accept far less than banks. If you cannot find an individual you think is suitable for handling your assets and do not have enough property to be managed by a financial institution, you may be better off not creating a trust.

Also, it is common for banks to manage the assets of all trusts worth less than $1 million as part of one large fund, while charging fees as if they were individually managed. Any noninstitutional trustee who invests trust money in a conservatively run mutual fund can normally do at least as well at a fraction of the cost.

Examples of Property Management

Here are some examples of how the Quicken WillMaker Plus property management options might be selected. The following scenarios are only intended as suggestions. Remember, if you live in South Carolina or Vermont, you cannot create an UTMA custodianship.

EXAMPLE 1: Married, adult children age 25 and older. You want to leave all your property, worth $250,000, to your spouse and name surviving children as alternate beneficiaries. As long as you think the children are all sufficiently mature to handle their shares of the property if your spouse does not survive you, answer no when Quicken WillMaker Plus asks if you wish to set up property management.

EXAMPLE 2: Married, children aged two, five and nine. You want to leave all your property, which is worth $250,000, to your spouse and name your children as alternate beneficiaries. You use the property management feature and select the UTMA option to manage the property if it passes to your children. You name your wife's mother—the same person you have named as personal guardian—as custodian, and name your brother as alternate personal guardian and alternate custodian. The property will be managed by the custodian until the age set by your state's law.

You also name your wife's mother as property guardian if management is needed for property your minor children receive outside of your will.

Later, when your children are older and you have accumulated more property, you may wish to make a new will and switch from the UTMA management approach to a pot trust so that the property can be used to meet the children's needs as required.

EXAMPLE 3: Single or married; two minor children from a previous marriage and one minor child with your present partner. You want to leave all your property, which is worth $250,000, directly to your children. You can use the UTMA, set up the trust for each child or create a pot trust. You should also name a property guardian to manage any property your minor child might get outside of your will. Consider naming your spouse to manage the children's property, and choose another trusted adult as an alternate.

> ⊘ **CAUTION**
>
> **Beware property rights of spouses and domestic partners.** If you are married or in a registered domestic partnership, your spouse or partner may have a right to claim a portion of your property, so it is usually unwise to leave it all to your children unless your spouse or partner agrees with that plan. (See "Property Ownership Rules for Married People" in Chapter 5.)

EXAMPLE 4: Single or married; two adult children from a previous marriage—ages 23 and 27—and one minor child with your present partner. You decide to divide $300,000 equally among the children. To accomplish this, you establish a trust for each child from the previous marriage and put the termination age at 30. You name your current spouse, who gets along well with the children, as trustee and a local trust company as alternate trustee. Because your third child is an unusually mature teenager, you choose the UTMA for this child and select 21 as the age at which this child takes any remaining property outright. You appoint your wife as custodian and your sister as successor custodian.

EXAMPLE 5: Married or single; one daughter, age 32, and three minor grandchildren. You want to leave $50,000 directly to each of the grandchildren. You establish a custodianship under the UTMA for each grandchild and name your daughter as custodian and her husband as successor custodian.

Choosing an Executor

You should name an executor to wrap up your will. After your death, that person will have legal responsibility for safeguarding and handling your property, seeing that debts and taxes are paid and distributing what is left to your beneficiaries as your will directs.

Some states use the term "personal representative" instead of "executor," but it means the same thing. If you live in one of these states, you will see the term "personal representative" in your will.

> **TIP**
>
> **Make your will and records accessible.** You can help with the executor's first task: locating your will. Keep the original in a fairly obvious place—such as a desk or file cabinet. Make sure your executor knows where it is and has access to it.

Duties of an Executor

Serving as an executor can be fairly easy, or it can require a good deal of time and patience—depending on the amount of property involved and the complexity of the plans for it.

The Executor's Job

Your executor will have a number of duties, most of which do not require special expertise and can usually be accomplished without outside help. An executor typically must:

- obtain certified copies of the death certificate
- locate will beneficiaries
- examine and inventory the deceased person's safe deposit boxes
- collect the deceased person's mail
- cancel credit cards and subscriptions
- notify Social Security and other benefit plan administrators of the death
- learn about the deceased person's property—which may involve examining bankbooks, deeds, insurance policies, tax returns and many other records

- get bank accounts released or, in the case of pay-on-death accounts, get them transferred to their new owner, and
- collect any death benefits from life insurance policies, Social Security, veterans benefits and other benefits due from the deceased's union, fraternal society or employer.

In addition to these mundane tasks, the executor will typically have to:

- file papers in court to start the probate process and obtain the necessary authority to act as executor
- handle the probate court process—which involves transferring property and making sure the deceased's final debts and taxes are paid, and
- prepare final income tax forms for the deceased and, if necessary, file estate tax returns for the estate.

Note for Texas Residents: Independent Administration

Like many states, Texas offers a simplified probate process. In the Lone Star State, it's called "independent administration" and it gives an executor broad powers to act without supervision of the probate court. For example, an independent executor can pay final bills and distribute property without the court's oversight.

Unlike other states, Texas requires a will to contain a bit of special language to request this simplified process. That's why your Quicken WillMaker Plus will refers to your executor as your "independent executor" and includes the required language that permits the independent administration of your estate.

 SEE AN EXPERT

When to see a lawyer. We've designed your will to request independent administration because it saves money and speeds up probate. If you want your executor to work under the close supervision of a court, see an experienced estate planning attorney for advice.

For these tasks, it may be necessary to hire outside professionals who will be paid out of the estate's assets—a lawyer to initiate and handle the probate process and an accountant to prepare the necessary tax forms. But in some states, because of simplified court procedures and adequate self-help law materials, even these tasks can be accomplished without outside assistance.

For help with the task of educating your executor, you can print out documents titled Letter to Executor and Letter to Alternative Executor, which you can give to those you name to serve. These documents offer guidance on the executor's duties.

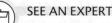

RESOURCE

More help for executors. For a complete guide to an executor's duties and details about how to wrap up an estate, see *The Executor's Guide: Settling a Loved One's Estate or Trust*, by Mary Randolph (Nolo).

Posting a Bond

Sometimes, a probate court asks an executor to post a bond—an insurance policy that protects beneficiaries if the executor is dishonest or incompetent. Some probate courts require bonds for all executors, while others only require bonds for out-of-state executors. However, many courts won't demand a bond if the will says that no bond is required.

The will you make with Quicken WillMaker Plus expressly states that no bond is necessary. As long as you choose an executor you trust, there's no reason to require your executor to post a bond. Furthermore, the cost of the bond—usually about 10% of its face amount—comes out of your estate, so your beneficiaries receive less than they would if no bond was purchased.

SEE AN EXPERT

If you want to require a bond. If you're less than confident about your executor's competence or you feel that the extra insurance of a bond is worth the cost, see an experienced estate planning attorney who can draft your will to require your executor to post a bond.

Getting Paid

The laws of every state provide that an executor may be paid out of the estate. Depending on your state law, this payment may be:

- based on what the court considers reasonable
- a small percentage of the gross or net value of the estate, or
- set according to factors specified in your state's statutes.

An executor who either stands to get a large portion of the estate or is a close family relative commonly does the work without being paid. Some will makers opt to leave their executors a specific bequest of money in appreciation for serving.

However, outside experts will almost always be paid out of the estate. The amount experts—including lawyers—are paid is totally under the control of the executor. However, a few states set out fees that may be charged by lawyers and other professionals—usually a percentage of the value of the estate.

> **CAUTION**
>
> **Beware of lawyers' fees.** Lawyers commonly imply that the fee allowed by statute is the fee that they are required to charge for their services. In fact, lawyers are perfectly free to charge by the hour or to set a flat fee that is unrelated to the size of the estate. One of the most important tasks that your executor can perform is to negotiate a reasonable fee with any lawyer he or she may pick to help probate your estate. Be sure you explain this to your choice for executor.

Naming an Executor

Glancing through the list of the executor's duties mentioned above should tip you off about who might be the best person for the job.

The prime characteristics are honesty, skill at organizing and finesse in keeping track of details. For many tasks, such as collecting mail and finding important records and papers, it may be most helpful to name someone who lives nearby or who is familiar with your business matters.

Choosing Your Executor

The most important guideline in naming an executor is to choose someone you trust enough to have access to your personal records and finances after your death. Many people choose someone who is also named to get a substantial amount of property under the will. This is sensible, because a person with an interest in how your property is distributed—a spouse, partner, child or close family member—is also likely to do a conscientious job as executor. And he or she will probably also come equipped with knowledge of where your records are kept and an understanding of why you want your property split up as you have directed.

Following are a few more things you may want to consider when making your choice. Whomever you choose, make sure the person you select is willing to do the job. Discuss the possible duties involved with your choice for executor before naming him or her in your will.

Naming Someone Who Lives Out of State

As a practical matter, it's wise to name an executor who lives close to you. It will be more difficult for the executor to handle day-to-day matters from a distance. But if the best person for the job lives far away, there's no law against naming that person in your will. Every state allows out-of-state executors to serve, though most states impose special rules on them. The table below sets out the details.

Naming More Than One Person

While you may name two executors or two alternate executors to serve together, doing so is often not wise. Joint executors may act without each other's consent—and if they ever disagree, your estate may be the loser because of lengthy probate delays and court costs.

Restrictions on Out-of-State Executors	
Alabama	Nonresident can be appointed executor only if already serving as executor of same estate in another state. (Ala. Code § 43-2-22)
Arkansas	Nonresident executor must appoint an in-state agent to accept legal papers. (Ark. Code Ann. § 28-48-101(b)(6))
Connecticut	Nonresident executor must appoint in-state probate court judge as agent to accept legal papers. (Conn. Gen. Stat. Ann. § 52-60)
Delaware	Nonresident executor must appoint county Register of Wills as the agent to accept legal papers. (Del. Code Ann. Tit. 12, § 1506)
District of Columbia	Nonresident executor must publish notices in a newspaper and appoint the probate register as agent to accept legal papers. (D.C. Code Ann. §§ 20-303, 20-343)
Florida	Nonresident can be appointed executor only if he or she is related by blood, marriage or adoption to person making will. (Fla. Stat. Ann. § 733.304)
Illinois	Nonresident executor may be required to post bond, even if will expressly states bond not required. (755 Ill. Comp. Stat. § 5/6-13)
Indiana	Nonresident can serve as executor if resident appointed coexecutor and nonresident posts a bond. Nonresident can serve alone if he or she posts a bond, files a written notice of acceptance and appoints an in-state agent to accept legal papers. (Ind. Code Ann. § 29-1-10-1)
Iowa	Nonresident can serve as executor only if resident appointed coexecutor, unless court allows nonresident to serve alone. (Iowa Code § 633.64)
Kansas	Nonresident executor must appoint an in-state agent to accept legal papers. (Kan. Stat. Ann. § 59-1706)
Kentucky	Nonresident can be appointed executor only if he or she is related by blood, marriage or adoption to person making will. (Ky. Rev. Stat. Ann. § 395.005)

Restrictions on Out-of-State Executors (continued)	
Maryland	Nonresident executor must publish notices in a newspaper and appoint an in-state agent to accept legal papers. (Md. Code Ann. [Est. & Trusts]. §§ 5-105, 5-503)
Massachusetts	Nonresident executor must appoint an in-state agent to accept legal papers. (Mass. Gen. Laws ch. 195, § 8)
Missouri	Nonresident executor must appoint an in-state agent to accept legal papers. (Mo. Rev. Stat. § 473.117)
Nevada	Nonresident can serve as executor only with a resident coexecutor or with court approval. (Nev. Rev. Stat. Ann. § 139.010)
New Hampshire	Nonresident executor must be approved by probate judge and must appoint an in-state agent to accept legal papers. (N.H. Stat. §§ 553:5, 553:25)
New Jersey	Nonresident must post bond unless will waives the requirement. (N.J. Stat. Ann. § 3B:15-1)
North Carolina	Nonresident executor must appoint an in-state agent to accept legal papers. (N.C. Gen. Stat. § 28A-4-2)
Ohio	Nonresident can be appointed executor only if he or she is related by blood, marriage or adoption to person making will—or if he or she lives in a state that permits nonresidents to serve. (Ohio Rev. Code Ann. § 2109.21)
Oklahoma	Nonresident executor must appoint an in-state agent to accept legal papers. (Okla. Stat. Ann. tit. 58, § 162)
Pennsylvania	Nonresident can serve as executor only with permission of register of wills. Nonresident executor must file an affidavit stating that estate has no known debts in Pennsylvania, and that he or she will not perform any duties prohibited in home state. (20 Pa. Cons. Stat. Ann. §§ 3157, 4101)
Rhode Island	Nonresident executor must be approved by a judge and must appoint an in-state agent to accept legal papers. (R.I. Gen. Laws §§ 33-8-7, 33-18-9)

Restrictions on Out-of-State Executors (continued)

Tennessee	Nonresident executor must appoint secretary of state as agent to accept legal papers and may be required to post bond. Nonresident can also serve if resident appointed coexecutor. (Tenn. Code Ann. § 35-50-107)
Texas	Nonresident executor must appoint an in-state agent to accept legal papers. (Tex. Prob. Code Ann. § 78)
Vermont	Nonresident executor must appoint an in-state agent to accept legal papers. Nonresident executor can be appointed only with court approval; court must approve nonresident executor upon request of surviving spouse or civil union partner, adult children or parents or guardians of minor children. (Vt. Stat. Ann. tit. 14, § 904)
Virginia	Nonresident executor must post a bond and appoint an in-state agent to accept legal papers. Bond without a guarantee is permitted. (Va. Code Ann. § 26-59)
Washington	Nonresident executor must post a bond and appoint an in-state agent to accept legal papers. If nonresident is surviving spouse and sole beneficiary of will, or if will expressly states so, bond is not required. (Wash. Rev. Code Ann. §§ 11.28.185, 11.36.010)
West Virginia	Nonresident executor may serve if clerk of the county commission of the county where the probate is conducted serves as nonresident's agent. Nonresident must post bond unless will says otherwise. (W.Va. Code Ann. § 44-5-3)
Wisconsin	Nonresident executor must appoint an in-state agent to accept legal papers. At court's discretion, nonresident executor can be removed or refused appointment solely on grounds of residency. (Wis. Stat. Ann. § 856.23)
Wyoming	Nonresident executor must appoint an in-state agent to accept legal papers. (Wyo. Stat. § 2-11-301)

Naming an Institution

While it is almost always best to choose a trusted person for the job, you may not know anyone who is up to the task of winding up your estate—especially if your estate is large and complicated and your beneficiaries are either very old, very young or just inexperienced in financial matters. If so, you can select a professional management firm to act as your executor. (Banks often provide this service.)

If you are considering naming an institution as executor, be sure the one you choose is willing to accept the job—most won't unless your estate is fairly large. Also, institutions charge a hefty fee for acting as executor. They may charge both a percentage of the value of property to be managed and a number of smaller fees for routine services, such as buying and selling property.

If You Do Not Name an Executor

If you do not name an executor in your will, the document will still be valid. But your decision will not have been a wise one. It will most often mean that a court will have to scurry to come up with a willing relative to serve. If that fails, the court will probably appoint someone to do the job who is likely to be unfamiliar with you, your property and your beneficiaries. People appointed by the court to serve are usually called administrators.

The laws in many states provide that anyone who is entitled under the will to take over half a person's property has first priority to serve as executor. If no such person is apparent, courts will generally look for someone to serve among the following groups of people, in the following order:

- surviving spouse or registered domestic partner
- children
- grandchildren
- great-grandchildren
- parents
- brothers and sisters
- grandparents

- uncles, aunts, first cousins
- children of a deceased spouse or partner
- other next of kin
- relatives of a deceased spouse or partner
- conservator or guardian
- public administrator
- creditors, and
- any other person.

Naming an Alternate

In case you name someone to serve as executor who dies before you do or for any other reason cannot take on the responsibilities, you should name at least one alternate to serve instead.

You may name up to two levels of alternate executors—called your first alternate and second alternate:

- **First alternate.** Your first alternate will serve only if your primary executor(s) cannot. We recommend that you name just one person to serve as first alternate, but if you feel it is necessary, you may name two people to serve together. (See "Naming More Than One Person," above, for the pitfalls of naming coexecutors.)
- **Second alternate.** Your second alternate will serve only if your executor(s) and first alternate(s) cannot. You can name only one second alternate.

EXAMPLE: Marsha names Bill and Jane as her coexecutors. She then names Susan as first alternate and Keith as second alternate. When Marsha dies, if either Bill or Jane is unavailable to be the executor of her estate, the other will serve alone. If both Bill and Jane are unavailable, Susan will serve. In the unlikely event that Bill, Jane and Susan are all unavailable, it will be up to Keith to wrap up Marsha's estate.

In choosing an alternate executor, consider the same factors you did in naming your first choice. (See "Choosing Your Executor," above.)

Debts, Expenses and Taxes

Money matters have a way of living on—even after your death. But you can easily guide your survivors through the vexing process of dealing with your debts and expenses by including clear instructions in your will.

In your will, you can:

- forgive debts that others owed you during your lifetime
- designate what property should be used to pay debts you owe at death, and
- designate what property should be used to pay state and federal death taxes owed by your estate or due on the property in it.

> **TIP**
>
> **Keeping track of your debts, expenses and taxes.** At your death, your executor and other survivors may need to learn about the debts you owed and that others owed to you during your life. For help collecting and recording this information, use the Quicken WillMaker Plus Information for Caregivers and Survivors form.

Forgiving Debts Others Owe You

You can release anyone who owes you a debt from the responsibility of paying it back to your estate after you die. You can cancel any such debt—oral or written. If you do, your forgiveness functions much the same as giving a gift; those who were indebted to you will no longer be legally required to pay the money they owed.

Keep in mind that releasing people or institutions from the debts they owe you may diminish the property that your beneficiaries receive under your will.

Quicken WillMaker Plus prompts you to describe any debt you wish to cancel—including the name of the person who owes it, the approximate date the debt was incurred and the amount you wish to forgive. This information is important so that the debt can be properly identified.

Explaining Your Intention

If you forgive a debt, it is likely to come as a pleasant surprise to those living with the expectation that they must repay it. And you will probably give the gesture considerable thought before including such a direction in your will. While the final document will contain a brief clause stating your intention, you may wish to explain your reasoning beyond this bald statement. If you wish to do so, it is best to write your explanation in a brief letter that you attach to your will. (See Chapter 12.)

CAUTION

Caution for married or legally partnered people. If you want to use your will to forgive a debt and the debt was incurred while you were married or legally partnered, you may only have the right to forgive half the debt. There is a special need to be cautious about this possibility in community property states. If your debt is a community property debt, you cannot cancel the whole amount due unless your spouse or partner agrees to allow you to cancel his or her share of the debt—and puts that agreement in writing.

Liabilities at Your Death

If you live owing money, chances are you will die owing money. If you do, your executor will be responsible for rounding up your property and making sure all your outstanding debts are satisfied before any of the property is put in the hands of those you have named to get it. The property you own at your death—or your estate—may be liable for several types of debts, expenses and taxes.

Debts You Owe

When you leave this credit-happy world, you will likely go out with debts you have not fully paid—personal loans, credit card bills, mortgage loans or income taxes. Whether such debts pass to the beneficiary along with the property, or must be paid out of the estate, depends upon how the debt is characterized. (See "Types of Debts," below.)

Expenses Incurred After Your Death

There are several expenses incurred after you die—including the costs of a funeral, burial or cremation and probate—which may take your survivors by surprise if you do not plan ahead for paying them.

Funeral and burial expenses, for example, typically cost several thousand dollars. And for those who do not plan ahead, the costs may soar even higher. In addition, probate and estate administration fees typically run about 5% to 7% of the value of the property you leave to others in your will.

Estate and Inheritance Taxes

Estate tax is a concern for few people. The tax is levied on the property you own at death—but a large amount of property is exempt from taxation. (See "Estate and Inheritance Taxes," below.)

Unless you specify otherwise in your will, in most states, these taxes will normally be paid proportionately out of the estate's liquid assets. This means that a beneficiary's property will be reduced by the percentage that the property bears to the total liquid assets. Liquid assets include bank accounts, money market accounts and marketable securities. Real estate and tangible personal property, such as cars, furniture and antiques are not included. This could cause a problem if, for example, you left your bank account with $50,000 in it to a favorite nephew and your tax liability—most of which resulted from valuable real property left to another beneficiary—gobbled up all or most of it.

Quicken WillMaker Plus provides several options for dealing with any estate or inheritance taxes your estate may owe. See "Estate and Inheritance Taxes," below."

When You Need Not Worry—And When You Should

Typically, you do not need to leave instructions about debts if any of the following are true:

- Your debts and expenses are likely to be negligible—or to represent only a tiny fraction of a relatively large estate.
- You are leaving all your property to your spouse or partner or specifying that it should be shared among a very few beneficiaries, without dividing it into specific bequests.
- You understand and approve of how your state law deals with debts and expenses.

On the other hand, you may need to be concerned about covering your debts and death taxes when your will-making plan involves dividing up your property among a number of beneficiaries.

And you need to plan more carefully if debts payable by your estate are likely to be large enough to cut significantly into bequests left to individuals and charitable institutions. The danger, of course, is that unless you plan carefully, the people whose bequests are used to pay debts and expenses may be the very people whom you would have preferred to take your property free and clear.

EXAMPLE: Ruth has $40,000 in a money market account and several valuable musical instruments, also worth $40,000. She makes a will leaving the money market account to her daughter and the instruments to her musician son but does not specify how her debts and expenses should be paid. Due to medical bills and an unpaid personal loan from a friend, Ruth dies owing $35,000. After Ruth's death, her executor must follow state law, which first requires that debts be paid out of the residuary estate. But because there is no residuary—all property is used up by specific bequests—a second rule applies that requires that debts be paid out of liquid assets. As a result, the executor pays the $35,000 out of the money market account, leaving the daughter with only $5,000. The son receives the $40,000 worth of musical instruments.

Types of Debts

There are two basic kinds of debts to think about when making a will—secured and unsecured.

Secured Debts

Secured debts are any debts owed on specific property that must be paid before title to that property fully belongs to its owner.

One common type of secured debt occurs when a major asset, such as a car, appliance or business, is paid for over a period of time. Usually, the lender of credit will retain some measure of legal ownership in the asset—termed a security interest—until it is paid off.

Another common type of secured debt occurs when a lender, as a condition of the loan, takes a security interest in property already owned by the person applying for the money. For instance, most finance companies require their borrowers to agree to pledge "all their personal property" as security for the loan. The legal jargon for this type of security interest is a non-purchase-money secured debt—that is, the debt is incurred for a purpose other than purchasing the property that secures repayment.

Other common types of secured debts are mortgages and deeds of trust owed on real estate in exchange for a purchase or equity loan, tax liens and assessments that are owed on real estate and, in some instances, liens or legal claims on personal and real property created as a result of litigation or home repair.

If you are leaving property in your will that is subject to a secured debt, you may be concerned about whether the debt will pass to the beneficiary along with the property, or whether it must be paid by your estate.

Debts on Real Estate

Quicken WillMaker Plus passes all secured debts owed on real estate along with the real estate.

EXAMPLE 1: Paul owes $50,000 under a deed of trust on his home, signed as a condition of obtaining an equity loan. He leaves the home to his children. The deed of trust is a secured debt on real property and passes to the children along with the property.

EXAMPLE 2: Sonny and Cati, a married couple, borrow $100,000 from the bank to purchase their home and take out a deed of trust in the bank's favor as security for the loan. They still owe $78,000 and are two years behind in property tax payments. In separate wills, Sonny and Cati leave their ownership share to each other and name their children as alternates to take the home in equal shares. The deed of trust is a purchase money secured debt and, if the children get the property, they will also get the mortgage—and responsibility for paying the past-due amount in taxes.

When the Debt Exceeds the Property Value

Because the property is usually worth more than any debt secured by it, a person who takes the property at your death but does not want to owe money can sell the property, pay off the debt and pocket the difference. However, at times, relying on this approach is not satisfactory—especially when it comes to houses.

For example, if you leave your daughter your house with the hope that it will be her home, you will probably not want her to have to sell the house because she cannot meet the mortgage payments. If you think a particular beneficiary will need assistance with paying a debt owed on property, try to leave the necessary money or valuable assets to him or her as well.

Debts on Personal Property

All debts owed on personal property pass to the beneficiaries of the property.

EXAMPLE: Phil owns a Ferrari. Although the car is registered in Phil's name, the bank holds legal title pending Phil's payment of the outstanding $75,000 car note. Phil uses Quicken WillMaker Plus to leave the car to his companion, Paula. The car note is a secured debt and will pass to Paula with the car.

Unsecured Debts

Unsecured debts are all debts not tied to specific property. Common examples are medical bills, most credit card bills, utility bills and probate fees. Your executor must pay these debts and expenses out of property from your estate. A student loan is another common example of an unsecured debt. However, most student loans can be canceled if the borrower dies before the loan is paid off, so the borrower's estate will owe nothing.

Paying Debts and Expenses

Quicken WillMaker Plus offers two options for paying debts, including the expenses of probate. You can:

- designate a particular asset or assets to be used or sold to pay debts and expenses, or
- choose not to designate specific assets, which will mean that your executor will pay the debts and expenses as required by the laws of your state.

Designating Specific Assets

One helpful approach to taking care of debts and expenses is to designate one or more specific assets that your executor must use to pay them. For example, if you designate a savings or money market account to be used for paying off your debts and expenses, and the amount in the account is sufficient to meet these obligations, the other bequests you make in your will won't be affected by your estate's indebtedness.

If you select specific assets to pay your debts and expenses, you'll probably want to select liquid assets over nonliquid assets. Liquid assets are those easily converted into cash at full value: bank and deposit accounts, money market accounts, stocks and bonds. On the other hand, tangible assets, such as motor vehicles, planes, jewelry, stamp and coin collections, electronic items and musical instruments, must be sold to raise the necessary cash. Hurried sales seldom bring in anywhere near the full value, which means the net worth of your estate will also be reduced.

> **EXAMPLE:** Harry writes mystery books for a living. He has never produced a blockbuster but owns 15 copyrights, which produce royalties of about $70,000 a year. During his life, Harry has traveled widely and collected artifacts from around the world. They have a value of $300,000 if sold carefully to knowledgeable collectors. Harry makes a will leaving his copyrights to his spouse and the artifacts to his children. He also designates that the artifacts should be used to pay his debts and expenses—which total $150,000 at death. Harry's executor, who is not a collector and has little time or inclination to sell the artifacts one by one, sells them in bulk for $140,000—less than half of their true value. To raise the extra $10,000, two of the copyrights are sold, again at less than their true value. As a result, Harry's children receive nothing and his spouse gets less than Harry intended.

Avoid designating property you have left to specific beneficiaries. It is important to review your specific bequests before designating assets to pay debts and expenses. If possible, designate liquid assets that have not been left to specific beneficiaries. Only as a last resort should you earmark a tangible item also left in a specific bequest for first use to pay debts and expenses.

One exception to this general recommendation occurs if you believe you are unlikely to owe much when you die and that the expenses of probate will be low. Then, it makes sense for you to designate a substantial liquid asset left as a specific bequest to also pay debts and expenses.

Covering Your Debts With Insurance

One way to deal with the problem of large debts and small assets is to purchase a life insurance policy in an amount large enough to pay your anticipated debts and expenses and have the proceeds made payable to your estate. You can then specify in your will that these proceeds should be used to pay your debts and expenses—with the rest going to your residuary beneficiary or a beneficiary named in a specific bequest.

But be careful. If large sums are involved, talk with an estate planner or accountant before adopting this sort of plan. Having insurance money paid to your estate subjects that amount to probate. A better alternative may be to provide that estate assets be sold, with the proceeds used to pay the debts. Then have the insurance proceeds made payable directly to your survivors free of probate.

Of course, if the source you specify is insufficient to pay all the bills, your executor will still face the problem of which property to use to make up the difference. For this reason, it is often wise to list several resources and specify the order in which they should be used. Also, make sure that they are worth more than what is likely to be required.

EXAMPLE 1: Ella, a widow, makes a will that contains the following bequests:

- My house at 1111 Soto Street in Albany, New York, to Hillary Bernette. (The house has an outstanding mortgage of $50,000, for which Hillary will become responsible.)
- My coin collection (appraised at $30,000) to Stanley, Mark and Belinda Bernette.
- My three antique chandeliers to Herbert Perkins.
- The rest of my property to Denise Everread. Although not spelled out in the will, this property consists of a savings account ($26,000), a car ($5,000), a camera ($1,000) and stock ($7,000).

Using Quicken WillMaker Plus, Ella specifies that her savings account and stock be used in the order listed to pay debts and expenses. When Ella dies, she owes $8,000; the expenses of probating her estate total $4,000. Following Ella's instructions, her executor would close the savings account, use $12,000 of it to pay debts and expenses and turn the rest over to Denise along with the stock and camera.

EXAMPLE 2: Now suppose Ella has only $6,000 in the savings account. When she dies, her executor, following the same instructions, would close the account ($6,000) and sell enough stock to make up the difference ($6,000). The remaining $1,000 worth of stock, the camera and the car would pass to Denise.

> CAUTION
> **Describe property consistently.** If you designate property both as a specific bequest and as a source for paying your debts, be sure to describe it exactly the same in both instances to avoid confusion.

If You Don't Specify Assets

If you do not specify how you want your debts and expenses to be paid, your executor will need to follow your state's laws, and your Quicken WillMaker Plus will instructs him or her to do so.

Some states leave it up to your executor to make good decisions about how to pay your debts and expenses. Other states require that debts and expenses be paid first out of property in your estate that does not pass under your will. In other states, your debts and expenses must first be paid out of liquid assets, such as bank accounts and securities, then from tangible personal property and, as a last resort, from real estate.

Estate and Inheritance Taxes

Before you concentrate on how you want your estate or inheritance taxes to be paid, consider whether you need to be concerned about these types of taxes at all. Most people do not.

These taxes are imposed on the transfer of property after someone dies. Some people confuse probate-avoidance devices, such as living trusts and joint tenancy, with tax-savings. But avoiding probate does not reduce these taxes.

Whether or not your estate will be required to pay taxes depends on two factors:

• the value of your taxable estate—that is, your net estate minus any gifts or expenses that are tax exempt, and
• the laws of the state in which you live.

Federal Estate Taxes

Only a small fraction of estates end up owing federal estate tax. Primarily, that's because a large amount of property is exempt from the tax. For deaths in 2011 or 2012, the exemption is $5 million, so only estates worth more than $5 million will owe federal estate taxes.

Planning for estate taxes can be quite complicated. If you think your estate might be large enough to owe estate tax, see Chapter 13, which explains the system.

State Inheritance and Estate Taxes

State taxes normally do not take a deep enough bite to cause serious concern unless your estate is large. However, because of recent changes to federal and state tax laws, an increasing number of estates owe some state tax. (Some estates may have to pay state tax even if they aren't large enough to owe federal estate tax.) If you own a lot of property—say, more than $500,000 worth—and you're concerned about it, you may want to check with an estate planning or tax lawyer who can bring you up to date on the laws in your state.

SEE AN EXPERT

Getting help with large estates. As you might imagine, financial planning experts have devised many creative ways to plan for paying estate and inheritance taxes. If your estate is large enough to warrant concern about possible federal or state taxes, it is large enough for you to afford a consultation with an accountant, estate planning specialist or lawyer specializing in estates and trusts.

Choosing How to Pay Taxes

Quicken WillMaker Plus offers the following options for paying estate and inheritance taxes. You can:

- pay them from all property you own at death
- designate specific assets, or
- choose not to specify how your taxes will be paid, leaving that matter up to state law.

If the value of your estate is well below the federal and state estate tax range, and you have no reasonable expectation that your estate will grow much larger before your death, you may want to skip this discussion of your options for paying taxes and choose the option "Don't specify."

If you are a relatively young, healthy person and you expect your estate to owe only a small amount of tax, you may want to adopt one of the Quicken WillMaker Plus tax payment options now and worry about more sophisticated tax planning later. After all, by the time you die, federal and state tax rules may have changed many times.

Paying Taxes From All Property You Own

For the purpose of computing estate and inheritance tax liability, your estate consists of all property you legally own at your death, whether it passes under the terms of your will or outside of your will—such as a joint tenancy, living trust, savings bank trust or life insurance policy. Because your estate's tax liability will be computed on the basis of all this property, you may wish to have the beneficiaries of the property share proportionately in the responsibility for paying the taxes.

EXAMPLE: Julie Johanssen, a widow, owns a house (worth $1 million), stocks ($400,000), jewelry ($150,000) and investments as a limited partner in a number of rental properties ($900,000). To avoid probate, Julie puts the house in a living trust for her eldest son, Warren; puts the stocks in a living trust for another son, Alain; and uses her will to leave the jewelry to a daughter, Penelope, and the investments to her two surviving brothers, Sean and Ivan. She specifies that all beneficiaries of property in her taxable estate share in paying any estate and inheritance taxes.

When Julie dies, the net worth of her estate, which consists of all the property mentioned, is over the amount of the estate tax exemption in the year of her death, so there is federal estate tax liability.

Each of Julie's beneficiaries will be responsible for paying a portion of this liability. Each portion will be measured by the proportion that beneficiary's inheritance has to the estate as a whole.

Designating Specific Assets

As with payment of debts and expenses, it may be a good approach to designate one or more specific property items to satisfy the amount you owe in taxes. Again, if you designate a bank, brokerage or money market account to be used for paying taxes, and the amount in the account is adequate to meet these obligations, the other bequests you make in your will should not be affected.

Of course, if the resource you specify for payment of your estate and inheritance taxes is not sufficient to cover the amount due, your executor will still face the problem of which property will be used to make up the difference. So, again, it is a good idea to list several resources that should be used to pay estate and inheritance taxes.

> CAUTION
>
> **Guidance for selecting specific assets.** If you do choose to select specific assets to be used to pay your taxes, follow the general rules set out in "Paying Debts and Expenses," above.

If You Don't Specify a Method of Payment

If you choose this option, your will directs your executor to pay your estate and inheritance taxes as required by the laws of your state. As with your debts and expenses, your state law controls how your executor is to approach this issue if you do not establish your own plan. Some states leave the method of payment up to your executor, while others provide that all beneficiaries must share the tax burden. Depending on your financial and tax situation and the law of your state, more variables set in than can reasonably be covered here. If you are concerned about the possible legal repercussions of choosing this option, consider researching your state's law. (See Chapter 17.)

Make It Legal: Final Steps

Once you have proceeded through all the Quicken WillMaker Plus screens and responded to all the questions the program poses, your will is nearly finished. There are just a few more steps you must take to make it legally effective so that the directions you expressed in it can be carried out after your death.

No Accents or Umlauts

If your name contains accent marks, umlauts or other special characters, you can type them into Quicken WillMaker Plus. *However, those characters will not show up correctly in your printed document unless you change the default font* (Times New Roman). Common Windows fonts that will correctly print special characters include:

- Georgia (serif), and
- Verdana (sans serif).

For details on how to change the fonts of printed documents, see "Changing How Your Document Looks" in Part 4 of the Users' Manual. You can find the Users' Manual under the Help menu on any screen in the program.

Checking Your Will

Before you sign your will, take some time to scrutinize it and make sure it accurately expresses your wishes. You can do this either by previewing it in the program or by printing out a draft copy. (Consult the Users' Manual if you need additional guidance.)

Having an Expert Check Your Will

You may want to have your will checked by an attorney or a tax expert. This makes good sense if you are left with nagging questions about the legal implications of your choices, or if you own a great deal of property or have a complicated idea of how you want to leave it. But keep in mind that you are your own best expert on most issues and decisions involved in making a will—what property you own, your relation to family members and friends and your own favorite charities. Also, some attorneys don't support the self-help approach to making a will, so you may have to find one who is cooperative. (See Chapter 17.)

Signing and Witnessing Requirements

To be valid, a will must be legally executed. This means that you must sign your will in front of two witnesses. Each witness must sign the will not only in your presence, but also in the presence of the other witnesses.

Requirements for Witnesses

There are a few legal requirements for witnesses. The witnesses need to be of sound mind. In most states, the witnesses need to be 18 or older. Many states also require that the witnesses not be people who will take property under the will. Thus, we require that you not use as a witness someone to whom you leave property in your will, even as an alternate or residuary beneficiary.

As a matter of common sense, the people you choose to be witnesses should be easily available when you die. While this bit of future history is impossible to foretell with certainty, it is usually best to choose witnesses who are in good health, are younger than you are and likely to remain in your geographic area. However, the witnesses do not have to be residents of your state.

The Self-Proving Option

For a will to be accepted by a probate court, the executor must show that the document really is the will of the person it purports to be—a process called proving the will. In the past, all wills were proved either by having one or two witnesses come into court to testify or swear in written, notarized statements called affidavits that they saw you sign your will.

Today, most states allow people to make their wills self-proving—that is, they can be admitted in probate court without the hassle of herding up witnesses to appear in court or sign affidavits. This is accomplished when the person making the will and the witnesses all appear before a notary public and sign an affidavit under oath, verifying that all necessary formalities for execution have been satisfied.

If you live in a state that offers the self-proving option, Quicken WillMaker Plus automatically produces the correct affidavit for your state, with accompanying instructions. With the exception of New Hampshire, the self-proving affidavit is not part of your will, but a separate document. To use it, you and your witnesses must first sign the will as discussed above. Then, you and your witnesses must sign the self-proving affidavit in front of a notary public. This may be done any time after the will is signed but, obviously, it is easiest to do it while all your witnesses are gathered together to watch you sign your will. Most notaries will charge at least a minimal amount for their services—and will require you and your witnesses to present some identification verifying that you are who you claim to be.

Many younger people—who are likely to make a number of wills before they die—decide not to make their wills self-proving, due to the initial trouble of getting a notary at the signing. If you are one of these people, file the uncompleted affidavit and instructions in a safe place in case you change your mind later.

Note for California and Indiana Readers

In California or Indiana, the self-proving feature does not require a separate affidavit. Instead, the fact that the witnesses sign the will under the oath printed above their signatures is sufficient to have the will admitted into probate, unless a challenge is mounted. There is no need to take further steps to make a California or Indiana will self-proving.

States Without Self-Proving Laws

The self-proving option is not available in the District of Columbia, Maryland, Ohio or Vermont. In these states, your executor will be required to prove your will.

Signing Procedure

You need not utter any magic words when signing your will and having it witnessed, but a few legal requirements suggest the best way to proceed:

- Gather all witnesses together in one place.
- Inform your witnesses that the papers you hold in your hand are your last will and testament. This is important, because the laws in many states specifically require that you acknowledge the document as your will before the witnesses sign it. The witnesses need not read your will, however, and there is no need for them to know its contents. If you want to ensure that the contents of the will stay confidential, you may cover all but the signature portion of your will with a separate sheet of paper while the witnesses sign.
- Initial each page of the will at the bottom on the lines provided. The purpose of initialing is to prevent anyone from challenging the will as invalid on the grounds that changes were made to it by someone else.

- Sign the last page on the signature line while the witnesses watch. Use the same form of your name that you stated in your will.
- Ask each of the witnesses to initial the bottom of each page on a line there, then watch as they sign and fill in their addresses on the last page where indicated. Their initials act as evidence if anyone later claims you changed your will without going through the proper legal formalities.

Changing Your Quicken WillMaker Plus Will

Once you have signed your will and had it witnessed, it is extremely important that you do not alter it by inserting handwritten or typed additions or changes. Do not even correct misspellings. The laws of most states require that after a will is signed, any additions or changes to it, even clerical ones, must be made by following the same signing and witnessing requirements as for an original will.

Although it is legally possible to make handwritten corrections on your will before you sign it, that is a bad idea since, after your death, it will not be clear to the probate court that you made the corrections before the will was signed. The possibility that the changes were made later may throw the legality of the whole will into question.

If you want to make changes after your will has been signed and witnessed, there are two ways to accomplish it: You can either make a new will or make a formal addition, called a codicil, to the existing one. Either approach requires a new round of signing and witnessing.

One of the great advantages of Quicken WillMaker Plus is that you can conveniently keep current by simply making a new will. This does away with the need to tack on changes to the will in the form of a codicil and involves no need for additional gyrations. Codicils are not a good idea when using Quicken WillMaker Plus because of the possibility of creating a conflict between the codicil and the original will. It is simpler and safer to make a revised Quicken WillMaker Plus will, sign it and have it witnessed. (See "How to Make a New Will" in Chapter 11.)

Storing Your Will

Once your will is properly signed and witnessed, be sure that your executor can easily locate it at your death. Here are some suggestions:

- Store your printed and witnessed will in an envelope on which you have typed your name and the word "Will."
- Place the envelope in a fireproof metal box, file cabinet or home safe. An alternative is to place the original will in a safe deposit box. But before doing that, learn the bank's policy about access to the box after your death. If, for instance, the safe deposit box is in your name alone, the box can probably be opened only by a person authorized by a court, and then only in the presence of a bank employee. An inventory may even be required if any person enters the box or for state tax purposes. All of this takes time, and in the meantime, your document will be locked away from those who need it.

Helping Others Find Your Will

Your will should be easy to locate at your death. You want to spare your survivors the anxiety of having to search for your will when they are already dealing with the grief of losing you. Make sure your executor and at least one other person you trust know where to find your will.

Making Copies of Your Will

Some people are tempted to prepare more than one signed and witnessed original of their wills in case one is lost. While it is legal in most states to prepare and sign duplicate originals, it is never a good idea. Common sense tells you why: If you later want to change your will, it can be difficult to locate all the old copies to destroy them.

That said, it is sometimes a good idea to make several unsigned copies of your current will. You may want to give one to your executor or other loved ones, so they know your plans.

To share your will, print multiple copies when you finalize your document. Print these copies with a "duplicate" watermark; see Part 4 of the Users' Manual for instructions. Sign your original will and distribute the unsigned copies. We also recommend that you store one unsigned copy with your original will.

If you need more copies later, you can photocopy the unsigned will or print copies from your computer by returning to the program.

Of course, you aren't required to disclose the contents of your will to anyone. If you prefer to keep your will confidential until your death, do not make any copies.

Updating Your Will

Your will is an extremely personal document. Information such as your marital status, where you live, the property you own and whether you have children—all are examples of life choices that affect what you include in your will and what laws will be applied to enforce it.

Life wreaks havoc on even the best-laid plans. You may sell one house and buy another. You may divorce. You may have or adopt children. Eventually you will face the grief of losing a loved one. Not all life changes require you to change your will. However, significant ones often do. This chapter tells you when it's necessary to make a new will.

When to Make a New Will

The following occurrences signal that it is time for you to make a new will.

Marrying or Divorcing

Suppose that after you use Quicken WillMaker Plus to leave all or part of your property to your spouse, you get divorced. Under the law in many states, the divorce automatically cancels the bequest to the former spouse. The alternate beneficiary named for that bequest or, if there is none, your residuary beneficiary, gets the property. In some states, however, your former spouse would still be entitled to take your property as directed in the will. If you remarry, state legal rules become even more murky. (In a few states, these rules also apply to registered domestic partners.)

Rather than deal with all these complexities, follow this simple rule: Make a new will if you marry, divorce, are separated and seriously considering divorce or if you register or dissolve a domestic partnership.

SEE AN EXPERT

Beware of state laws on spouses' shares. If you leave your spouse or registered domestic partner out of your will because you are separated, and you die before you become divorced, it is possible that the spouse or partner could claim a statutory share of your estate. (See "Your Spouse's Right to Inherit From You" in Chapter 5.) Consult a lawyer to find out how the laws of your state apply to this situation. (See Chapter 17.)

Getting or Losing Property

If you leave all your property in a lump to one or more persons or organizations, there is no need to change your will if you acquire new items of property or get rid of existing ones. Those individuals or organizations take all of your property at your death, without regard to what it is.

But if you have made specific bequests of property that you no longer own, it is wise to make a new will. If you leave a specific item—a particular Tiffany lamp, for example—to someone, but you no longer own the item when you die, the person named in your will to receive it may be out of luck. In most states, that person is not entitled to receive another item or money instead. In some states, however, the law presumes that you wanted the beneficiary to have something—and so gives him or her the right to a sum of money equal to the value of the gift. While this may be what you want, it could still disrupt your plan for how you want your property distributed. The legal word for a bequest that fails to make it in this way is ademption. People who do not get to take the property in question are often heard to use an earthier term.

However, in some circumstances, if a specific item has merely changed form, the original beneficiary may still have a claim to it. Examples of this are:

- a promissory note that has been paid and for which the cash is still available, and
- a house that is sold in exchange for a promissory note and deed of trust.

A problem similar to ademption occurs when there is not enough money to go around. For example, if you leave $50,000 each to your spouse and two children, but there is only $90,000 in your estate at your death, the gifts in the will must all be reduced. In legal lingo, this is called an abatement. How property is abated under state law is often problematic.

You can avoid these problems if you revise the type and amount of your bequests to reflect reality—a task that requires the commitment to make a new will periodically.

Adding or Losing Children

Each time a child is born or legally adopted into your family, the new child should be named in the will—where you are asked to name your children—and provided for according to your wishes. If you do not do this, the child might later challenge your will in court, claiming that he or she was overlooked as an heir and is entitled to a substantial share of your property. (See "Your Children" in Chapter 4.)

If any of your children die before you and leave children, you should name those grandchildren in your will. If they are not mentioned in your will, they might later be legally entitled to claim a share of your estate. (See "Your Grandchildren" in Chapter 4.)

Moving to a Different State

Quicken WillMaker Plus applies several state-specific laws when it helps you create your will. These laws are especially important in two situations:

- If you have set up one form of management for young beneficiaries and then move to a different state, you may find when making a new will that Quicken WillMaker Plus presents you with different management options. This is because some states have adopted the Uniform Transfers to Minors Act and others have not. If you want to see whether your new state offers different management options, see "The Uniform Transfers to Minors Act" in Chapter 7.
- If you are married and do not intend to leave all or most of your property to your spouse, review "Property Ownership Rules for Married People" in Chapter 5, which discusses the rules if you move from a community property state to a common law state or vice versa.

Losing Beneficiaries

If a beneficiary you have named to receive a significant amount of property dies before you, you should make a new will. It is especially important to do this if you named only one beneficiary for a bequest and did not name an alternate—or if the alternate you named is no longer your first choice to get the property.

Losing Guardians or Property Managers

The first choice or alternate named to serve as a personal guardian for your minor children or those you have named to manage their property may move away, become disabled or simply turn out to be unsuitable for the job. If so, you will probably want to make a new will naming a different person.

Losing an Executor

The executor of your estate is responsible for making sure your will provisions are carried out. If you decide that the executor you originally named is no longer suitable—or if he or she dies before you do—you should make a new will in which you name another person for the job.

Losing Witnesses

The witnesses who sign your will are responsible for testifying that the signature on your will is valid and that you appeared capable of making a will when you did so. If two or more of your witnesses become unable to fulfill this function, you may want to make a new will with new witnesses—especially if you have some inkling that anyone is likely to contest your will after you die. But a new will is probably not necessary if you have made your will self-proving. (See "The Self-Proving Option" in Chapter 10.)

How to Make a New Will

It is easy to make a new will using Quicken WillMaker Plus. In fact, a subsequent swoop through the program will proceed even more quickly than the first time through, since you will know what to expect and will likely be familiar with many of the legal concepts you had to learn at first.

If you review your will and wish to change some of your answers, the program will automatically alert you to specific changes that may signal different laws applying to your situation. These include changes in:

- your marital or domestic partner status
- your state of residence
- the number of children you have, and
- your general approach to will making—from simple to complex, or vice versa.

If you make a new will, even if it only involves a few changes, you must follow the legal requirements for having it signed and witnessed just as if you were starting from scratch. If you choose to make your will self-proving, you must also complete a new affidavit.

> CAUTION
>
> **In with the new, out with the old.** As soon as you print, sign and have your new will witnessed, it will legally replace all wills you have made before it. But to avoid possible confusion, you should physically destroy all other original wills and any copies of them.

Explanatory Letters

n addition to the tasks that you can accomplish in a Quicken WillMaker Plus will, you may also wish to:

- explain why you are giving property to certain beneficiaries and not to others
- explain disparities in bequests
- express positive or negative sentiments about a beneficiary
- express wishes about how to care for a pet
- leave instructions for your digital legacy
- explain how shared gifts should be divided, or
- leave your loved ones a statement about your personal experiences, values or beliefs.

Quicken WillMaker Plus does not allow you to do these things in your will for one important reason: The program has been written, tested and tested again with painstaking attention to helping you make your own legal and unambiguous will. If you add general information, personal statements or reasons for making or not making a bequest, you risk the possibility of producing a document with conflicting, confusing or possibly even illegal provisions.

Fortunately, there is a way you can have a final say about personal matters without seriously risking your will's legal integrity. You can write a letter to accompany your will expressing your thoughts to those who survive you.

Since what you put in the letter will not have legal effect as part of your will, there is little danger that your expressions will tread upon the time-tested legal language of the will or cause other problems later. In fact, if your will is ambiguous and your statement in the letter sheds some light on your intentions, judges may use the letter to help clarify your will. However, if your statements in the letter fully contradict provisions in your will, you may create interpretation problems after your death. For example, if you don't leave anything to your daughter in your will and also state in a letter attached to the will that she is your favorite child and that is why you are leaving her the family home, you are setting the stage for future confusion.

Keeping these cautions in mind, writing a letter to those who survive you to explain why you wrote your will as you did—and knowing they will read your reasoning at your death—can give you a great deal of peace of mind during life. It may also help explain potential slights and hurt feelings of surviving friends and family members. This chapter offers some guidance on how you can write a clear letter that expresses your wishes without jeopardizing the legality of your will.

An Introduction for Your Letter

A formal introduction to the letter you leave can help make it clear that what you write is an expression of your sentiments and not intended as a will—or an addition to or interpretation of your will.

After the introduction, you are free to express your sentiments, keeping in mind that your estate may be held liable for any false, derogatory statements you make about an individual or organization.

One suggested introduction follows.

To My Executor:

This letter expresses my feelings and reasons for certain decisions made in my will. It is not my will, nor do I intend it to be an interpretation of my will. My will, which I signed, dated and had witnessed on _____ , is the sole expression of my intentions concerning all my property and other matters covered in it.

Should anything I say in this letter conflict with, or seem to conflict with, any provision of my will, the will shall be followed.

I request that you give a copy of this letter to each person named in my will to take property, or act as a guardian or custodian and to anyone else you determine should receive a copy.

Expressing Sentiments and Explaining Choices

There is little that a manual such as this can say to guide you in personal expressions of the heart. What follows are some suggestions about topics you might wish to cover.

Explaining Why Gifts Were Made

The Quicken WillMaker Plus requirement that you must keep descriptions of property and beneficiaries short and succinct may leave you unsatisfied. You may have thought hard and long about why you want a particular person to get particular property—and feel frustrated that you are constrained in your will to listing your wishes in a few simple words. You can remedy that by explaining your feelings in a letter.

EXAMPLE 1:

> [Introduction]
>
> The gift of my fishing boat to my friend Hank is in remembrance of the many companionable days we enjoyed fishing together on the lake. Hank, I hope you're out there for many more years.

EXAMPLE 2:

> [Introduction]
>
> Julie, the reason I have given you the farm is that you love it as much as I do and I know you'll do your best to make sure it stays in the family. But please, if the time comes when personal or family concerns mean that it makes sense to sell it, do so with a light heart—and knowing that it's just what I would have done.

Explaining Disparities in Gifts

You may also wish to explain your reasons for leaving more property to one person than another. While it is certainly your prerogative to make or not make bequests as you wish, you can also guess that in a number of family situations, unbalanced shares may cause hurt feelings or hostility after your death.

Ideally, you could call those involved together during your life, explaining to them why you plan to leave your property as you do. However, if you wish to keep your property plans private until after you die—or would find such a meeting too painful or otherwise impossible—you can attach a letter of explanation to your will.

EXAMPLE 1:

[Introduction]

I love all my children equally. The reason I gave a smaller ownership share in the house to Tim than to my other children is that Tim received family funds to purchase his own home, so it is fair that my other two children receive more of my property now.

EXAMPLE 2:

[Introduction]

I am giving the bulk of my property to my son Jason for one reason: Because of his health problems, he needs it more.

Ted and Ellen, I love you just as much, and I am extremely proud of the life choices you have made. But the truth is that you two can manage fine without a boost from me, and Jason cannot.

Offering Suggestions for Shared Gifts

If you are leaving a shared gift that contains a number of specific items—such as "my household furnishings" or "my art collection"—you may have some thoughts on how you'd like your beneficiaries to divide up the property. Of course, you can use your will to control the size of the share that each beneficiary gets, but that that still leaves your survivors to figure out who gets which specific assets. For example, if you leave your entire estate to be shared equally by your three children, how should your executor decide who gets the house, who gets the bank accounts and who gets the cars?

You can use a letter to make suggestions to your executor about how you want your property divided. Your suggestions will not have any legal weight; your executor is required to follow the terms of your will, not the terms of your letter. However, your letter can give your executor valuable guidance about how to distribute property, within the terms of your will.

Even if you don't particularly care who gets which things, you may want to suggest a fair way of figuring it out, such as a lottery for the highly coveted items.

Whatever suggestions you give, be very careful not to contradict any of the gifts you make in your will.

EXAMPLE:

[Introduction]

I have left my library equally to my grandchildren. I know each of them has enjoyed many of the books over the years and I want to make sure that each receives a few favorites. I suggest that you hold a drawing to determine the order in which each grandchild will choose a book, with each then taking a volume in turn until their favorites are spoken for. The rest of the library can be distributed—taken or given away—in whatever manner they choose.

Expressing Positive or Negative Sentiments

Whatever your plans for leaving your property, you may wish to attach a letter to your will in which you clear your mind of some sentiments you formed during life. These may be positive—thanking a loved one for kind acts. Or they may be negative—explaining why you are leaving a person out of your will.

EXAMPLE 1:

[Introduction]

The reason I left $10,000 to my physician Dr. Buski is not only that she treated me competently over the years, but that she was unfailingly gentle and attentive. I always appreciated that she made herself available—day or night—and took the time to explain my ailments and treatments to me.

EXAMPLE 2:

[Introduction]

I am leaving nothing to my brother Malcolm. I wish him no ill will. But over the years, he has decided to isolate himself from me and the rest of the family and I don't feel I owe him anything.

Supporting Your Same-Sex Marriage

If you and your partner got married and then moved to a state that doesn't recognize your marriage, you may want to attach a signed letter to your will that expresses your wish that your partner be treated in all ways as your legal spouse. This letter won't change how your property is distributed by your will, but it will make your intention clear. The note is simply a way to avoid confusion by stating that you were legally married and you consider your partner to be your spouse. It can be as brief as the sample below, or you can write more if you'd like to express your feelings about your relationship or its legal status.

EXAMPLE:

[Introduction]

Jennifer Jones and I were legally married on March 12, 2007, in the state of Massachusetts. In 2009, we moved to Kansas, which does not currently recognize our marriage. No matter where we live, I consider Jennifer my legal spouse, and it is my wish that she be treated for all purposes, including inheritance, as my legal spouse.

Instructions for Your Digital Legacy

As discussed in Chapter 5, you may want to leave instructions about your digital legacy—your online accounts, information, identities, and files—that will be left when you die. If you know what you want to happen with them, you can leave guidance and log-in information in your explanatory letter.

EXAMPLE:

[Introduction]

For many years I have been blogging about my experiences as a stay-at-home mom. I am thankful to have a large online following, I consider many of the people in that community to be my friends, and I would like them to be notified of my death. Please log in to my account and post a brief message about my passing. Also, please leave the blog live for at least a year (it's paid for) and save as much of the content as you can—I hope the kids might enjoy reading it someday. You can access the account at http://homemakermom. blogspot.com. My log-in name is my email account—homemakermom@ gmail.com and the password is 8tle1oAK.

Explaining Choices About Your Pet

As discussed in Chapter 4, the best way to provide a home for your pet is to use your will to name a caretaker for your pet and leave some money to that person to cover the costs of your pet's care. If you like, you can use your explanatory letter to say why you chose a particular person to watch over your animals after your death.

EXAMPLE:

[Introduction]

I have left my dog Cessna to my neighbor Belinda Mason because she has been a loving friend to him, taking care of him when I was on vacation or unwell. I know that Belinda and her three children will provide a caring and happy home for Cessna when I no longer can.

Leaving Details About Your Pet's Care

You may want to provide your pet's caretaker with information and suggestions about your pet's habits and needs. We recommend that you use the Quicken WillMaker Plus Information for Survivors and Caregivers form for this purpose. It allows you to leave specifics about each animal, including health needs, food and exercise requirements and sleeping habits. You can also use the document to describe memorial plans or final arrangements for your pet.

Describing Personal Experiences and Values

Many people are interested in leaving behind more than just property. If you wish, you can also leave a statement about the experiences, values and beliefs that have shaped your life. This kind of letter or document is often known as an "ethical will," and it can be of great worth to those who survive you.

While you could legally include an ethical will statement in your regular will—that is, the one you make to leave your property to others—we recommend that you include these sentiments in your explanatory letter or in a separate document. The reasons are the same as those mentioned earlier: It's better to avoid including anything potentially confusing or ambiguous in your legal will.

As long as you don't contradict the provisions of your legal will, your options for expressing yourself are limited only by the time and energy you have for the project. You could do something as simple as use your explanatory letter to set out a concise description of your basic values. Or, if you feel inspired, you may leave something much more detailed for your loved ones. Many survivors are touched to learn about important life stories, memories and events. You might also consider including photographs or other mementos with your letter. If writing things down seems like too much effort, you could use an audio or video to talk to those who are closest to you. A little thought will surely yield many creative ways to express yourself to those you care for.

RESOURCE

More information about ethical wills. If you want to go beyond writing down some of your experiences and values in your explanatory letter, there is a growing body of websites and literature that can help you explore different ways of making an ethical will. You might begin by Googling "ethical will" and exploring some of the resources available on the Internet.

When You May Need More Than a Will

f you have little to leave your survivors you probably don't need to do any planning beyond making a basic will, powers of attorney and health care directives (all of which you can make with Quicken WillMaker Plus). If that's your situation, you can skip this chapter altogether.

On the other hand, you may want to take another look at your situation and possibly do some additional estate planning to:

- avoid probate
- reduce estate taxes, or
- control how property left to one or more beneficiaries can be used.

If your estate is moderate to large, you should think about planning to avoid probate. Putting to work even a few simple probate avoidance devices can save your inheritors a bundle.

The next step—tax planning—is more complicated, but it's also something you won't need to worry about unless you have a very large estate.

Finally, if you have reason to want to place controls on the property you leave, you'll most likely want to see a good estate planning lawyer. At the end of this chapter, we'll talk a bit about your options.

Avoiding Probate

You may have heard or read that you ought to avoid probate—and that if you don't take steps to do so, your survivors will surely waste a lot of time and money after your death. This section will help you understand what probate is and why you may want to steer your estate away from it.

What Is Probate?

Probate is the legal process that includes filing a deceased person's will with a court, locating and gathering assets, paying debts and taxes and eventually distributing what's left as the will directs. Unless the estate qualifies as "small" under the terms of a state's law, all property left by will must go through probate. If there is no will and no probate avoidance devices are used, property is distributed according to state law—and it still must go through probate.

Fortunately, there are many devices you can use to keep property out of probate, including revocable living trusts, joint tenancy, pay-on-death beneficiary designations, and others. Property transferred by any of these methods can be given directly to the people slated to get it at your death—no court proceedings required.

Why Avoid Probate?

Probate has many drawbacks and few advantages. It's usually costly, involving fees for attorneys, appraisers, accountants and the probate court. The cost of probate varies widely from state to state, but fees can eat up about 5% of your estate, leaving that much less to go to the people you want to get it. If the estate is complicated, the fees can be even larger.

The Cost of Probate	
If you leave property worth:	**Probate may cost about:**
$200,000	$10,000
$500,000	$25,000

At least as bad as the expense of probate is the delay it causes. In many states, probate can take a year or two, during which time beneficiaries generally get nothing unless the judge allows the immediate family a small "family allowance."

If you own real estate in more than one state, it's usually necessary to have a whole separate probate proceeding in each state. That means the surviving relatives must probably find and hire a lawyer in each state and pay for multiple probate proceedings.

From the family's point of view, probate's headaches are rarely justified. If the estate contains common kinds of property—a house, stocks, bank accounts, a small business, cars—and no relatives or creditors are fighting about it, the property merely needs to be handed over to the new owners. In the vast majority of cases, the probate process entails nothing more than tedious paperwork, and the attorney is nothing more than a very highly paid clerk.

Living Trusts: A Popular Way to Avoid Probate

If you've heard something about living trusts but wonder exactly what they are and how they work, this section will give you a quick lesson.

First of all, what's a trust? It's an arrangement under which one person, called the trustee, owns property on behalf of someone else, called the beneficiary. You can create a trust simply by preparing and signing a document called a declaration of trust.

What, then, is a living trust? It's a trust that you set up during your lifetime to avoid probate. Living trusts sometimes go by a Latin name— "inter vivos" (among the living)—because they're created while you're alive, not at your death like some other kinds of trusts. They're also sometimes called "revocable living trusts" because you can revoke them at any time.

You can make an individual living trust or a trust that is shared with your spouse or partner.

How a Living Trust Works

A basic living trust does, essentially, what a will does: leaves your property to the people you want to inherit it. But because a trustee owns your property, your assets don't have to go through probate at your death.

When you create a living trust, you appoint yourself trustee, with full power to manage trust property. Then you transfer ownership of some or all of your property to yourself as trustee. You keep absolute control over the property held in trust. You can:

- sell, mortgage or give away property held in trust
- put ownership of trust property back in your name
- add property to the trust

- change the beneficiaries
- name a different successor trustee, or
- revoke the trust completely.

More Advantages of Living Trusts

In addition to avoiding probate, a living trust offers other benefits.

Avoiding the need for a conservator or guardianship. A living trust can be useful if you become incapacitated and unable to manage your own financial affairs. That's because the person you name as trustee (or the other grantor, if you make a shared trust) can take over management of trust assets, watching over the property for your benefit.

If there is no living trust and you haven't made other arrangements for someone to take over your finances if you become incapacitated, such as preparing a durable power of attorney for finances, a court will have to appoint someone to do the job. Typically, the spouse or adult child of the person seeks this authority and is called a conservator or guardian.

Keeping your estate plan confidential. When your will is filed with the probate court after you die, it becomes a matter of public record. A living trust, on the other hand, is a private document in most states. Because the living trust document is never filed with a court or other government entity, what you leave to whom remains private. (There is one exception: Records of real estate transfers are always public.)

Some states require you to register your living trust with the local court, but there are no penalties if you don't. The only way your trust might become public is if—and this is very unlikely—someone files a lawsuit to challenge the trust or collect a court judgment you owe.

If you and your spouse or partner create a trust together, both of you must consent to changes, although either of you is permitted to revoke the entire trust.

After you die, the person you named in your trust document to be "successor trustee" takes over. This person transfers the trust property to the relatives, friends or charities you named as the trust beneficiaries. No probate is necessary for property that was held in trust. In most cases, the whole thing can be handled within a few weeks. When the property has all been transferred to the beneficiaries, the living trust ceases to exist.

If any of your beneficiaries inherit trust property while still young, the successor trustee (or the surviving grantor of a shared trust) will probably have more responsibility, following instructions you leave in the trust to manage the property until the beneficiaries are old enough to inherit it outright.

Do You Really Need a Living Trust?

Here are some factors to think about when deciding whether a living trust is right for you:

Your age. If you're under 60 and healthy, it often makes sense to prepare a will, use simple probate-avoidance devices, such as joint tenancy and pay-on-death bank accounts, for some property and leave the more complicated estate planning until later.

The size of your estate. The bigger your estate, the bigger the potential probate cost and the less likely that your estate will qualify for simplified probate proceedings, discussed below. Often it makes good sense to concentrate effort on making sure that major assets, such as real estate or business assets, are owned in a way that will avoid probate.

The type of property you own. You don't need a trust to avoid probate for assets like your bank and retirement accounts and many other types of property. Take some time to learn a little bit about other types of probate avoidance devices before you jump into preparing a living trust; see "Other Ways to Avoid Probate," below.

Why You Still Need a Will

A living trust cannot completely replace a will. Even if you want to use a living trust to pass all of your property, there are reasons why you need a will, too.

Naming a guardian for minor children. You can't nominate a personal guardian for your young children in a living trust; you need a will in which to do this. (See "Personal Guardians for Your Minor Children" in Chapter 4.)

Passing property not included in the trust. A living trust works to pass only property you transfer to the trust's name. Property you may receive after you make the trust won't be transferred unless you add it to the living trust later. For example, if you have inherited property from a relative that is still tied up in probate, or you expect to receive money from the settlement of a lawsuit, you need a will in case something happens to you tomorrow. And because you cannot accurately predict what property you might receive shortly before death, it's smart to back up a living trust with a will.

RESOURCE

How to make your own living trust. Nolo offers several tools that allow you to make your own individual or shared basic living trust:

- *Nolo's Online Living Trust*, available at www.nolo.com. We'll walk you step-by-step through the process of making a living trust online. You can print your trust and all the instructions you need to finalize it and make it legal.
- *Living Trust Maker.* If you'd rather make your trust with downloadable software, this is the option for you. You can find *Living Trust Maker* on Nolo's website at www.nolo.com.
- *Make Your Own Living Trust*, by Denis Clifford. This bestselling book with CD-ROM shows you how to make the right living trust for your situation. Find it at www.nolo.com or through your favorite bookseller.

Other Ways to Avoid Probate

Here are some methods you might want to investigate, to use with or instead of a living trust.

Pay-on-Death Bank Accounts

Payable-on-death bank accounts offer one of the easiest ways to keep money—even large sums of it—out of probate. All you need to do is fill out a simple form, provided by the bank, naming the person you want to inherit the money in the account at your death.

As long as you are alive, the person you named to inherit the money in a payable-on-death (POD) account has no rights to it. You can spend the money, name a different beneficiary or close the account. At your death, the beneficiary just goes to the bank, shows proof of the death and of his or her identity and collects whatever funds are in the account. The probate court is never involved.

Transfer-on-Death Registration of Securities

Almost all states have adopted a law (the Uniform Transfer-on-Death Securities Registration Act) that lets you name someone to inherit your stocks, bonds or brokerage accounts without probate. It works very much like a payable-on-death bank account. When you register your ownership, either with the stockbroker or the company itself, you make a request to take ownership in what's called "beneficiary form." When the papers that show your ownership are issued, they will also show the name of your beneficiary.

After you register ownership this way, the beneficiary has no rights to the stock as long as you are alive. You are free to sell it, give it away or name a different beneficiary. But on your death, the beneficiary can claim the securities without probate, simply by providing proof of death and some identification to the broker or transfer agent. (A transfer agent is a business that is authorized by a corporation to handle stock transfers.)

Transfer-on-Death Deeds for Real Estate

In Arizona, Arkansas, Colorado, Indiana, Kansas, Minnesota, Missouri, Montana, Nevada, New Mexico, Ohio, Oklahoma and Wisconsin, you can prepare a deed now but have it take effect only at your death. These transfer-on-death deeds must be prepared, signed, notarized and recorded (filed in the county land records office) just like a regular deed. But unlike a regular deed, you can revoke a transfer-on-death deed. The deed must expressly state that it does not take effect until death.

Check your state's statute for the rules. Several of the statutes provide deed forms. Nolo also offers transfer on death deed forms—and instructions on how to use them—at www.nolo.com.

Transfer-on-Death Registration for Vehicles

Arizona, California, Connecticut, Indiana, Kansas, Missouri, Nebraska, Nevada, Ohio and Vermont offer vehicle owners the sensible option of naming a beneficiary, right on the certificate of title or title application, to inherit a vehicle. If you do this, the beneficiary you name has no rights as long as you are alive. You are free to sell or give away a car or name someone else as the beneficiary.

To name a transfer-on-death beneficiary, all you do is apply for registration in "beneficiary form." The new certificate lists the name of the beneficiary, who will automatically own the vehicle after your death. You can find more information on the website of your state's motor vehicles department.

Retirement Plans

Retirement plans, such as IRAs, 401(k)s and Keoghs, don't have to go through probate. All you need to do is name a beneficiary to receive the funds at your death, and no probate will be necessary.

Life Insurance

Life insurance proceeds are subject to probate only if the beneficiary named in the policy is your estate. That's done occasionally if the estate will need immediate cash to pay debts and taxes, but it's usually counterproductive because doing so could greatly increase probate fees.

Joint Tenancy

Joint tenancy is an efficient and practical way to transfer some kinds of property without probate.

Joint tenancy is a way two or more people can hold title to property they own together. All joint owners (called joint tenants) must own equal shares of the property. (Vermont and Connecticut are exceptions;

joint owners there may own unequal shares.) When one joint owner dies, the surviving owners automatically get complete ownership of the property. This is called the "right of survivorship." The property doesn't go through probate court—there is only some simple paperwork to fill out to transfer the property into the name of the surviving owner.

A will doesn't affect who inherits joint tenancy property. So, even if your will leaves your half-interest in joint tenancy property to someone else, the surviving owners will still inherit it.

This rule isn't as ironclad as it may sound. You can, while still alive, break the joint tenancy by transferring your interest in the property to someone else (or, in some states, to yourself, but not as a joint tenant).

Joint tenancy often works well when couples acquire real estate or other valuable property together. If they take title in joint tenancy, probate is avoided when the first owner dies—though not (unlike a living trust) when the second owner dies.

Joint tenancy is usually a poor estate planning device when an older person, seeking only to avoid probate, puts solely owned property into joint tenancy with someone else. If you make someone else a co-owner, in joint tenancy, of property that you now own yourself, you give up half ownership of the property. The new owner has rights that you can't take back. For example, the new owner can sell or mortgage his or her share. And federal gift tax may be assessed on the transfer.

There can also be serious problems if one joint tenant becomes incapacitated and cannot make decisions. The other owners must get legal authority to sell or mortgage the property. That may mean going to court to get someone (called a conservator or guardian, in most states) appointed to manage the incapacitated person's affairs. (This problem can be partially dealt with if the joint tenant has signed a durable power of attorney. See Chapter 14.) With a living trust, if you (the grantor) become incapacitated, the successor trustee (or the other spouse, if you made a trust together) takes over and has full authority to manage the property. No court proceedings are necessary.

Several states have abolished or restricted joint tenancy; see below.

State Restrictions on Joint Tenancy	
Alaska	No joint tenancies for real estate, except for husband and wife, who may own property as tenants by the entirety. (See below.)
Oregon	A transfer of real estate to husband and wife creates a tenancy by the entirety, not joint tenancy. All other transfers in joint tenancy create a tenancy in common. (See "Property You Own With Others," in Chapter 5.)
Tennessee	A transfer of real estate to husband and wife creates a tenancy by the entirety, not joint tenancy. All other transfers in joint tenancy create a tenancy in common. (See "Property You Own With Others," in Chapter 5.)
Texas	A joint tenancy can be created only if you sign a separate written agreement.
Wisconsin	No joint tenancies between spouses after January 1, 1986. If spouses attempt to create a joint tenancy, it will be treated as community property with right of survivorship. (See below.)

Tenancy by the Entirety

"Tenancy by the entirety" is a form of property ownership that is similar to joint tenancy. About half the states offer it, and it is limited to married couples or same-sex couples who have registered with the state (in states that allow this).

Tenancy by the entirety has many of the same advantages and disadvantages of joint tenancy and is most useful in the same kind of situation: when a couple acquires property together. When one owner dies, the surviving co-owner inherits the property. The property doesn't go through probate.

If property is held in tenancy by the entirety, neither spouse or partner can transfer his or her half of the property alone, either while alive or by will or trust. It must go to the survivor. (This is different from joint tenancy; a joint tenant is free to transfer his or her share to someone else during his or her life.)

States That Allow Tenancy by the Entirety		
Alaska[1]	Maryland	Oklahoma
Arkansas	Massachusetts	Oregon[1]
Delaware[1]	Michigan	Pennsylvania
District of Columbia	Mississippi	Rhode Island
Florida	Missouri	Tennessee
Hawaii	New Jersey	Utah[1]
Illinois[1]	New York[1]	Vermont
Indiana[1]	North Carolina[1]	Virginia
Kentucky[1]	Ohio[2]	Wyoming

[1] For real estate only.

[2] For real estate only, and only if created before April 4, 1985.

EXAMPLE: Fred and Ethel hold title to their house in tenancy by the entirety. If Fred wanted to sell or give away his half-interest in the house, he could not do so without Ethel's signature on the deed.

Community Property With Right of Survivorship

In a few states, married couples (and in California, registered domestic partners) can own property together "as community property with right of survivorship." When one spouse dies, the other automatically inherits the property, without probate. The states that offer this option are Alaska, Arizona, California, Nevada and Wisconsin.

Simplified Probate Proceedings

Many states have begun, slowly, to dismantle some of the more onerous parts of probate. They have created categories of property and beneficiaries that don't have to go through a full-blown probate court proceeding. If your family can take advantage of these procedures after your death, you may not need to worry too much about avoiding probate.

Almost every state has some kind of simplified (summary) probate or out-of-court transfer process for one or more of these categories:

Small estates. Most states offer streamlined probate court procedures for small estates; what qualifies as a small estate varies widely from state to state. In many states, even if your total estate is too large to qualify as a small estate, your heirs can still make use of the simplified procedures if the amount that actually goes through probate is under the limit.

Personal property. If the estate is small, many states also let people collect personal property (that's anything but real estate) they've inherited by filling out a sworn statement (affidavit) and giving it to the person who has the property. Typically, the beneficiary must also provide some kind of proof of his or her right to inherit, such as a death certificate and copy of the will.

Property left to the surviving spouse. In some states, if a surviving spouse inherits less than a certain amount of property, no probate is necessary.

> **RESOURCE**
>
> **More information about avoiding probate.** To learn more about saving your family the costs and hassles of probate, see *8 Ways to Avoid Probate*, by Mary Randolph (Nolo).

Reducing Estate Taxes

Estate taxes are imposed after your death, on property you leave at your death. Because everyone is entitled to a large estate tax exemption, only a small number of estates end up owing it.

The Federal Estate Tax

The vast majority of Americans do not need to worry about federal estate tax, because under the current rules, only very very large estates owe this tax. Here's why:

The personal estate tax exemption. The personal exemption allows a set dollar amount of property to pass tax free, no matter who inherits it. For deaths in 2011 or 2012, the personal exemption is $5 million. So if your estate is worth less than $5 million, it won't owe federal estate tax when you die. If you have made taxable gifts during your life, the amount of the personal exemption will be reduced by the amount of those taxable gifts.

The marital deduction. All property left to a surviving spouse passes free of estate tax. (The marital deduction does not apply to noncitizen spouses or to married same-sex spouses.)

The charitable deduction. All property left to a tax-exempt charity is also free of estate tax.

Special rules for married couples. For deaths in 2011 or 2012, a surviving spouse gets a big tax break. If the deceased spouse didn't use up his or her $5 million tax exemption, the survivor can use what's left. That gives the couple a total $10 million exemption, split between them in any way that provides the greatest tax benefit. (This rule does not apply to married same-sex spouses.)

> **EXAMPLE:** Juan dies and leaves $4 million to his widow Janice. Because property left to a spouse is tax free, no estate tax is owed and none of Juan's personal exemption is used.
>
> Then Janice dies, leaving $7 million (her own $3 million plus the $4 million she inherited from her husband) to her children. Her estate won't own any estate tax either—here's why: The first $5 million is covered by her own $5 million exemption. The remaining $2 million is covered by Juan's completely unused $5 million exemption. Janice's estate would not have owed any tax even if it had grown to $10 million.

These rules will probably change again in 2013, but they will almost certainly continue to allow average-sized estates to pass tax free. So unless you plan to leave several million dollars worth of property, you don't need to give federal estate taxes a second thought. If you do expect to leave a very large estate, consult a tax professional or estate planning attorney to discuss tax planning.

State Estate and Inheritance Taxes

Even if your estate isn't big enough to owe federal estate tax, the state may still take a bite.

Estate tax. About half the states collect estate tax and your estate may owe state estate tax even if it doesn't owe federal estate taxes. However, the rates are usually relatively low, so the state tax rarely takes a large bite out of the estate.

Inheritance tax. Some states impose a separate tax on a deceased person's property, called an inheritance tax. The tax rate depends on who inherits the property; usually, spouses and other close relatives pay nothing or at a low rate.

If you live in a state that imposes an estate or inheritance tax, there's not much you can do to avoid it, save moving to another state. For each state's rules, see *The Executor's Guide: Settling a Loved One's Estate or Trust*, by Mary Randolph (Nolo).

Ways to Reduce Federal Estate Tax

If you have a very large estate, here are some tax-saving strategies you may want to talk about with a tax advisor or estate planning attorney. Each can be used alone or in combination with other methods.

Annual Tax-Exempt Gifts

If you don't need all your income and property to live on, making sizable gifts while you're alive can be a good way to reduce eventual federal estate taxes before that tax is repealed. Currently, only gifts larger than $13,000 made to one person or organization in one calendar year count toward the personal estate tax exemption. You can give smaller gifts tax-free.

> **EXAMPLE:** Allen and Julia each give each of their two daughters $13,000 every year for four years. They have transferred $208,000 without becoming liable for gift tax.

Other Tax-Exempt Gifts

Other gifts are exempt regardless of amount, including:

- gifts between spouses who are U.S. citizens (gifts to spouses who are not U.S. citizens are exempt only up to $136,000 per year)
- gifts paid directly for medical bills or school tuition, and
- gifts to tax-exempt charitable organizations.

AB Living Trusts

AB living trusts are designed to help couples with very large estates reduce or eliminate estate tax. However, for married couples, the new federal estate tax rules (see above) make this type of trust useful only if their combined estate is greater than $10 million. Needless to say most married couples do not need an AB trust under these new rules.

That said, you might still consider making an AB trust if:

- You and your spouse or partner have a large estate and are worried that you might owe tax under the *next* set of estate tax laws—those that Congress writes for 2013 and beyond. In this case, you might consider making an AB *disclaimer* trust. AB disclaimer trusts provide flexibility under changing tax laws.
- You and your partner aren't legally married or if you are a legally married same-sex couple. In these situations, you won't qualify for the special rules for married couples described above and an AB trust could be useful if you and your partner have a combined estate worth more than $5 million.

Keep in mind that AB trusts limit the surviving spouse's ability to use trust property, can be expensive to create, and in some situations can cause stress among family members. So, if you think that an AB trust might be useful for you, do some more research on your own or discuss your options with an experienced estate planning attorney.

> **RESOURCE**
> **More information about AB trusts.** To learn more about AB trusts or to make your own AB disclaimer trust, see *Make Your Own Living Trust*, by Denis Clifford (Nolo), or consult a knowledgeable estate planning lawyer.

Charitable Trusts

If you want to make a big contribution to a charitable cause you care about—and, at the same time, cut your income taxes now and guarantee some income for life—then a charitable trust may be for you. They're not just for the very rich; you can contribute to a "pooled" charitable trust with as little as $5,000.

QTIPs and QDOTs

These trusts, known by their catchy acronyms (easier to say than Qualified Terminable Interest Property trust, you have to admit), are mainly used by married couples concerned about estate tax. A QTIP lets couples postpone paying estate tax until the second spouse's death and also locks in, while both are still alive, who inherits the property at the second spouse's death. A QDOT is useful when a spouse who is not a U.S. citizen stands to inherit a large amount of property.

Life Insurance Trusts

Although the proceeds of a life insurance policy don't go through probate, they are included in your estate for federal estate tax purposes. You can reduce the tax bill by giving ownership of the policy to a life insurance trust (or to the beneficiary directly) at least three years before your death. But like other estate tax-saving strategies, this one will have to be reassessed in light of changes in the estate tax exemption.

Using Trusts to Control Property

Most people are content to leave their property to their survivors outright, without trying to control what they do with it. However, there are times, especially for people with very large estates, when it can make sense to impose controls on what people can do with property you leave them. We discuss the most common situations here.

Children and Young Adults

Many people who leave property to children or young adults want to delay the age at which the beneficiaries will receive the property. You can set up this kind of property management in your will. See Chapter 7.

Second or Subsequent Marriages

Some people enter into second, third or fourth marriages unconcerned about estate planning. If each spouse has enough property of his or her own to live comfortably, there may be no need to combine assets and create the problems that can arise as a result. In such cases, the simplest solution is often to make a prenuptial agreement making it clear that separate property stays separate; then each can make an independent estate plan for that property.

But in many second or subsequent marriages, one or both spouses may feel conflicted about estate planning. On one hand, a surviving spouse may need the income from, or the use of, the other spouse's property to live comfortably. On the other hand, either spouse may want to provide an inheritance for children from a former marriage. This situation becomes even more complicated when a current spouse and children from a former marriage don't get along well.

One possible solution is to set up a trust—often called a "marital property control trust"—to try to balance the interests and needs of all concerned. Essentially, this type of trust gives the surviving spouse some use of or income from the trust property, then leaves the property outright to children from a prior marriage when the surviving spouse dies.

A marital property control trust is very different from an AB trust (discussed above) intended only to reduce estate taxes. With an AB trust, the surviving spouse is usually granted the maximum rights allowed under IRS rules to use trust property. In contrast, a marital property control trust is designed to protect the trust principal, so that most of it still exists when the surviving spouse dies.

Trusts like these are tricky, and you'll need an experienced lawyer to help you set one up. To learn more about the unique concerns of couples in second or subsequent marriages, and how to solve them, you might want to turn to Nolo's book, *Estate Planning for Blended Families: Providing for Your Spouse & Children in a Second Marriage*, by Richard E. Barnes.

Beneficiaries With Special Needs

A person with a physical or mental disability may not be able to handle property, no matter what age. And gifts left directly to a beneficary with special needs will jeopardize that person's access to public benefits. The solution is often to establish a trust—called a "special needs trust"—to manage the property while preserving the beneficiary's eligibility for government benefits. You can learn more about this kind of trust by reading *Special Needs Trusts: Protect Your Child's Financial Future*, by Stephen Elias and Kevin Urbatsch (Nolo).

Big Spenders

If you want to leave a substantial amount of property to someone who is known to be irresponsible with money, a good estate planning lawyer can help you establish what's known as a "spendthrift trust." In it, you can empower a trusted person or institution to dole out the money a little at a time.

Groups of Beneficiaries

For any number of reasons, you may want the exact division of your estate to be determined after your death, instead of directing the division in a will or trust.

The usual way to accomplish this is to create what is called a "sprinkling trust." Usually, the trust creator names the beneficiaries of the trust during life, but does not specify what share each is to receive. That is done by the trustee, after the creator dies, under whatever terms the trust dictates. Again, you'll need an experienced lawyer to set up this kind of trust.

SEE AN EXPERT

How to find a good lawyer. Many of the estate planning strategies discussed in this chapter require a lawyer's help. For tips on finding the expert you need, see Chapter 17.

Durable Power of Attorney for Finances

M any people fear that they may someday become seriously ill and unable to handle their own financial affairs—that they might be unable to pay bills, make bank deposits, watch over investments or collect insurance and government benefits. As you grow older or face the possibility of an incapacitating illness, it's wise to plan for such a contingency. Fortunately, there's a simple way to do so: preparing a durable power of attorney for finances.

A durable power of attorney for finances is an inexpensive, reliable legal document. In it, you name someone who will make your financial decisions if you become unable to do so yourself.

This person is called your attorney-in-fact, or in some states, your agent. (Your document will include the correct term for your state.)

If you ever do become incapacitated, the durable power of attorney will likely appear as a minor miracle to those who are close to you.

Important Terms

- **Principal.** The person who creates and signs the power of attorney document, authorizing someone else to act for him or her. If you make a durable power of attorney for finances, you are the principal.
- **Attorney-in-Fact.** The person who is authorized to act for the principal. In many states, the attorney-in-fact is also referred to as an agent of the principal—and some states use the term "agent" exclusively. Your power of attorney will include the correct term for your state.
- **Alternate Attorney-in-Fact.** The person who takes over as attorney-in-fact if your first choice cannot or will not serve. Also called successor attorney-in-fact or successor agent, depending on the state.
- **Durable Power of Attorney.** A power of attorney that will remain in effect even if the principal becomes incapacitated. This is the kind of power of attorney you make with this program.
- **Incapacitated.** Unable to handle one's own financial matters or health care decisions. Also called disabled or incompetent in some states. Usually, a physician makes the determination.

CAUTION

The perils of forging a signature. If someone becomes incapacitated, panicky family members may consider just faking the signatures necessary to carry on routine financial matters. It may seem perfectly acceptable to sign Aunt Amanda's name to a check if the money is used to pay her phone bill.

But this is forgery—and it's a crime. The law is strict in this area to guard against dishonest family members who might loot a relative's assets.

Forging a signature on checks, bills of sale, tax returns or other financial documents may work for a while, but it will probably be discovered eventually. And then the court proceeding everyone was trying to avoid will be necessary— and a judge will not be eager to put a proven liar in charge of a relative's finances.

TIP

Keeping track of information for your attorney-in-fact. The attorney-in-fact you name may need to know a vast number of details about your property and how you deal with it. With Quicken WillMaker Plus, you can make an Information for Caregivers and Survivors form to help with this task. With this document, you can provide a comprehensive guide of the details of your life—ranging from information about your property and your financial accounts, to the names and addresses of people you want contacted in the event of your illness—to the person who will care for you in the event of your incapacity. To find out more, click on My Documents and select Information for Caregivers and Survivors from the list.

What Quicken WillMaker Plus Can Do

Quicken WillMaker Plus allows you to create your own durable power of attorney for finances. Using this program, you can:

- name your attorney-in-fact
- appoint someone to replace your attorney-in-fact if he or she cannot serve, and
- state exactly how much authority you want your attorney-in-fact to have over your finances.

In addition to your durable power of attorney for finances, Quicken WillMaker Plus prints out a number of related documents. The first of these is an information sheet for you to give to your attorney-in-fact, explaining what his or her responsibilities will be. There are also several forms designed to make your attorney-in-fact's job easier—including forms for delegating tasks to others and resigning from the job if that becomes necessary. Finally, we provide a form that you can use to revoke your durable power of attorney if you change your mind. Each document is explained in this chapter.

What a Durable Power of Attorney for Finances Can Do

Almost everyone with property or an income can benefit from a durable power of attorney for finances. It's particularly important, however, to have a durable power of attorney if you fear that health problems may make it impossible for you to handle your financial matters.

The main reason to make a durable power of attorney for finances is to avoid court proceedings if you become incapacitated. If you don't have a durable power of attorney, your relatives or other loved ones will have to ask a judge to name someone to manage your financial affairs. These proceedings are commonly known as conservatorship proceedings. Depending on where you live, the person appointed to manage your finances is called a conservator, guardian of the estate, committee or curator.

If You Are Married

If you are married, don't assume that your spouse will automatically be able to manage all of your finances if you cannot do so.

Your spouse does have some authority over property you own together —for example, your spouse may pay bills from a joint bank account or sell stock in a joint brokerage account. There are significant limits, however, on your spouse's right to sell property that both of you own. For example, in most states, both spouses must agree to the sale of co-owned real estate or cars. Because an incapacitated spouse can't consent to such a sale, the other spouse's hands are tied.

And when it comes to property that belongs only to you, your spouse has no legal authority. You must use a durable power of attorney to give your spouse authority over your property.

> **EXAMPLE 1:** New York residents Michael and Carrie have been married for 47 years. Their major assets are a home and stock. They own the home in both their names as joint tenants. The stock was bought only in Michael's name, and the couple has never transferred it into shared ownership. Michael becomes incapacitated and requires expensive medical treatment. Without a durable power of attorney, Carrie cannot sell the stock to pay for medical costs.

> **EXAMPLE 2:** Janice's husband, Hal, is incapacitated and living in a nearby nursing home. Janice wants to raise money by selling Hal's old car, which he can no longer drive, but she can't because she doesn't have a durable power of attorney and the title is in Hal's name.

If You Have a Living Trust

A central purpose of a revocable living trust is to avoid probate. But the trust can also be useful if you become incapable of taking care of your financial affairs. That's because the person who will distribute trust property after your death—called the successor trustee—can also, in most cases, take over management of the trust property if you become incapacitated.

But few people transfer all their property to a living trust, and the successor trustee has no authority over property that the trust doesn't own. So although a living trust may be helpful, it is not a complete substitute for a durable power of attorney for finances.

The two documents work well together, however, especially if you name the same trusted person to be your attorney-in-fact and the successor trustee of your living trust. That person will have authority to manage property both in and out of your living trust. You can also give your attorney-in-fact the power to transfer items of your property into your living trust. (See "Specific Financial Powers," below.)

> **EXAMPLE:** Consuela, a widow, owns all the stock of a prosperous clothing manufacturing corporation. To avoid probate, she transfers the stock into a living trust, naming her brother, Rodolfo, as successor trustee. If Consuela becomes incapacitated, Rodolfo will become acting trustee and manage the stock in the trust for Consuela's benefit.
>
> Consuela also prepares a durable power of attorney for finances and names Rodolfo as her attorney-in-fact. That gives him authority over assets she does not transfer to the trust—for example, her bank accounts and car. In her durable power of attorney, she also gives Rodolfo the power to transfer property into her living trust, if he feels that's in her best interest.

Avoiding Conservatorship Proceedings

Conservatorship proceedings can be complicated, expensive and even embarrassing. Your loved ones must ask the court to rule that you cannot take care of your own affairs—a public airing of a very private matter. Court proceedings are matters of public record; in some places, a notice may even be published in a local newspaper. If relatives fight over who is to be the conservator, the proceedings will surely become even more disagreeable, sometimes downright nasty. And all of this causes costs to mount up, especially if lawyers must be hired.

If a judge decides to appoint a conservator, there is no guarantee that the person who gets the job will be the person you would have chosen. A judge may ask you to express a preference for conservator—and will strongly consider what you say—but even this will not ensure that your

Avoiding Conservatorship Proceedings (continued)

choice will serve. To increase the chances that your wishes will be followed, you can use the durable power of attorney you make with this program to name your attorney-in-fact as conservator, if a court must ever appoint one. (See "Nominating a Conservator or Guardian," below.)

If you don't name a conservator in your power of attorney document, state law generally provides a priority list for who should be appointed. For example, a number of states make the person's spouse or registered domestic partner the first choice as conservator, followed by an adult child, parent and brother or sister. In many states, the law allows the court to appoint whoever it determines will act in your best interests.

The appointment of a conservator is usually just the beginning of court proceedings. Often the conservator must:

- post a bond—a kind of insurance policy that pays if the conservator steals or misuses property
- prepare detailed financial reports—or hire a lawyer or accountant to prepare them and periodically file them with the court, and
- get court approval for certain transactions, such as selling real estate or making slightly risky investments.

All of this, of course, costs money—your money.

A conservatorship isn't necessarily permanent, but it may be ended only by the court.

You can probably avoid the troubles of a conservatorship if you take the time to create a durable power of attorney for finances now. When you make a durable power of attorney, you give your attorney-in-fact full legal authority to handle your financial affairs. A conservatorship proceeding would be necessary only if no one were willing to serve as attorney-in-fact, if the attorney-in-fact wanted guidance from a court or a close relative thought the attorney-in-fact wasn't acting in your best interests.

If You Own Joint Tenancy Property

Joint tenancy is a way that two or more people can own property together. The most notable feature of joint tenancy is that when one owner dies, the other owners automatically get the deceased person's share of the property. But if you become incapacitated, the other owners have very limited authority over your share of the joint tenancy property.

For example, if you and someone else own a bank account in joint tenancy, and one of you becomes incapacitated, the other owner is legally entitled to use the funds. The healthy joint tenant can take care of the financial needs of the incapacitated person simply by paying bills from the joint account. But the other account owner has no legal right to endorse checks made out to the incapacitated person. In practice, it might be possible—if not technically legal—to get an incapacitated person's checks into a joint account by stamping them "For Deposit Only," but that's not the easiest way to handle things.

Matters get more complicated with other kinds of joint tenancy property. Real estate is a good example. If one owner becomes incapacitated, the other has no legal authority to sell or refinance the incapacitated owner's share.

In a durable power of attorney, you can give your attorney-in-fact authority over property you own in joint tenancy—including real estate and bank accounts.

What a Durable Power of Attorney for Finances Cannot Do

The expense and intrusion of a conservatorship are rarely desirable. In a few situations, however, special concerns justify the process. For example, you may not know anyone who could handle the job of managing your finances—or you may expect disgruntled family members to cause trouble for the person you choose as your attorney-in-fact. In these situations, it's probably better not to make a durable power of attorney for finances. In some other situations, a document other than a durable power of attorney for finances will better meet your needs.

Provide Court Supervision of Your Finances

If you can't think of someone you trust enough to appoint as your attorney-in-fact, with broad authority over your property and finances—and who is willing to take on the responsibility—don't create a durable power of attorney. A conservatorship, with the safeguard of court supervision, may be worth the extra cost and trouble for this purpose.

Protect Against Family Fights

A durable power of attorney is a powerful legal document. Once you've finalized yours, anyone who wants to challenge your plans for financial management will face an uphill battle in court. But if you expect that family members will challenge your document or make continual trouble for your attorney-in-fact, a conservatorship may be preferable. Your relatives may still fight, but at least the court will be there to keep an eye on your welfare and your property.

> **SEE AN EXPERT**
>
> **Help if your family is feisty.** If you expect family fights and feel uncomfortable making a durable power of attorney for finances, you may want to talk with a knowledgeable lawyer. He or she can help you weigh your concerns and options and decide whether a durable power of attorney is the best option for you. (See Chapter 17.)

Authorize Health Care Decisions

A durable power of attorney for finances does not give your attorney-in-fact legal authority to make health care decisions for you. To make sure that your wishes for health care are known and followed, you should use Quicken WillMaker Plus to create a health care directive. (See Chapter 15.)

Authorize Decisions About Marriage, Adoption, Voting or Wills

You cannot authorize your attorney-in-fact to marry, adopt, vote in public elections or make a will on your behalf. These acts are considered too personal to delegate to someone else.

Give Powers Delegated to Others

If you've already given someone legal authority to manage some or all of your property, you cannot delegate that authority to your attorney-in-fact.

For example, if you become incapacitated, your attorney-in-fact will not be able to:

- control property in a living trust you created giving the successor trustee power over that property, or
- manage your interest in a partnership business if you have a signed agreement giving your partners authority to do so.

Create, Modify or Revoke a Trust

The power of attorney you make with this program doesn't allow you to give your attorney-in-fact permission to create, modify or revoke a trust on your behalf—with one exception. If you've already set up a revocable living trust, you may give your attorney-in-fact the power to transfer property to that trust. (See "If You Have a Living Trust," above.)

About Your Attorney-in-Fact

This section explains more about the responsibilities the person you name as attorney-in-fact will have toward you and your property.

Possible Powers

Commonly, people give an attorney-in-fact broad power over their finances. But it's up to you. Using this program, you can give your attorney-in-fact authority to do some or all of the following:

- use your assets to pay your everyday expenses and those of your family
- handle transactions with banks and other financial institutions
- buy, sell, maintain, pay taxes on and mortgage real estate and other property
- file and pay your taxes
- manage your retirement accounts
- collect benefits from Social Security, Medicare or other government programs or civil or military service
- invest your money in stocks, bonds and mutual funds
- buy and sell insurance policies and annuities for you
- operate your small business
- claim or disclaim property you get from others
- make gifts of your assets to organizations and individuals that you choose
- transfer property to a living trust you've already set up, and
- hire someone to represent you in court.

(These powers are discussed in detail a little later in this chapter.)

You can tailor your durable power of attorney for finances to fit your needs by choosing which powers you grant and placing certain conditions and restrictions upon the attorney-in-fact. For example, you can give your attorney-in-fact authority over your real estate, with the express restriction that your house may not be sold.

Legal Responsibilities

The attorney-in-fact you appoint in your durable power of attorney is a fiduciary—someone who holds a position of trust and must act in your best interests. The law requires your attorney-in-fact to:

- handle your property honestly and prudently
- avoid conflicts of interest
- keep your property completely separate from his or her own, and
- keep adequate records.

These standards do not present problems in most simple situations. For example, if you just want your attorney-in-fact to sign for your pension check, deposit it in your bank account and pay for your basic needs, there is little possibility of uncertainty or dispute.

Sometimes, however, these rules impose unnecessary hardships on an attorney-in-fact. For example, your property may already be mixed with that of your attorney-in-fact, and it may make good sense for that to continue. We allow you to insert clauses in your power of attorney document that permit your attorney-in-fact to deviate from some of the rules above, so that the attorney-in-fact's freedom isn't unnecessarily fettered. (See "Additional Duties and Responsibilities," below.)

When Court Supervision May Be Required

An attorney-in-fact is not directly supervised by a court; that's the whole point of naming one. The attorney-in-fact is not required to file reports with any courts or government agencies.

But a court may become involved if someone close to you fears that the attorney-in-fact is acting dishonestly or not in your best interests. It's rare, but close relatives or friends may ask a court to order the attorney-in-fact to take certain actions. Or they may ask the court to terminate the power of attorney and appoint a conservator to look after your affairs. If a conservator is appointed for you, the attorney-in-fact will have to account to the conservator—or the conservator may revoke your durable power of attorney altogether. As mentioned above, you can use your durable power of attorney for finances to name your attorney-in-fact as your first choice for conservator.

Some states have statutes that set out specific procedures for such court actions. For example, a California statute authorizes any interested person, including relatives and friends of the principal, to ask a court to resolve questions relating to the durable power of attorney. Tennessee law provides that the next of kin can petition a court to require an attorney-in-fact to post a bond—something like an insurance policy, generally issued by a surety company.

Even if your state does not have a statute specifically authorizing court actions, someone interested in your welfare and upset with the attorney-in-fact could still go to court and ask for a conservator to be appointed.

Liability for Mistakes

Your attorney-in-fact must be careful with your money and other property. State laws require an attorney-in-fact to act as a prudent person would under the circumstances. That means the primary goal is not to lose your money.

The attorney-in-fact may, however, make careful investment moves on your behalf. For example, if your money is in a low-interest bank account, the attorney-in-fact might invest the money in government bonds, which pay higher interest but are still very safe.

Because most people choose a spouse, close relative or friend to be attorney-in-fact, your power of attorney makes your attorney-in-fact liable only for losses resulting from intentional wrongdoing or extreme carelessness—not for a well-meaning decision that turns out badly.

Record-Keeping Responsibilities

Your attorney-in-fact is legally required to keep accurate and separate records for all transactions made on your behalf. Good records are particularly important if the attorney-in-fact ever wants to resign and turn the responsibility over to another person.

Record keeping isn't an onerous requirement. The attorney-in-fact must simply be able to show where and how your money has been spent. In most instances, it's enough to have a balanced checkbook and receipts for bills paid and claims made. And because the attorney-in-fact will probably file tax returns on your behalf, income and expense records may be necessary.

> **EXAMPLE:** Keiji appoints Kathryn, his niece, to serve as his attorney-in-fact. Keiji receives income from his savings, two IRAs, Social Security and stock dividends. Kathryn must keep records of the income for bank and tax purposes.

You and your prospective attorney-in-fact should discuss and agree on what record keeping is appropriate. The attorney-in-fact may also want to review your current records now to make sure they're in order. If you don't have clear records, the attorney-in-fact may have to spend a lot of time sorting things out later.

As part of managing your finances, the attorney-in-fact may hire a bookkeeper, accountant or other financial adviser and pay for the services from your property.

> **TIP**
>
> **Getting help with organizing.** If, like many people, you keep records in haphazardly labeled shoe boxes and file folders, this may be a good time to get organized. For help, use the Quicken WillMaker Plus Information for Caregivers and Survivors form.

The Basics of Your Durable Power of Attorney

In almost every state, you can create a valid power of attorney if you are at least 18 years old and of sound mind. (In Alabama, you must be at least 19 years old. In Nebraska, you must be at least 19 or married.) This mental competency requirement isn't hard to meet. Generally, you must understand what a durable power of attorney for finances is and does—and you must understand that you are making one.

To make your durable power of attorney with this program, you must enter some basic identifying information about yourself. This section explains the questions the program poses, in the order they appear.

Your Name

If you have already used Quicken WillMaker Plus to prepare your will, health care directives or final arrangements, your name will automatically appear on the screen that requests this information.

If it does not, enter your name the way it appears on formal business documents, such as your driver's license, bank accounts or real estate deeds. This may or may not be the name that appears on your birth certificate.

If you have used different names in important documents, you can list all of them on the screen, separated by aka, which stands for "also known as." Be sure to enter all names in which you hold bank accounts, stocks, bonds, real estate and other property. This will make it far easier for your attorney-in-fact to get his or her job done.

If you use more than one name and you're up for some extra work, you may also consider settling on one name for your power of attorney document, and then changing your other documents to conform. That will clean up your records and save your attorney-in-fact some trouble later on. To change your name on official documents and records—for example, bank accounts, deeds or Social Security records—you'll have to contact the appropriate government office or financial institution to find out what documentation they'll need.

Your Social Security Number

Your Social Security number can be very useful for your attorney-in-fact. It may help him or her to obtain your financial information and take care of your affairs. However, we do not ask you to include the number in your document. Growing concerns about identity theft make it important for you to protect this sensitive piece of information. Some states even forbid Social Security numbers on documents that will be placed in the public records. That said, you should be sure that your attorney-in-fact knows your Social Security number. Write it down and ask your attorney-in-fact to keep it safe.

Your Gender

We ask whether you are male or female so that your durable power of attorney document will include the correct gender pronoun instead of the awkward "he or she" and "his or her."

Your Address

Enter the complete address of your residence. If during the course of the year you live in more than one state, use the address in the state where you vote, register vehicles, own valuable property, have bank accounts or run a business. If you've already made a will or health care directive, be consistent: Use the same address for every document.

When Your Document Takes Effect

Your durable power of attorney for finances is effective as soon as you sign it. This means that your attorney-in-fact can start acting on your behalf whenever you choose. If you need someone to help you keep an eye on your finances, you may want your attorney-in-fact to start acting for you right away. On the other hand, you may prefer that your attorney-in-fact use the document only if you are unable to handle matters yourself, either because you are temporarily ill or injured or because of long-term incapacity.

If you want your attorney-in-fact to use the document only if you become incapacitated and unable to take care of your finances, be sure to clearly convey those wishes to the person you name. If you don't trust that your attorney-in-fact will refrain from using the document unless and until you are incapacitated, consider naming someone else to do the job.

SEE AN EXPERT

Springing powers of attorney. You may have heard of "springing" powers of attorney—that is, documents that become effective only if you are incapacitated. Many people like the idea of these documents, because no one can take action regarding your finances until at least one doctor certifies that you're not well enough to manage them yourself. Unfortunately, there are many inconveniences involved in making a springing document and getting it accepted. Because of the hassles involved, many experts advise that you make an immediately effective power of attorney document. If you feel strongly that you want a springing document instead, consult an attorney.

Choosing Your Attorney-in-Fact

We ask you to name your attorney-in-fact. This is the most important decision you must make when you create a durable power of attorney.

Depending on the powers you grant, the attorney-in-fact may have tremendous power over your property. You need to choose someone you trust completely. Fortunately, most of us know at least one such person—usually a spouse, relative or close friend. If there's no one you trust completely with this authority, a durable power of attorney isn't for you.

Remember that you can't count on anyone to keep an eye on the attorney-in-fact once he or she takes over your finances. If your attorney-in-fact handles your affairs carelessly or dishonestly, the only recourse would be a lawsuit—usually not a satisfactory approach. Lawsuits are burdensome and expensive and would entangle your loved ones in all the legal red tape a power of attorney is designed to avoid. And there's no guarantee that money an incompetent attorney-in-fact lost would ever be recovered. This reality is not intended to frighten you needlessly, but simply to underscore the need to make a careful choice about who will represent you.

Any competent adult can serve as your attorney-in-fact; the person most definitely doesn't have to be a lawyer. But don't appoint someone without first discussing it with that person and making sure he or she accepts this serious responsibility. If you don't, you may well cause problems down the line. The person you've chosen may not want to serve, for a variety of reasons. And even if the person would be willing, if your choice doesn't know about the document, confusion and delay are inevitable if you become incapacitated.

TIP

Getting help. Your power of attorney prints out with an information sheet you can give to your attorney-in-fact explaining the responsibilities of the job. You can use this document to help you remember the main issues when talking with your attorney-in-fact.

In most situations, the attorney-in-fact does not need extensive experience in financial management; common sense, dependability and complete honesty are enough. If necessary, your attorney-in-fact can get professional help—from an accountant, lawyer or tax preparer, perhaps—and pay for it out of your assets.

Sometimes it's tough to know whom to choose. Perhaps your spouse or partner is ill or wouldn't be a good choice for other reasons. Or you may not know anyone that you feel entirely comfortable asking to take over your financial affairs. Or, if you have an active, complex investment portfolio or own a business, you might decide that your attorney-in-fact needs business skills, knowledge or management abilities beyond those of the people closest to you.

If you're not sure whom your attorney-in-fact should be, read the rest of this section and discuss the issue with those close to you. If you can't come up with a family member or close friend to name, you may want to consider asking your lawyer, business partner or banker to serve as attorney-in-fact. If you really know and trust the person, it may be a good option for you. Keep in mind that it's better not to make a durable power of attorney than to entrust your affairs to someone in whom you don't have complete confidence.

Discussing Your Wishes

Set aside time to talk with your attorney-in-fact about when to start taking care of financial tasks for you. You can agree that your attorney-in-fact should not exercise any authority under the document unless you become completely unable to take care of yourself and your property—or unless you otherwise direct. With respect to exercising authority under the document, your attorney-in-fact is legally required to follow your wishes.

If you become dissatisfied with your attorney-in-fact's actions, and you are still of sound mind, you can revoke the durable power of attorney and end your attorney-in-fact's power to act for you.

CAUTION

Avoiding family conflict. If there are long-standing feuds among family members, they may object to your choice of attorney-in-fact or the extent of the authority delegated. If you foresee any such conflicts, it's wise to try to defuse them in advance. A discussion with the people who are leery of the power of attorney might help. If you still feel uncomfortable after talking things over, you may want to discuss the troubles with a knowledgeable lawyer. A lawyer can review your estate planning documents and might help you feel reassured that your plans will be carried out as you wish.

Avoiding Poor Choices for Attorney-in-Fact

Here are some suggestions to help you avoid problems when choosing an attorney-in-fact:

- To carry out duties and responsibilities properly and promptly, it's usually best that the attorney-in-fact live nearby. Although overnight mail, faxes, email and other technological wonders have made it easier to conduct business long distance, it's still best for your attorney-in-fact to be close at hand—or at least willing to travel and spend time handling your affairs when needed. After all, this is the person who will be responsible for day-to-day details of your finances: opening your mail, paying bills, looking after property and so on. Of course, many families are spread across the country these days. If there's only one person you trust enough to name as attorney-in-fact, and that person lives far away, you may have to settle for the less than ideal situation.

- Don't name an institution, such as a bank, as attorney-in-fact. It isn't legal in some states, and it's definitely not desirable. Serving as attorney-in-fact is a personal responsibility, and there should be personal connection and trust between you and your attorney-in-fact. If the person you trust most happens to be your banker, appoint that person, not the bank.

If You Are Married or Partnered

If you're married or partnered, you'll probably want to name your spouse as your attorney-in-fact unless there is a compelling reason not to do so. There are powerful legal and practical reasons, in addition to the emotional ones, for appointing your spouse. The main one is that naming anyone else creates the risk of conflicts between the attorney-in-fact and your spouse over how to manage property that belongs to both spouses.

> **EXAMPLE:** Henry and Amelia, a married couple, each create a durable power of attorney for finances. Henry names Amelia as his attorney-in-fact, but Amelia names her sister Anna. Later, Amelia becomes unable to manage her financial affairs, and Anna takes over as her attorney-in-fact. Soon Anna and Henry are arguing bitterly over what should be done with the house and investments that Henry and Amelia own together. If they can't resolve their differences, Henry or Anna may have to go to court and ask a judge to determine what is in Amelia's best interests.

However, if your spouse is ill, quite elderly or simply not equipped to manage your financial affairs, you may have to name someone else as attorney-in-fact. The wisest course is for you and your spouse to agree on whom the attorney-in-fact should be, perhaps one of your grown children.

 SEE AN EXPERT

Divorce may not end your spouse's authority. In many states, if your spouse is your attorney-in-fact, that designation does not automatically end if you get divorced. Wherever you live after a divorce, you should revoke the power of attorney and create a new one, naming someone else as your new attorney-in-fact.

If You Have a Living Trust

If you have created a revocable living trust, the successor trustee you named in the trust document will have power over the trust property if you become incapacitated. If you and your spouse made a living trust together, the trust document almost certainly gives your spouse authority over trust property if you become incapacitated.

Creating a durable power of attorney for finances doesn't change any of this. Your attorney-in-fact will not have authority over property in your living trust. To avoid conflicts, it is usually best to have the same person managing both trust property and nontrust property if you become incapacitated. So, normally, you'll name the same person as successor trustee and as your attorney-in-fact.

> **EXAMPLE:** Carlos, a widower, prepares a revocable living trust to avoid probate and a durable power of attorney for finances in case he becomes incapacitated. He names his son, Jeffrey, as successor trustee of the living trust and attorney-in-fact under the durable power of attorney.
>
> Several years later, Carlos has a stroke and is temporarily unable to handle his everyday finances. Jeffrey steps in to deposit his father's pension checks and pay monthly bills, using his authority as attorney-in-fact. As successor trustee, he also has legal authority over the property Carlos transferred to his living trust, including Carlos's house.

Appointing More Than One Person

In general, it's a bad idea to name more than one attorney-in-fact, because conflicts between them could disrupt the handling of your finances. Also, some banks and other financial institutions prefer to deal with a single attorney-in-fact.

Still, it is legal to name more than one person—and we allow you to name up to three people to serve together. But if you're tempted to name more than one person simply so that no one feels hurt or left out, think again. It may be better to pick one person for the job and explain your reasoning to the others now. If you name more than one person and they don't get along, they may wind up resolving their disputes in court. The result might be more bad feelings than if you had just picked one person to be attorney-in-fact and explained your choice in the first place.

Making Decisions

If you name more than one attorney-in-fact, you'll have to grapple with the question of how they should make decisions. You can require coagents to carry out their duties in one of two ways:

- they must all reach agreement before they take any action on your behalf, or
- they may make decisions independent of one another.

Both methods have strengths and pitfalls, and there's no hard-and-fast rule on which is better. Choose the approach that feels more comfortable to you.

Requiring your attorneys-in-fact to act jointly ensures that decisions are made carefully and with the knowledge of everyone involved, but coordinating multiple decision makers can be burdensome and time-consuming. On the other hand, allowing your attorneys-in-fact to act separately makes it easy to get things done, but allowing two or three people to make independent decisions about your finances can lead to poor record keeping and general confusion. For example, your attorneys-in-fact may independently take money out of your bank accounts or buy and sell stock without full knowledge of what the others are doing to manage your investments.

If There Is a Disagreement

If your attorneys-in-fact get into a dispute that interferes with their ability to represent you properly, they may need help working things out. Getting help could mean submitting the dispute to mediation or arbitration—or going to court to have a judge decide what's best. Your attorneys-in-fact can decide how they want to handle the matter, keeping in mind that their foremost responsibility is to act in your best interest. The downside of all this is not just that there could be confusion and delays in handling your finances, but that you'll probably be the one to pay the costs of settling the dispute. All these are reasons to name just one attorney-in-fact.

If One or More Cannot Serve

If you name more than one attorney-in-fact, and one of them can't serve, the others will continue to serve. If none of them can serve, an alternate can take over.

> **SEE AN EXPERT**
>
> **If you want to name more than three people.** The best approach is usually to choose just one attorney-in-fact. But this program allows you to name up to three people to serve together. Asking two or three people to manage your finances may prove unwieldy enough—counting on more than three to coordinate their actions on your behalf would be a logistical nightmare. If you want to name more than three attorneys-in-fact, talk with a lawyer.

Naming Alternates

It's a good idea to name someone to take over as your attorney-in-fact in case your first choice can't serve or needs to resign. This program allows you to name up to two alternate attorneys-in-fact, officially called successors. Your first alternate would take over if your initial choice can't serve. The second alternate would take the job only if your first and second choices can't keep it.

When naming alternates, use the same criteria that you used to make your first choice for attorney-in-fact. Your alternates should be every bit as trustworthy and competent. If you don't know anyone you trust well enough to name as a first or second alternate, skip the matter altogether.

Someone who is asked to serve as an alternate attorney-in-fact may be worried about possible liability for the acts of the original attorney-in-fact. To protect against this, your power of attorney will state that a successor attorney-in-fact is not liable for any acts of a prior attorney-in-fact.

You can also authorize your attorney-in-fact to appoint someone to serve if all those you named cannot. You do this by giving your attorney-in-fact permission to delegate tasks to others. (See "Additional Duties and Responsibilities," below.) Allowing your attorney-in-fact to delegate his or her job to someone else eliminates the risk that the position might become vacant because of the original attorney-in-fact's disability or resignation. If this occurs, and you haven't named a successor or none of your successors are available, your durable power of attorney would be useless. There would have to be a conservatorship proceeding to find someone to manage your finances.

If You Name More Than One Attorney-in-Fact

If you name more than one attorney-in-fact, the person you name as a first alternate will take over only if all of your attorneys-in-fact must give up the job. If any number of your first choices can continue to serve, they may do so alone, without the addition of your alternate.

If you name a second alternate, that person will take over only in the extremely unlikely event that all of your named attorneys-in-fact and your first alternate cannot serve.

Specific Financial Powers

Using this program, you can give your attorney-in-fact up to 15 specific financial powers. The powers may put an enormous amount of control over your finances into the hands of your attorney-in-fact, and it's important that you understand exactly what each power authorizes your attorney-in-fact to do. To that end, we walk you through each power, one at a time, asking whether you want to grant it or not.

If you grant all the powers, your attorney-in-fact will be able to handle your investments, real estate, banking and other financial tasks. The attorney-in-fact can use your assets to pay your debts and expenses— including home maintenance, taxes, insurance premiums, wage claims, medical care, child support, alimony and your personal allowance. The attorney-in-fact can sign deeds, make gifts, pay school expenses and endorse and deposit checks.

As you go through the list of powers, you may find yourself feeling concerned about how much power you're putting in someone else's hands.

These feelings are not unusual, as the lists of actions your attorney-in-fact can take are long, exhaustive and perhaps a bit overwhelming. As reassurance, keep in mind your attorney-in-fact's overriding legal duty to act carefully—and always with your best interests at heart. (See "About Your Attorney-in-Fact," above.) If you still find yourself feeling uncomfortable, take some time to reflect on your choice of attorney-in-fact; be sure you've chosen the best person for the job.

Each of the financial powers is explained here. They are presented as they appear in the program.

The New York Statutory Gifts Rider

When you empower your attorney-in-fact to make significant transfers of property on your behalf, New York requires your durable power of attorney to include an additional form—called the New York Statutory Gifts Rider. The rider is required when you give your attorney-in-fact the power to:

- transfer property to your living trust
- modify the title of bank accounts held jointly with someone other than the attorney-in-fact
- modify the beneficiaries of pay-on-death (Totten trust) bank accounts
- modify life insurance or retirement plan beneficiaries
- use the power of attorney for personal benefit
- commingle property, or
- give gifts in excess of $500.

If required, the rider will print out with your durable power of attorney. You will need to initial some of the clauses, sign it in front of a notary public and have it witnessed. Detailed signing instructions will print out with your document.

Real Estate Transactions

This power puts the attorney-in-fact in charge of any real estate you own. Your attorney-in-fact must, for example, use your assets to pay your mortgage and taxes and arrange for necessary repairs and maintenance to your home. Most important, the attorney-in-fact may sell, mortgage, partition or lease your real estate.

The attorney-in-fact may also take any other action connected to real estate. For example, your attorney-in-fact may:

- buy or lease real estate for you
- refinance your mortgage to get a better interest rate
- pay off legal claims on your property
- buy insurance for your property
- build, remodel or remove structures on your property
- grant easements over your property, and
- bring or defend lawsuits over real estate.

Restricting the Sale of Your Home

Losing your home, especially if you've lived there many years, can be a disturbing prospect. Some people feel strongly that the attorney-in-fact should not sell their home—no matter what happens. If you want to grant the real estate power but forbid your attorney-in-fact from selling or mortgaging your home, we allow you to include that restriction.

But think carefully before you tie the hands of your attorney-in-fact in this way. You certainly don't want to lose your home—but a financial emergency may make it necessary. Ideally, you'll trust the person you name as your attorney-in-fact to use discretion to make the decision based on your best interests—particularly if you have named your spouse or other co-owner of your home to serve as your attorney-in-fact.

Personal Property Transactions

Personal property here means physical items of property—for example, cars, furniture, jewelry, computers and stereo equipment. It does not include real estate or intangible kinds of property such as stocks or bank notes.

If you grant this power, your attorney-in-fact can buy, sell, rent or exchange personal property on your behalf. Your attorney-in-fact can also insure, use, move, store, repair or pawn your personal things. Again, all actions must be taken in your best interest.

> **EXAMPLE:** Paul names his wife, Gloria, as his attorney-in-fact for financial matters. When he later goes into a nursing home, his old car, which he can no longer use, becomes an expense Gloria cannot afford. As Paul's attorney-in-fact, she has legal authority to sell the car.

Stock, Bond, Commodity and Option Transactions

This power gives your attorney-in-fact the power to manage your securities—including stocks, bonds, mutual funds, certificates of deposit, commodities and call and put options. Your attorney-in-fact can buy or sell securities on your behalf, accept or transfer certificates or other evidence of ownership and exercise voting rights.

> CAUTION
>
> **Brokers may use different forms.** Many brokerage houses have their own durable power of attorney forms. If yours does, it's a good idea to use it in addition to the power of attorney you make with this program. Using your broker's form will make things easier for your attorney-in-fact, because your broker will have no need to investigate your power of attorney and quibble over its terms. The broker will already have its form on file and will understand exactly what your attorney-in-fact is authorized to do.

Banking and Other Financial Institution Transactions

One of the most common reasons for making a durable power of attorney is to arrange for someone to handle banking transactions. If you give your attorney-in-fact authority to handle your bank accounts, your bills can be paid, and pension or other checks can be deposited in your accounts even if you can no longer take care of these matters yourself.

EXAMPLE: Virginia, who is in her 70s, is admitted to the hospital for emergency surgery. She's too weak to even think about paying her bills or depositing her Social Security check—and, anyway, she can't get to the bank. Fortunately, she earlier created a durable power of attorney for finances, naming her niece Marianne as her attorney-in-fact. Marianne can deposit Virginia's check and sign checks to pay the bills that come while Virginia is in the hospital.

Your attorney-in-fact may open and close accounts with banks, savings and loans, credit unions or other financial institutions on your behalf. The attorney-in-fact may write checks on these accounts, endorse checks you receive and receive account statements. The attorney-in-fact also has access to your safe deposit box, to withdraw or add to its contents.

In most states, the attorney-in-fact may also borrow money on your behalf and pledge your assets as security for the loan.

Signing Checks and Other Documents

Many people wonder how the attorney-in-fact signs checks and other documents on behalf of the principal. Exact procedures vary depending on both local custom and the procedures of a particular financial institution or government agency. In some places, after establishing authority with a particular institution or agency, the attorney-in-fact will sign his or her own name to checks and documents, followed by "POA" or other language such as "under power of attorney dated June 15, 2011." In other locations, the attorney-in-fact will first sign your name and then his or her own name, followed by the "POA" designation.

CAUTION

Financial institutions may use different forms. Many banks and other financial institutions have their own durable power of attorney forms. Even though granting this program's banking power will give your attorney-in-fact authority to act on your behalf at any financial institution, it's a good idea to use the financial institution's form in addition to the form you make with this program. Using the form that your financial institution is most familiar with will make it easier for your attorney-in-fact to get things done.

TIP
New York Statutory Gifts Rider. If you live in New York and you grant this power, your durable power of attorney will include an additional form. See "The New York Statutory Gifts Rider," above.

Business Operating Transactions

This power gives your attorney-in-fact authority to act for you in operating a business that you own yourself or that you run as a partnership, limited liability company or corporation. Subject to the terms of a partnership agreement, an operating agreement or corporate rules set out in the bylaws and shareholders' agreements, your attorney-in-fact may:

- sell or liquidate the business
- merge with another company
- prepare, sign and file reports, information and returns with government agencies
- pay business taxes
- enforce the terms of any partnership agreement in court, and
- exercise any power or option you have under a partnership agreement.

If your business is a sole proprietorship, the attorney-in-fact may also:

- hire and fire employees
- move the business
- change the nature of the business or its methods of operation, including selling, marketing, accounting and advertising
- change the name of the business
- change the form of the business's organization—that is, enter into a partnership agreement or incorporate the business
- continue or renegotiate the business's contracts

- enter contracts with lawyers, accountants or others, and
- collect and spend money on behalf of the business.

If you're a sole proprietor, a durable power of attorney is a very useful way to let someone else run the business if you become unable to do so. No court proceedings are required for the attorney-in-fact to take over if you become incapacitated, so there should be no disruption of your business. Be sure to work out a business plan with the person you plan to appoint as your attorney-in-fact; explain what you want for your business and how you expect it to be managed.

> **CAUTION**
>
> **Check your existing agreements.** If you operate your business with other people as a partnership, limited liability company or closely held corporation, your business agreement should cover what happens if a partner or shareholder becomes incapacitated. Typically, the other business owners can operate the business during the incapacitated person's absence or even buy out his or her share. A durable power of attorney will not affect these rules you already have in place.

> **EXAMPLE:** Mike wants his wife, Nancy, to be his attorney-in-fact to manage his finances if he becomes incapacitated. Mike, a house painter, runs the M-J Painting Co. with his equal partner, Jack. Their agreement provides that if one partner becomes incapacitated, the other has exclusive authority to operate the business.
>
> If Jack and Nancy have conflicts over money, however, there could be some problems. Mike, Jack and Nancy should think through the arrangement carefully and may want to consult a lawyer. Whatever they decide on should be spelled out in detail in the partnership agreement. They may also want to create a customized durable power of attorney, with the lawyer's help, that sets out the details of the business arrangements.

Insurance and Annuity Transactions

This power allows your attorney-in-fact to buy, borrow against, cash in or cancel insurance policies or annuity contracts for you and your spouse, children and other dependent family members. The attorney-in-fact's authority extends to all your policies and contracts, whether they name you or someone else as the beneficiary—that is, the person who will receive any proceeds of the policy when you die.

The one exception to this rule covers insurance policies you own with your spouse. Under these policies, your spouse must consent to any transaction that affects the policy. So, if your attorney-in-fact is not your spouse, he or she will have to obtain your spouse's permission before taking action. Especially in community property states, even policies that are in one spouse's name may, in fact, be owned by both spouses. (See "Property Ownership Rules for Married People" in Chapter 5.) If you have questions about who owns your insurance policies, consult a lawyer. (See Chapter 17.)

If you already have an insurance policy or annuity contract, your attorney-in-fact can keep paying the premiums or cancel it—whichever he or she decides is in your best interests.

Your attorney-in-fact is also permitted to change and name the beneficiaries of your insurance policies or annuity contracts. This is a broad power, and it's a good idea to discuss your wishes about it with your attorney-in-fact. If you don't want your attorney-in-fact to change your beneficiary designations, make that clear. If you have strong feelings about whom the designated beneficiary of any new policies should be, you can discuss that as well.

> **TIP**
>
> **New York Statutory Gifts Rider.** If you live in New York and you grant this power, your durable power of attorney will include an additional form. See "The New York Statutory Gifts Rider," above.

Estate, Trust and Other Beneficiary Transactions

This power authorizes your attorney-in-fact to act on your behalf to claim or disclaim property you get from any other source. For example, if you were entitled to money from a trust fund, your attorney-in-fact could go to the trustee—the person in charge of the trust—and press your claim on your behalf. Or, if you didn't really need the money and it would cause your eventual estate tax bill to increase, your attorney-in-fact could turn down the cash.

Transferring Property to Your Living Trust

A revocable living trust is a legal structure you create by preparing and signing a document that specifies who will receive certain property at your death. Living trusts are designed to avoid probate, though some may also help you save on estate taxes or set up long-term property management.

If you've already set up a living trust, this power gives your attorney-in-fact the authority to transfer items of your property to that trust. But your attorney-in-fact can transfer property into your living trust only if you've given him or her authority over that type of property elsewhere in your document. For example, if you want your attorney-in-fact to be able to transfer real estate into the living trust, you must also grant the real estate power. And if you want your attorney-in-fact to transfer bank accounts to your living trust, you must also grant the banking transactions power.

> **TIP**
>
> **New York Statutory Gifts Rider.** If you live in New York and you grant this power, your durable power of attorney will include an additional form. See "The New York Statutory Gifts Rider," above.

Legal Actions

This provision allows your attorney-in-fact to act for you in all matters that involve courts or government agencies. For example, your attorney-in-fact can bring or settle a lawsuit on your behalf. He or she can also accept court papers intended for you and hire an attorney to represent you in court, if necessary. Unless your attorney-in-fact is a lawyer, he or she may not actually represent you in court but must hire someone to do so. If you lose a lawsuit, the attorney-in-fact can use your assets to pay the winner whatever you owe.

Personal and Family Care

This is an important power. It gives the attorney-in-fact the authority to use your assets to pay your everyday expenses and those of your family. The attorney-in-fact can spend your money for your family's food; shelter; education; cars; medical and dental care; membership dues for churches, clubs or other organizations; pets; vacations; and travel. The attorney-in-fact is allowed to spend as much as it takes to maintain the standard of living to which you, your spouse, children and anyone else you usually support are accustomed.

If you regularly take care of others—for example, you are the primary caretaker for a disabled sibling or parent—your attorney-in-fact can use your assets to continue to help those people.

Pet Care

A properly executed power of attorney that includes the standard powers discussed in this section—for example, the banking power and the personal and family care power—should permit your attorney-in-fact to spend money to take care of your pets. But because the law isn't explicit about pets, you can grant this special pet care power to ensure that your attorney-in-fact has complete authority to provide care for your animals.

This power guarantees that your attorney-in-fact can pay for the ongoing care of your pets or animals, including food, veterinary care, grooming, toys, day care and temporary boarding or pet-sitting fees. Your attorney-in-fact will be permitted to care for your pets or animals in the same way as you have done.

Government Benefits

This power allows your attorney-in-fact to apply for and collect any benefits you may be entitled to from Social Security, Medicare, Medicaid or other government programs or civil or military service. To collect most government benefits, your attorney-in-fact must send the government office a copy of the durable power of attorney to prove his or her authority. Social Security is an exception, however. (See below.)

Social Security Benefits

If you collect your Social Security benefits by direct deposit (as will be required by May 2013), your attorney-in-fact will have access to those funds as long as you've given that person access to the bank account where the funds are deposited.

However, if you still receive a Social Security check through the mail, to collect your benefits, your attorney-in-fact will have to take the power of attorney document to a local Social Security office. A representative will interview the attorney-in-fact and establish him or her as your "representative payee"—that is, someone entitled to receive your Social Security checks for you.

If you're creating a power of attorney that's effective immediately, you can save your attorney-in-fact some work by simply contacting the Social Security Administration and naming your attorney-in-fact as your representative payee. However, that means your attorney-in-fact will start receiving your Social Security checks right away, and you may not want that. If it's not yet time for the attorney-in-fact to take control under your power of attorney, you're better off granting the government benefits power and letting the attorney-in-fact deal with the Social Security Administration when the time comes.

In addition to granting the government benefits power, you might also consider having your Social Security check deposited directly into a bank account where your attorney-in-fact will have access to the funds without the hassles of dealing with the SSA. You can set up a direct deposit arrangement at any time, as long as you are of sound mind.

To appoint a representative payee or arrange for direct deposit of your benefits, contact the SSA at 800-772-1213.

Retirement Plan Transactions

This power gives your attorney-in-fact authority over retirement plans such as IRAs and Keogh plans. The attorney-in-fact may select payment options and designate beneficiaries—the people who will take any money left in the fund at your death. He or she can also change current beneficiary designations, make voluntary contributions to your plan, change the way the funds are invested and roll over plan benefits into other retirement plans. The attorney-in-fact may also perform any other actions authorized by the plan, including borrowing from it.

CAUTION

This power is powerful. The power to change the beneficiaries of your retirement funds is a drastic one. Talk with your attorney-in-fact to be sure he or she understands your wishes with respect to this power.

TIP

New York Statutory Gifts Rider. If you live in New York and you grant this power, your durable power of attorney will include an additional form. See "The New York Statutory Gifts Rider," above.

Tax Matters

This provision gives your attorney-in-fact authority to act for you in all state, local and federal tax matters. The attorney-in-fact can prepare and file tax returns and other documents, pay tax due, contest tax bills and collect refunds. To file a tax return on your behalf, the attorney-in-fact must include a copy of the power of attorney with the return. The attorney-in-fact is also authorized to receive confidential information about you from the IRS.

The IRS Power of Attorney Form

The IRS has its own power of attorney form, but you don't need to use it. It is primarily designed to allow attorneys, accountants and other professionals to receive confidential tax information on behalf of clients. It is not a comprehensive, durable power of attorney for tax matters. The form you make with this document gives your attorney-in-fact the power to receive confidential information from the IRS, plus the authority to handle any tax matters that arise.

Making Gifts

This last financial power allows your attorney-in-fact to make gifts of your property. You may already know that you want your attorney-in-fact to be able to give away your property under some circumstances. On the other hand, allowing your attorney-in-fact to make gifts might feel like giving up too much control.

Note for New York Readers

In New York, your agent is permitted to continue gifts that you regularly make to charities or individuals, so long as no one person or charity receives gifts worth more than $500 in one calendar year. If you want to allow your agent to make larger gifts, you'll need to grant the power discussed in this section. If you do grant this power, your durable power of attorney will include an additional form. See "The New York Statutory Gifts Rider," above.

Reasons to Allow Gifts

There are many reasons why you might want to permit your attorney-in-fact to make gifts of your property. Here are a few of the most common.

Estate tax savings. If you have substantial assets and are concerned about your eventual estate tax liability, you may be planning to reduce estate taxes by giving away some of your property while you are still alive. If you have set up this sort of gift-giving plan, you'll probably want to authorize your attorney-in-fact to continue it.

Other gift-giving plans. There are lots of reasons to give gifts that have nothing to do with estate planning and avoiding taxes. You may, for example, want to donate regularly to your church or a favorite charity. Or perhaps you've made a commitment to help a family member with college or starting up a business.

Family emergencies. All of us are occasionally caught off guard by unexpected financial troubles. You may want your attorney-in-fact to be able to help out if a loved one faces such an emergency.

Possible Gift Tax Consequences

If your attorney-in-fact gives away more than a certain amount—currently $13,000—to any one person or organization in one calendar year, a federal gift tax return will probably have to be filed.

Several kinds of gifts, however, are not taxable regardless of amount: gifts to your spouse, gifts that directly pay for medical expenses or tuition and gifts to tax-exempt charities. Gift tax may eventually have to be paid, but unless you make hundreds of thousands of dollars' worth of taxable gifts during your life, no tax will actually be due until after your death. Because your attorney-in-fact is required to act in your best interest, making large gifts could create a conflict. On one hand, your attorney-in-fact may feel that you would want to make a sizable gift—even if it's a taxable one—to a particular person or organization. On the other hand, if you have a very large estate that is likely to owe estate tax at your death, your attorney-in-fact won't want to increase your eventual tax liability.

For this reason, if you do permit your attorney-in-fact to make gifts, it's particularly important that you explain, ahead of time, what you intend and whether you have any limits.

RELATED TOPIC

More information about estate taxes. If you want to learn more about estate and gift taxes, see Chapter 13. For help beyond this book, see *Plan*

Your Estate, by Denis Clifford (Nolo). It's a detailed guide to estate planning, including all major methods of reducing or avoiding estate and gift taxes. If you still have questions, talk with a knowledgeable attorney.

Gifts to the Attorney-in-Fact

First, you must decide whether you want to allow your attorney-in-fact to make gifts to himself or herself. Because this raises some unique issues, you must consider it separately from the question of gifts to other people.

If you want to allow gifts to your attorney-in-fact, you must place an annual limit on them. This is because of a tricky legal rule called a general power of appointment. If your attorney-in-fact has an unlimited power to give your property to himself or herself and happens to die before you do, the attorney-in-fact could become the legal owner of all your property. In this case, your attorney-in-fact would be subject to taxes based not only on his or her own assets, but on yours as well.

To avoid this problem, you must limit the amount of money your attorney-in-fact may accept in any given year. To avoid trouble with gift taxes, you may want to let the current gift tax threshold be your guide and set the limit at $13,000 or less. Whatever amount you choose, be sure it's far less than what you're worth. If you set the limit too high, you may inadvertently create a general power of appointment.

Gifts to the Alternate Attorney-in-Fact

You may want to allow your primary attorney-in-fact to receive gifts of your property, but not your alternate attorney-in-fact. We allow you to include this restriction in your power of attorney document. If you allow gifts to your first-choice attorney-in-fact, and you've also named an alternate attorney-in-fact, the program will ask you whether or not your alternate is allowed to receive gifts of your property.

If you wish to allow your alternate to accept gifts of your property, that's fine, too. If you do allow gifts to your alternate, the annual gift limit will be the same as the amount you set for your first-choice attorney-in-fact.

Gifts to Others

After you've decided whether you want to allow gifts to your attorney-in-fact, we ask you about gifts to other people and organizations. If you're comfortable giving your attorney-in-fact broad authority, you can allow gifts to anyone your attorney-in-fact chooses. Or, you can specify the people and organizations to whom your attorney-in-fact may give your property.

If you give your attorney-in-fact broad authority to make gifts, be sure to discuss your intentions. Your attorney-in-fact should have a sound understanding of your plans for giving gifts—including the recipients you have in mind, under what circumstances gifts should be made and in what amounts.

Forgiving Loans

When you give your attorney-in-fact the power to make gifts, you also give the power to forgive or cancel debts others owe you. If anyone owes you money and you've authorized your attorney-in-fact to make gifts to them, be sure you let your attorney-in-fact know which debts you want to be paid and which may be forgiven.

If you've authorized gifts to your attorney-in-fact and he or she owes you money, your attorney-in-fact can forgive those debts, too. But for these debts, your attorney-in-fact can't cancel amounts worth more than his or her maximum gift amount in any calendar year. For example, your son, whom you've named as attorney-in-fact, owes you $20,000. You've placed the annual gift limit at $7,000. He can forgive his debt to you at the rate of $7,000 per year.

Remember that any gifts your attorney-in-fact makes must be in your best interest or according to your explicit instructions. For example, your attorney-in-fact may make annual gifts to each of your three children to reduce your estate tax liability—or periodic gifts to your niece because you promised to help her with college costs. Your attorney-in-fact should follow the guidelines you have set out in the power of attorney document.

Talk With Your Attorney-in-Fact

It's critically important that you talk with your attorney-in-fact, not just to be sure your choice is willing to take on the job of handling your finances, but to be sure your representative understands what that job entails. Sit down and discuss the list of powers you grant, being especially careful to cover those areas where your attorney-in-fact might exercise a lot of personal discretion.

Now is the time to clarify any special needs or concerns that you have. For example, if there are certain items of personal property you'd never want your attorney-in-fact to sell, note them down and let your attorney-in-fact know how you feel. Or, if you are allowing your attorney-in-fact to make gifts to help out family members or other loved ones who need help, talk frankly about whom you'd feel comfortable helping, as well as when and to what extent.

There is one caveat here: While it is wise to let your attorney-in-fact know what your wishes are, it's generally a bad idea to create a lot of complicated restrictions. There is no way to know what the future will bring—and, ideally, your attorney-in-fact will have enough flexibility to take whatever actions are necessary to take care of you. It is important to let your attorney-in-fact know what you want, but also to trust your choice enough to make the right decisions when the time comes.

Additional Duties and Responsibilities

After you've named your attorney-in-fact and decided which financial powers to grant, you have just a few more choices to make about how your attorney-in-fact will carry out the job. These last few questions include:

- whether you want your attorney-in-fact to make periodic reports to anyone about your finances

- whether you want to allow your attorney-in-fact to delegate tasks to others
- whether your attorney-in-fact may benefit financially from actions taken on your behalf
- whether the attorney-in-fact must keep his or her property separate from yours, and
- whether you want to pay your attorney-in-fact.

Periodic Reports

This program lets you require the attorney-in-fact to issue reports to people you name. Unless you require it, your attorney-in-fact doesn't have to report to anyone about your finances. In most cases, that arrangement is fine.

But in some circumstances, you may want to require reports. For example, if the attorney-in-fact is in charge of your business, investors may need to receive periodic financial statements, audited or reviewed by an accountant. Or perhaps you want to defuse a potentially explosive personal conflict by reassuring suspicious family members that they'll receive regular reports about your finances. We allow you to require quarterly or semiannual reports to people whom you name. (If you live in New York, this works a little differently. See the note just below.)

Note for New York Readers

In New York, instead of requiring reports, Quicken WillMaker Plus will ask you whether you want to designate one or more "monitors." If you do, any monitor may ask your attorney-in-fact for a copy of the power of attorney document and a record of all transactions your attorney-in-fact makes on your behalf.

As with requiring reports, naming monitors can place a substantial burden on your attorney-in-fact. See "About Reports," below, for help determining whether or not you really need to monitor your attorney-in-fact.

EXAMPLE: Theodore, who is ill, appoints his son, Jason, as his attorney-in-fact for finances. Theodore's two other children, Nancy and Ed, live out of state and aren't on the best of terms with Jason.

To prevent conflict between his children over Jason's handling of Theodore's finances, Theodore decides to require Jason to give Nancy and Ed semiannual reports of all financial transactions he engages in as attorney-in-fact.

About Reports

The idea of making your attorney-in-fact accountable to people may appeal to you. But before you enter a long list of names of people to whom your attorney-in-fact must make reports, ask yourself whether or not these reports are truly necessary.

One of the most important reasons for making a durable power of attorney is to give control of your finances to someone you trust completely, bypassing the court system. One big advantage of this tactic is that you spare your attorney-in-fact the hassle and expense of preparing reports and accountings for a court.

If you want someone to keep tabs on your attorney-in-fact, think again about whether you truly trust the person you've named.

This program's power of attorney document requires that all reports include income received by you and expenses incurred. If you want other details included, be certain your attorney-in-fact knows what they are.

Unless the timing of reports is governed by a business agreement or other legally binding document, you are free to require quarterly or semiannual reports. Weigh the need for the reports against the inconvenience to your attorney-in-fact and the expense of preparing the reports. If you have a very anxious relative, for example, you may want to authorize quarterly reports. Making these reports could be less hassle for your attorney-in-fact than dealing with constant interference from your family members. If the situation is not so tense, semiannual reports will probably do fine.

Special Requirements for Attorneys-in-Fact in Utah

If you live in Utah, your attorney-in-fact will have additional reporting responsibilities. These involve what the state calls "interested persons"— that is, anyone who may inherit property under your will or, if you don't make a will, your inheritors according to state law.

Here's what your attorney-in-fact must do:

- If you become incapacitated, your attorney-in-fact must notify all interested persons that he or she is your attorney-in-fact and provide them with his or her address. The attorney-in-fact has 30 days from the date of your incapacity to do this. However, since it is usually difficult to pin down the particular date on which someone becomes incapacitated, it is perhaps wiser for the attorney-in-fact to notify people within a month of first taking action under the power of attorney document.
- If any interested person requests it, your attorney-in-fact must provide a copy of the durable power of attorney.
- If any interested person requests it, your attorney-in-fact must provide an annual accounting of the assets to which the durable power of attorney applies, unless you specify that reports are not required, as this program permits you to do.
- Your attorney-in-fact must notify all interested persons when you die.
- If your attorney-in-fact turns over the job to an alternate, the new attorney-in-fact has ten days to notify inheritors of the change. The new attorney-in-fact must comply with all the reporting requirements listed above.

There are a couple of things you can do to help your attorney-in-fact comply with these requirements. First, give the attorney-in-fact the Information for the Attorney-in-Fact that prints out with your power of attorney document. It explains these reporting rules. Second, if you've made a will, give your attorney-in-fact a list of all the people to whom you are leaving property. It's not necessary to disclose exactly what you're leaving to each person, but without a simple list of names, your attorney-in-fact will have no sure way of knowing who needs to be contacted under

> ### Special Requirements for
> ### Attorneys-in-Fact in Utah (continued)
>
> law. (If you make your will using Quicken WillMaker Plus, there's an easy way to provide this list: It prints out at the end of the Letter to Executor that accompanies your will.)
>
> This Utah law is unusual because it places such strict reporting requirements on the attorney-in-fact. Before taking action under the power of attorney document, your attorney-in-fact may want to look at the Utah statutes to find out whether the requirements have changed. The law is contained in Sections 75-5-501(2) and (3) of the Utah Code, which can easily be found online. (See Nolo's Legal Research Center at www.nolo.com/legal-research.)

Delegating Powers

If your attorney-in-fact resigns from the job, the alternate you named will take over. But if there is no alternate available, or if your attorney-in-fact is only temporarily unavailable, the attorney-in-fact will need to find another person to do the job.

If you allow it, your attorney-in-fact can turn over all or part of his or her duties to someone else in this situation. This reassignment of duties is called delegation.

If you allow your attorney-in-fact to delegate tasks, he or she is free to turn over any or all of the job to a competent third person. This person may step in temporarily or permanently, depending on the situation.

> EXAMPLE 1: Caroline names her son, Eugene, as her attorney-in-fact for finances, effective immediately. She names a close friend, Nicole, as alternate attorney-in-fact. A year later, Eugene goes on vacation for three weeks, so he delegates his authority over Caroline's bank accounts to Nicole until he returns.

EXAMPLE 2: Anthony names his wife, Rosa, as his attorney-in-fact; his son Michael is the alternate attorney-in-fact. When Rosa declines to serve because of her own poor health, Michael takes over but soon finds that other responsibilities make it impossible to continue. He delegates all his authority to his sister, Theresa.

This program prints out a form that your attorney-in-fact can use to delegate authority to someone else. The new representative will use the signed form, along with your power of attorney document, to act on your behalf.

Exceptions to Legal Responsibilities

As discussed, your attorney-in-fact must always act in your best interests, must act honestly and prudently when managing your property and must keep good records. However, you may want to allow your attorney-in-fact to deviate from some standard legal duties, including:

- avoiding conflicts of interest, and
- keeping your property completely separate from his or her own.

Conflicts of Interest

In most states, an attorney-in-fact has no right to engage in activities from which he or she personally stands to benefit. Such activities, which create conflicts of interest between the principal and attorney-in-fact, are called self-dealing. The attorney-in-fact's motive is irrelevant. If the transaction is challenged in court, it is presumed fraudulent until the attorney-in-fact proves otherwise.

EXAMPLE: David is the attorney-in-fact for his elderly mother, Irene. After Irene's failing eyesight makes it impossible for her to drive, David decides to buy her car from her. He looks up the car's fair market value to make sure he is paying a fair amount, writes a check and deposits it in Irene's bank account.

This transaction is forbidden, even though David isn't cheating Irene, unless Irene's power of attorney specifically allows David to benefit from his management of her property and finances.

The ban on self-dealing is intended to protect you; after all, the attorney-in-fact is supposed to be acting on your behalf. It's quite sensible, however, to give the attorney-in-fact permission to self-deal if he or she is your spouse, a close family member, a business partner or another person whose finances are already intertwined with yours. We allow you to grant this permission in your power of attorney document.

EXAMPLE: Maurice wants Alice, his best friend, to serve as his attorney-in-fact. They have been involved in many real estate transactions together—including several current projects. Maurice doesn't want to risk disrupting these projects or curtailing Alice's ability to do business, so he specifically states in his durable power of attorney that Alice may benefit from transactions she undertakes on Maurice's behalf as his attorney-in-fact.

TIP

New York Statutory Gifts Rider. If you live in New York and you grant this power, your durable power of attorney will include an additional form. See "The New York Statutory Gifts Rider," above.

Making Gifts

When you grant financial powers to your attorney-in-fact, you may allow him or her to receive gifts of your property. (See "Making Gifts," above.) If you explicitly grant the gift-making power in your document, receiving permitted gifts is not considered a conflict of interest. In other words, it's perfectly fine to forbid your attorney-in-fact from using your power of attorney document for personal benefit while also allowing him or her to receive some of your property as a gift.

Mixing Funds

An attorney-in-fact is never allowed to mix or commingle your funds with his or her own unless the power of attorney specifically authorizes it. You will probably want to grant that authority if you appoint your spouse, mate or immediate family member as attorney-in-fact, and your finances are already thoroughly mixed together in joint bank or security accounts.

> EXAMPLE: Jim and Eduardo have been living together for 25 years. They have a joint checking account and share all basic living expenses. Each names the other as his attorney-in-fact. To avoid any possible problems, Jim and Eduardo both include, in their powers of attorney, specific provisions that allow commingling of funds.

TIP

New York Statutory Gifts Rider. If you live in New York and you grant this power, your durable power of attorney will include an additional form. See "The New York Statutory Gifts Rider," above.

Different Powers for Alternate Attorneys-in-Fact

While you might want to give your first-choice attorney-in-fact full power to benefit personally from transactions conducted on your behalf, or to mix your funds with his or hers, you may not feel comfortable giving an alternate attorney-in-fact the same authority. This is often the case for those who name a spouse or partner as attorney-in-fact and then name alternates with whom they are not so close or financially entwined. We allow you to specify whether an alternate attorney-in-fact should have the same power as your first choice, or whether you want to restrict the alternate's authority when it comes to personal benefit and mixing funds.

If You Named More Than One Attorney-in-Fact

Delegation becomes more complicated if you've named more than one attorney-in-fact.

Attorneys-in-Fact Who Must Act Jointly

If you require your attorneys-in-fact to act together in all that they do, it's a good idea to give them the power to delegate responsibilities. This is to avoid trouble in the event that one or more of your attorneys-in-fact becomes unable to act on your behalf. If this happens, the unavailable attorney-in-fact can use the delegation form to give his or her authority to the remaining attorneys-in-fact, temporarily or permanently. Your remaining attorneys-in-fact can use the delegation form to prove that they are permitted to act alone. If you don't grant the delegation power, an attorney-in-fact who will be unavailable will have to execute an affidavit—a sworn, notarized statement—that he or she cannot act for you. (If one of your attorneys-in-fact permanently resigns, he or she can sign a resignation form; the remaining attorneys-in-fact can use that form to prove their authority.)

In the unlikely event that all of your attorneys-in-fact will be temporarily unavailable, they can get together to choose a person to take over.

Attorneys-in-Fact Who May Act Separately

If you've authorized your attorneys-in-fact to act independently, allowing them to delegate tasks is probably not necessary or wise. The main reason for allowing delegation is to ensure that someone will always be on hand to take care of your finances. In your situation, if just one of your attorneys-in-fact is temporarily unable to act on your behalf, the others may simply act alone, without any special documents or fuss. And you can name up to two alternate attorneys-in-fact to take over if all of your attorneys-in-fact must step down. (See "Naming Alternates," above.)

Allowing delegation in your situation could, in fact, create much unnecessary confusion. Because your attorneys-in-fact may act independently, they could each delegate tasks to individuals that they choose—without consulting each other. When it comes to your finances, it's better not to open the door to that sort of chaos.

Paying Your Attorney-in-Fact

You can decide whether or not you want to pay your attorney-in-fact. If you do, you can specify your payment arrangement.

In family situations, an attorney-in-fact is normally not paid if the duties won't be complicated or burdensome. If your property and finances are extensive, however, and the attorney-in-fact is likely to devote significant time and effort managing them, it seems fair to offer compensation for the work. Discuss and resolve this issue with the proposed attorney-in-fact before you finalize your document.

If you decide to pay your attorney-in-fact something for managing your financial affairs, you can set your own rate—for example, $10,000 per year, $20 per hour or some other figure on which you agree. Or, if you don't want to decide on an amount right now, you can allow your attorney-in-fact to determine a reasonable wage when he or she takes over. No single strategy works best for everyone. Choose the approach—and the amount—that feels right to you.

EXAMPLE 1: Frederick is quite wealthy. He owns and operates a successful chain of convenience stores in a large city. He also owns a house, several pieces of investment property and a wide array of stocks. When he is diagnosed with a life-threatening illness, he creates a durable power of attorney for finances appointing his close friend Barbara as his attorney-in-fact. Because he expects Barbara to watch over his business as well as tend to his other financial affairs, he feels it's appropriate to pay her for her services. Frederick and Barbara settle on a rate of $20,000 per year for her services.

EXAMPLE 2: Martin creates a durable power of attorney naming his brother, Andrew, as attorney-in-fact. Martin owns a complex investment portfolio, and the brothers agree that Andrew should be paid if he has to manage Martin's finances. They consider an hourly wage but decide not to be that specific now. In his durable power of attorney, Martin states that Andrew may pay himself "reasonable" fees for his services.

If You Name More Than One Attorney-in-Fact

If you name more than one attorney-in-fact and you want to pay them, the amount you enter—for example, $5,000 per year or $18 per hour—applies to each one. If you want to allow your attorneys-in-fact to determine a reasonable amount for their services, each is allowed to set his or her own fee.

Nominating a Conservator or Guardian

It is possible, though highly unlikely, that a court proceeding could be brought to invalidate or overrule your durable power of attorney for finances. (See "Invalidation," below.) If your document is invalidated for any reason, a judge will appoint someone to manage your finances. This person is usually called a "guardian of your estate" or "conservator of your estate."

You can nominate your attorney-in-fact to serve as your financial guardian or conservator, if a court must appoint someone to that position. The court will follow your recommendation unless there is a compelling reason not to do so—for example, if someone has proved that your attorney-in-fact is mishandling your money. (Again, this type of outcome is very rare.)

If you do not nominate your attorney-in-fact to serve as the guardian or conservator of your estate, your power of attorney document will not mention the issue at all. In this case, the court would appoint a guardian or conservator by determining what would be in your best interests, but would do so without input from you.

Making It Legal

After you've done the hard work of putting together a durable power of attorney, you must carry out some simple tasks to make sure the document is legally valid and will be accepted by the people with whom your attorney-in-fact may have to deal. This section explains what to do.

Before You Sign

Before you finalize your power of attorney, you may want to show it to the banks, brokers, insurers and other financial institutions you expect your attorney-in-fact to deal with on your behalf.

Discussing your plans with people at these institutions before it is final—and giving them a copy of the durable power of attorney, after you sign it, if you wish—can make your attorney-in-fact's job easier. An institution may require that you include specific language in your durable power of attorney, authorizing the attorney-in-fact to do certain things on your behalf. You may have to go along if you want cooperation later. If you don't want to change your durable power of attorney, find another bank that will accept the document as it is.

Signing and Notarizing

A durable power of attorney is a serious document, and to make it effective you must observe certain formalities when you sign the document.

In all states but California, you must sign your durable power of attorney in the presence of a notary public for your state. (In California, you may choose whether to have your document notarized or witnessed. See "For California Residents: Making the Choice," below.) In many states, notarization is required by law to make the durable power of attorney valid. But even where law doesn't require it, custom usually does. A durable power of attorney that isn't notarized may not be accepted by people with whom your attorney-in-fact tries to deal.

The notary public watches you sign the durable power of attorney and then signs it, too, and stamps it with an official seal. The notary will want proof of your identity, such as a driver's license that bears your photo and signature. The notary's fee is usually inexpensive—around $10 in most places.

Finding a notary public shouldn't be a problem; many advertise in the yellow pages. Or check with your bank, which may provide notarizations as a service to customers. Real estate offices and title companies also have notaries.

If you are gravely ill, you'll need to find a notary who will come to your home or hospital room. To arrange it, call around to notaries listed in the yellow pages. Expect to pay a reasonable extra fee for a house call.

> **TIP**
>
> **In New York, you might need to sign twice.** If you live in New York and your power of attorney includes a New York Statutory Gifts Rider, you must sign and notarize both documents. See "The New York Statutory Gifts Rider," above.

Witnessing

Most states don't require the durable power of attorney to be signed in front of witnesses. (See "States That Require Witnesses," below.) Nevertheless, it doesn't hurt to have a witness or two watch you sign, and sign the document themselves. Witnesses' signatures may make the power of attorney more acceptable to lawyers, banks, insurance companies and other entities the attorney-in-fact may have to deal with. Part of the reason is probably that some other legal documents with which people are more familiar—including wills and health care directives—must be witnessed to be legally valid.

Witnesses can serve another function, too. If you're worried that someone may challenge your capacity to execute a valid durable power of attorney later, it's prudent to have witnesses. If necessary, they can testify that in their judgment, you knew what you were doing when you signed the document.

The witnesses must be present when you sign the document in front of the notary. Witnesses must be mentally competent adults, preferably ones who live nearby and will be easily available if necessary. The person who will serve as attorney-in-fact should not be a witness. In some states, the attorney-in-fact must sign the durable power of attorney document. (These states are listed below.)

State	No. of Witnesses	Other Requirements
States That Require Witnesses		
Arizona	1	Witness may not be your attorney-in-fact, the spouse or child of your attorney-in-fact or the notary public who acknowledges your document.
California	2	Witnesses are required only if your document is not notarized. The attorney-in-fact may not be a witness.
Connecticut	2	The attorney-in-fact may not be a witness.
Delaware	1	Witness may not be related to you by blood, marriage or adoption or be entitled to inherit a portion of your estate under your will or trust.
District of Columbia	2	Witnesses are necessary only if your power of attorney is to be recorded. (See "Recording," below.) The attorney-in-fact may not be a witness.
Florida	2	The attorney-in-fact may not be a witness.
Georgia	2	The attorney-in-fact may not be a witness. In addition, one of your witnesses may not be your spouse or blood relative.
Illinois	1	The witness may not be your agent, someone related to you or your agent by blood, marriage or adoption, a person who provides health services to you, or an owner or operator of a health care facility where you are a resident.
Maryland	2	Witnesses may not be your attorney-in-fact.
Michigan	2	Witnesses are necessary only if your power of attorney is to be recorded. (See "Recording," below.) The attorney-in-fact may not be a witness.

	States That Require Witnesses (continued)	
State	**No. of Witnesses**	**Other Requirements**
New York	2	Witnesses are necessary only if your power of attorney includes a statutory gifts rider. (See "The New York Statutory Gifts Rider," above.) Your agent may not be a witness, nor should any person who stands to benefit from your power of attorney document—for example, by receiving gifts you have authorized your agent to make.
Oklahoma	2	Witnesses may not be your attorney-in-fact, or anyone who is related by blood or marriage to you or your attorney-in-fact.
Pennsylvania	2	Witnesses are necessary only if the power of attorney is finalized with a mark (rather than a signature) or if it is signed by another person on behalf of and at the direction of the principal. Witnesses may not be your attorney-in-fact or the person who signs the document for you, if you can't sign it yourself.
South Carolina	2	The attorney-in-fact may not be a witness.
Vermont	1	Witness may not be your attorney-in-fact or the notary public who acknowledges your document.

For California Residents: Making the Choice

If you live in California, your durable power of attorney is valid if you have it notarized *or* if you sign it in front of two witnesses. Some people feel most comfortable using both methods together, but you are legally required to choose only one. We let you indicate how you want to finalize your document.

When choosing a method, there's one important consideration to keep in mind. If your power of attorney grants your attorney-in-fact authority over your real estate, you should absolutely have your document notarized. This is because you will have to put a copy of your document on file in the county recorder's office (see "Recording," below)—and in order to record your document, it must be notarized.

Obtaining the Attorney-in-Fact's Signature

In the vast majority of states, the attorney-in-fact does not have to agree in writing to accept the job of handling your finances. The exceptions to this rule are California, Georgia, Montana, New Hampshire, New York, Pennsylvania and Vermont.

California

In California, your attorney-in-fact must date and sign the durable power of attorney before taking action under the document. Ask the attorney-in-fact to read the Notice to Person Accepting the Appointment as Attorney-in-Fact at the beginning of the form. If your attorney-in-fact will begin using the power of attorney right away, he or she should date and sign the designated blanks at the end of the notice. If you've asked your attorney-in-fact not to use the document unless or until you become incapacitated, there's no need to obtain the signature now. Your attorney-in-fact can sign later, if it's ever necessary.

Georgia

In Georgia, your attorney-in-fact must sign the durable power of attorney document and complete an Acceptance of Appointment form. The acceptance form states that the attorney-in-fact understands the legal responsibilities involved in serving as an attorney-in-fact and agrees to carry out the duties to the best of his or her ability.

First, have your attorney-in-fact read and sign the acceptance form that prints out along with your power of attorney document. (After signing, the attorney-in-fact should attach the acceptance form to the original, finalized power of attorney document.) Then, ask the attorney-in-fact to sign the designated blank at the end of the power of attorney document itself, after your own signature.

If you've asked your attorney-in-fact not to use the document unless or until you become incapacitated, you don't have to obtain the attorney-in-fact's signatures right away. Keep the acceptance form together with the original power of attorney document. Your attorney-in-fact can complete it and sign the power of attorney later, if it ever becomes necessary to use the document.

Montana

If you live in Montana, we recommend that you ask your attorney-in-fact to sign the acceptance statement at the end of your durable power of attorney document. (You'll find it after the notary's acknowledgment.) It confirms that the attorney-in-fact willingly takes on the responsibilities of the job. Montana law states that having your attorney-in-fact sign this statement is optional, and that your attorney-in-fact becomes legally responsible simply by acting on your behalf. Nevertheless, the statement is included in Montana's official power of attorney form, and asking your attorney-in-fact to sign it will avoid any confusion about whether he or she understands the seriousness of the job.

Delaware, New Hampshire and Pennsylvania

In Delaware, New Hampshire and Pennsylvania, your attorney in fact must complete and sign an acknowledgment form. (Delaware calls it a certification.) This simple form ensures that your attorney-in-fact understands the legal responsibilities involved in acting on your behalf. When you print out your durable power of attorney, it will be accompanied by an acknowledgment form for your attorney-in-fact to sign.

If your attorney-in-fact will begin using the power of attorney right away, give the acknowledgment form to him or her along with the finalized, original power of attorney document. Your attorney-in-fact must complete the form and attach it to the power of attorney before taking action under the document.

If you've asked your attorney-in-fact not to use the power of attorney unless or until you become incapacitated, keep the acknowledgment form together with the original power of attorney document. Your attorney-in-fact can complete it later, if it ever becomes necessary to use the power of attorney.

New York and Vermont

If you live in New York or Vermont, your attorney-in-fact must sign the power of attorney before taking action under the document. If your attorney-in-fact will begin using the power of attorney right away, ask him or her to print and then sign his or her full name in the designated blanks at the end of the form. If you've asked your attorney-in-fact not to use the document unless or until you become incapacitated, there's no need to obtain the attorney-in-fact's signature now. He or she can sign the document later, if it's ever necessary.

Recording

You may need to put a copy of your durable power of attorney on file in the land records office of the counties where you own real estate, called the county recorder's or land registry office in most states. This is called "recording," or "registering" in some states.

Mandatory Recording

Just two states, North Carolina and South Carolina, require you to record a power of attorney for it to be durable—that is, for it to remain in effect if you become incapacitated.

Note for Illinois, Kentucky and Minnesota Readers

If you live in Illinois, Kentucky or Minnesota, when you review your power of attorney document, you'll notice a "preparation statement" at the very end of it. The preparation statement is a simple listing of the name and address of the person who prepared the document. We add this statement because, in these three states, you cannot record your document without it.

In most cases, the name of the principal and the name of the person who prepared the document will be the same: your own. Occasionally, however, someone may use this program to prepare a form for another person—an ailing relative, for example. In that case, the name and address of the person who stepped in to help should appear in the preparation statement.

> ## Note for North Carolina Readers
>
> In your state, a durable power of attorney must be:
> - recorded with the Register of Deeds, and
> - filed with the clerk of the Superior Court within 30 days after recording, unless the durable power of attorney waives the requirement that the attorney-in-fact file inventories and accountings with the court. Your power of attorney form waives this filing requirement.

In other states, you must record the power of attorney if it gives your attorney-in-fact authority over your real estate. Essentially, this means you must record the document if you granted the real estate power. In this case, if you don't record the document, your attorney-in-fact won't be able to sell, mortgage or transfer your real estate.

Recording makes it clear to all interested parties that the attorney-in-fact has power over the property. County land records are checked whenever real estate changes hands or is mortgaged; if your attorney-in-fact attempts to sell or mortgage your real estate, there must be something in the records that proves he or she has authority to do so.

There is no time limit on when you must record a durable power of attorney. So if you've created a document that won't be used unless and until you become incapacitated, you may not want to record it immediately. Your attorney-in-fact can always record the document later, if he or she ever needs to use it.

Even if recording is not legally required, you can do so anyway; officials in some financial institutions may be reassured later on by seeing that you took that step.

Where to Record

In most states, each county has its own office for a recorder or registry of deeds. If you're recording to give the attorney-in-fact authority over real estate, take the durable power of attorney to the office in the county where the real estate is located. If you want your attorney-in-fact to have authority over more than one parcel of real estate, record the power of attorney in each county where you own property. If you're recording for any other reason, take the document to the office in the county where you live.

How to Record

Recording a document shouldn't be complicated, though some counties can be quite fussy about their rules (See below.) You may even be able to record your document by mail, but it's safer to go in person. Typically, the clerk makes a copy of your document for the public records and assigns it a reference number. In most places, it costs less than $10 per page to record a document.

> (!) **CAUTION**
>
> **Check your county's recording procedures before you finalize your document.** Some counties will ask you to meet very particular requirements before they will put your power of attorney on file. Or, if you don't adhere to their rules, they will charge you an extra fee for filing the document.
>
> For example, in some counties, you may be required to file an original document, rather than a photocopy, with the land records office. In this case, you'll need to make a second original, being sure to have it signed, notarized and witnessed (if necessary), just like the first.
>
> And some counties require a margin of a certain number of inches at the top of the first page of a power of attorney. This is where they put the filing stamp when you record the document. Local customs vary widely here; some counties will accept a standard one-inch margin while others ask for a margin of two, three or even four inches. When you make your document, you can set the correct number of inches for the top margin of the first page.
>
> To avoid hassles and extra expenses, you should call the land records office before you finalize your power of attorney to make sure you're prepared to meet any special requirements for putting it on file.

What to Do With the Signed Document

Your attorney-in-fact will need the original power of attorney document, signed and notarized, to act on your behalf. So, if you want your attorney-in-fact to start using the document right away, give the original document to the attorney-in-fact.

If you named more than one attorney-in-fact, give the original document to one of them. Between them, they will have to work out the best way to prove their authority. For example, they may decide to visit some financial institutions or government offices together to establish themselves as your attorneys-in-fact. Or they may need to take turns with the document. Some agencies, such as the IRS, will accept a copy of the document, rather than the original: Such flexible policies make things easier on multiple attorneys-in-fact who need to share the original document.

Making and Distributing Copies

If you wish, you can give copies of your durable power to the people your attorney-in-fact will need to deal with—in banks or government offices, for example. If the durable power is in their records, it may eliminate hassles for your attorney-in-fact later because they will be familiar with the document and expecting your attorney-in-fact to take action under it.

If your power of attorney won't be used unless and until you become incapacitated, however, it may seem premature to contact people and institutions about a document that may never go into effect. It's up to you.

Be sure to keep a list of everyone to whom you give a copy. If you later revoke your durable power of attorney, notify each institution of the revocation. (See "Revoking Your Durable Power of Attorney," below.)

Keeping Your Document Up to Date

If you make a power of attorney that your attorney-in-fact won't use unless and until you become incapacitated, it's a good idea to revoke it and create a new one every five to seven years, especially if your circumstances have changed significantly. A durable power of attorney never expires, but if the document was signed many years before it is used, the attorney-in-fact may have more difficulty getting banks, insurance companies or people in government agencies to accept it.

What to Do With the Additional Documents

This program prints out several additional documents along with your durable power of attorney form. These are discussed throughout the chapter, but here is a quick summary of these documents and what you should do with them.

Information for an Attorney-in-Fact

This sheet is intended to help your attorney-in-fact understand the job. It discusses the attorney-in-fact's duties and responsibilities, including the duty to manage your property honestly and prudently and to keep accurate records. You should give a copy to the person you name in your document and take some time to talk together about the responsibilities involved.

Delegation of Authority

If you allow your attorney-in-fact to delegate tasks to others, he or she may want to use the Delegation of Authority form. Give a copy to your attorney-in-fact. Or, if your power of attorney won't be used right away, keep the form with your power of attorney document so your attorney-in-fact will have easy access to it later.

Resignation of Attorney-in-Fact

Your attorney-in-fact can use the Resignation of Attorney-in-Fact form to step down from the job. The attorney-in-fact should fill out the form and send it to the alternate attorney-in-fact. If you name more than one attorney-in-fact, the one who resigns may send the form to the others. Give a copy of this form to your attorney-in-fact along with your power of attorney document. Or, if your power of attorney won't be used right away, keep the forms together in a safe place known by your attorney-in-fact, who can obtain them if it becomes necessary.

Notice of Revocation of Durable Power of Attorney

If you ever want to revoke your power of attorney, prepare and sign a Notice of Revocation. Keep a copy of this form on file in case you need it later.

Notice of Revocation of Recorded Power of Attorney

If you record your power of attorney, then change your mind and want to cancel the document, you must also record a Notice of Revocation. To do this, you can use the Notice of Revocation of Recorded Power of Attorney form. Keep a blank copy on file for future use.

Revoking Your Durable Power of Attorney

After you make a power of attorney, you can revoke it at any time, as long as you are of sound mind. But to make the revocation legally effective, you must carefully follow all the procedures set out in this section.

If You Move to Another State

If you move to another state, it's best to revoke your old durable power of attorney as described below and create a new one, complying with all regulations of your new state. This is true even though your old power of attorney may be acceptable under your new state's laws.

If you don't make a new document, your attorney-in-fact may run into problems that are more practical than legal. For example, the document may need to be recorded with the local land records office in the new state. If the document does not meet certain requirements, the recorder's office in the new state may not accept it. Making a new document will ensure that things will go smoothly for your attorney-in-fact.

Who Can Revoke

Only you, or someone a court appoints to act for you, can revoke your power of attorney.

When You Can Revoke

You can revoke your durable power of attorney as long as you are of sound mind and physically able to do so. The sound mind requirement is not difficult to satisfy. If someone challenged the revocation, a court would look only at whether or not you understood the consequences of signing the revocation. (The competency requirement is the same as that required to create a valid power of attorney in the first place; see "Possible Challenges to Your Document," below.)

> **SEE AN EXPERT**
>
> **If you and your attorney-in-fact can't agree.** An attorney-in-fact who refuses to accept a revocation can create serious problems. If you get into such a dispute with your attorney-in-fact, consult a lawyer. (See Chapter 17.)

If a Conservator or Guardian Is Appointed

If your attorney-in-fact is satisfactorily handling your financial affairs while you can't, it's very unlikely that a court will need to appoint a conservator for you. And if it does become necessary, you can use your document to name your attorney-in-fact to the post. (See "Nominating a Conservator or Guardian," above.)

If, however, you or a family member objected to the attorney-in-fact's actions, a court might appoint someone else as conservator. In a few states, appointment of a conservator automatically revokes a durable power of attorney. In that case, the conservator would become solely responsible for your property and financial matters.

In many states, the conservator would have the legal authority to revoke your durable power of attorney. Someone appointed to take physical care of you—usually called a guardian or guardian of the person—not your property, may also, depending on state law, have the power to revoke a financial power of attorney.

When to Revoke

If you've prepared a power of attorney that won't be used unless you're incapacitated, years may elapse between the time you sign the durable power of attorney and when it is put to use. During that interval—or even after your attorney-in-fact starts using the document, as long as you are mentally competent—you may decide you need to revoke the durable power of attorney. Here are the most common situations in which you should revoke a power of attorney and start over.

Changing the Terms

There is no accepted way to amend a power of attorney. If you want to change or amend a durable power of attorney, the safe course is to revoke the existing document and prepare a new one. Don't go back and modify your old document with pen, typewriter or correction fluid—you could throw doubt on the authenticity of the whole thing.

> **EXAMPLE:** Tom signed a durable power of attorney several years ago. Now he is in declining health and wants to add to the authority he gave his attorney-in-fact, Sarah, giving her the power to sell his real estate if necessary. Tom should revoke his old durable power of attorney and create a new one, granting the additional authority.

Similarly, you should revoke your durable power of attorney if you change your mind about your choice of attorney-in-fact. If you create a durable power of attorney that won't be used until later, the person you named to be your attorney-in-fact may become unavailable before he or she is needed. Or you may simply change your mind. If that's the case, you can revoke the durable power of attorney before it is ever used.

Moving to Another State

If you move to a different state, your attorney-in-fact may run into some trouble getting others to accept the validity of a power of attorney signed in your old state. It's best to revoke your power of attorney and prepare a new one.

Losing the Document

If you lose your signed power of attorney document, it's wise to formally revoke it, destroy any copies and create a new one. Very few people are likely to accept your attorney-in-fact's authority if they can't look at the document granting the authority. By officially revoking the lost version, you reduce chances that the old power of attorney might someday resurface and confuse matters.

Marrying or Divorcing

If you get married after signing a durable power of attorney, you'll probably want to designate your new spouse to be your attorney-in-fact, if he or she wasn't the person you named originally.

If you name your spouse as your attorney-in-fact and later divorce, you will probably want to revoke the power of attorney and create a new one, naming someone else as the attorney-in-fact.

In a number of states, the designation is automatically ended if you divorce the attorney-in-fact. In that case, any alternate you named would serve as attorney-in-fact. You still may want to create a new power of attorney—one that doesn't mention your former spouse and lets you name another alternate attorney-in-fact.

Revoking Your Document

There are two ways to revoke your power of attorney. You can:
- prepare and sign a document called a Notice of Revocation, or
- destroy all existing copies of the document.

The first method is always preferable, because it creates proof that you really revoked the power of attorney.

Some states may allow you to revoke your power of attorney simply by preparing a new one. It's still advisable, however, to prepare a separate Notice of Revocation and notify everyone who needs to know about the revocation.

Preparing a Notice of Revocation

The purpose of a Notice of Revocation is to notify the attorney-in-fact and others that you have revoked the durable power of attorney.

This program prints out two kinds of Notice of Revocation forms for you to use. If you didn't record your durable power of attorney in the county land records office, choose the Notice of Revocation for an unrecorded document. If you did record the original durable power of attorney, you must also record the revocation; choose the Notice of Revocation for a recorded document.

Signing and Notarizing the Document

You must sign and date the Notice of Revocation. It need not be witnessed, but witnessing may be a prudent idea—especially if you have reason to believe that someone might later raise questions regarding your mental competence to execute the revocation. If you want witnesses' signatures, we offer that option. Choose the appropriate revocation document and indicate that you will have it witnessed.

Sign the Notice of Revocation in front of a notary public. (For more on notarization, see "Making It Legal," above.)

Recording the Document

If you recorded the original durable power of attorney at your local recorder of deeds office, you must also record the revocation.

But even if the original durable power of attorney was not recorded, you can record a revocation if you fear that the former attorney-in-fact might try to act without authorization. If the revocation is part of the public records, people who check those records in dealing with the real estate later will know that the former attorney-in-fact is no longer authorized to act on your behalf.

Note for North Carolina Readers

When you register the revocation in the Register of Deeds Office, it must be accompanied by a document showing that a copy of the revocation notice has been delivered to—or served on—the former attorney-in-fact. This document is called a proof of service.

The revocation must be served on the attorney-in-fact by the county sheriff or someone else authorized by law to serve legal papers.

Notifying Others

It's not enough to sign a revocation, or even to record it, for it to take effect; there's one more crucial step. You must notify the former attorney-in-fact and all institutions and people who have dealt or might deal with the former attorney-in-fact. Each of them must receive a copy of the Notice of Revocation.

If you don't give this written notification, people or institutions who don't know the durable power of attorney has been revoked might still enter into transactions with the former attorney-in-fact. If they do this in good faith, they are legally protected. You may well be held legally liable for the acts of your attorney-in-fact, even though you have revoked his or her authority. In other words, once you create a durable power of attorney, the legal burden is on you to be sure everyone knows you have revoked it.

Who Needs to Know?

When you're ready to send out revocation notices, try to think of everyone with whom the attorney-in-fact has had, or may have, dealings. These may include:

- banks
- mortgage companies
- title companies
- stockbrokers
- insurance companies
- Social Security offices
- Medicare or Medicaid offices
- military or civil service offices
- the IRS
- pension fund administrators
- post offices
- hospitals
- doctors
- schools
- relatives
- business partners
- landlords
- lawyers
- accountants
- real estate agents, and
- maintenance and repair people.

EXAMPLE: Before Michael undergoes a serious operation, he makes a durable power of attorney. After his convalescence, Michael revokes the power of attorney in writing. He sends a copy of the revocation to Colette, his attorney-in-fact, but neglects to send a copy to his bank. Colette, fraudulently acting as Michael's attorney-in-fact, removes money from Michael's accounts and spends it. The bank isn't responsible to Michael for his loss.

When the Power of Attorney Ends

A durable power of attorney for finances is valid until you revoke it, you die or there is no one to serve as your attorney-in-fact. A court can also invalidate a power of attorney, but that happens very rarely.

Revocation

As long as you are mentally competent, you can revoke a power of attorney for finances at any time, whether or not it has taken effect. All you need to do is fill out a simple form, sign it in front of a notary public and give copies to the attorney-in-fact and to people or institutions with whom the attorney-in-fact has been dealing. (See "Revoking Your Durable Power of Attorney," above.) You can use this program to print out a revocation form.

EXAMPLE: Susan prepares a durable power of attorney naming her closest friend, Tina, as her attorney-in-fact. Three years later, they have a bitter fight. Susan prepares a one-page document that revokes the durable power of attorney and gives Tina a copy. She destroys the old document and then prepares a new one, naming her sister Joan as her attorney-in-fact.

Invalidation

Even if you sign a durable power of attorney for finances, if you become incapacitated there is a remote possibility that a disgruntled relative could ask a court to appoint a conservator to manage your financial affairs.

It's rare, but a power of attorney could be ruled invalid if a judge concludes that you were not mentally competent when you signed the durable power of attorney or that you were the victim of fraud or undue influence. The power of attorney could also be invalidated for a technical error, such as the failure to sign your document in front of witnesses if your state requires it. If that happens, the judge could appoint a conservator to take over management of your property.

In most states, if a court appoints a conservator, the attorney-in-fact becomes accountable to the conservator—not just to you—and the conservator has the power to revoke your durable power of attorney if he or she doesn't approve of the way your attorney-in-fact is handling your affairs. In a few states, however, your durable power of attorney is automatically revoked, and the conservator assumes responsibility for your finances and property.

Divorce

In a handful of states, if your spouse is your attorney-in-fact and you divorce, your ex-spouse's authority is immediately terminated. If you named an alternate attorney-in-fact in your power of attorney, that person takes over as attorney-in-fact. If you didn't name an alternate, your power of attorney ends.

In any state, however, others may question the validity of a document created before a divorce that names the ex-spouse as attorney-in-fact. For this reason, if you get divorced you should revoke your durable power of attorney and make a new one.

No Attorney-in-Fact Is Available

A durable power of attorney must end if there's no one to serve as the attorney-in-fact. To avoid this, we let you name up to two alternate attorneys-in-fact, so someone will be available to serve if your first choice can't do the task.

For a bit of extra insurance, you can also allow the alternate attorney-in-fact to delegate his or her duties to someone else. (See "Delegating Powers," above.)

Death

A durable power of attorney ends when the principal dies. In most states, however, if the attorney-in-fact doesn't know of your death and continues to act on your behalf, his or her actions are still valid.

If you want your attorney-in-fact to have any authority over winding up your affairs after your death, grant that authority in your will—and in your living trust, if you make one. (See Chapter 8 for information about executors.)

Possible Challenges to Your Document

A common fear is that your durable power of attorney for finances will not be accepted by those around you. While rare, challenges are sometimes raised by people who feel you were not of sound mind when you signed the document or who fear that the document is not legally valid.

Your Mental State

You must be of sound mind when you create your durable power of attorney for finances. When you sign the document, no one makes a determination about your mental state. The issue will come up only if someone goes to court and challenges the durable power of attorney, claiming that you weren't mentally competent when you signed it. That kind of lawsuit is very rare.

Even in the highly unlikely event of a court hearing, the competency requirement is not difficult to satisfy. If you understood what you were doing when you signed your durable power of attorney, that's enough. To make this determination, a judge would probably question any witnesses who watched you sign the document and others who knew you well at the time. There would be no general inquiry into your life. It wouldn't matter, for example, that you were occasionally forgetful or absentminded around the time when you signed your power of attorney document.

Heading Off Problems

If you think someone is likely to challenge the legitimacy of your durable power of attorney, you can take several steps to head off problems:

- **See a lawyer.** An experienced estate planning lawyer can answer questions about your durable power of attorney and about your other estate planning documents as well. For example, you may also be expecting challenges to your will, a trust or health care wishes. The lawyer can put your fears to rest by answering your questions and reviewing or modifying your documents. He or she can help to ensure that your estate plan will hold up under the challenges of your stubborn relatives. Your attorney can also testify about your mental competency, should the need arise.

- **Sign your document in front of witnesses.** You can sign your document in front of witnesses, even if your state does not require it. (See "Making It Legal," above.) After watching you sign, the witnesses themselves sign a statement that you appeared to know what you were signing and that you signed voluntarily. If someone later challenges your competency, these witness statements will be strong evidence that you were of sound mind at the time you signed your document.

- **Get a doctor's statement.** You may also want to get a doctor's statement around the time you sign your durable power of attorney. The doctor should write, date and sign a short statement saying that he or she has seen you recently and believes you to be mentally competent. You can attach this statement to your power of attorney document. Then, if necessary, your attorney-in-fact can produce the statement as evidence that you were of sound mind when you signed your power of attorney.

- **Make a videotape.** You can also videotape a statement of your intent to make and sign the durable power of attorney. However, using a videotape could work against you if it shows any visible quirks of behavior or language that could be used as evidence that you were not in fact competent when you made your document. If you do make a videotape, keep it with your power of attorney document.

The Document's Validity

It's reasonable for someone to want to make sure that your durable power of attorney is still valid and hasn't been changed or revoked. To reassure other people, your attorney-in-fact can show that person the power of attorney document. To lay any fears to rest, it clearly states that any person who receives a copy of the document may accept it without the risk of legal liability—unless he or she knows that the document has been revoked.

Laws in most states also protect people who rely on apparently valid powers of attorney. For example, many states have laws stating that a written, signed power of attorney is presumed valid, and a third party may rely on it.

As a last resort, the attorney-in-fact can sign a sworn statement or affidavit in front of a notary public, stating that as far as he or she knows, the durable power of attorney has not been revoked and that you are still alive. Most states have laws that make such a statement conclusive proof that the durable power of attorney is in fact still valid.

The Powers Granted

Any other person who relies on a durable power of attorney must be sure that the attorney-in-fact has the power he or she claims to have. That means the person must examine the document to see what power it grants.

This program's power of attorney document is very specific about the attorney-in-fact's powers. For example, if you give your attorney-in-fact authority over your banking transactions, the document expressly states that the attorney-in-fact is empowered to write checks on your behalf. Your attorney-in-fact can point to the paragraph that grants that authority, so a doubting bank official can read it in black and white.

An attorney-in-fact who runs into resistance should seek, politely but insistently, someone higher up in the bureaucracy.

Health Care Directives

E very adult can benefit from making health care directives—that is, documents in which you express your health care wishes and appoint a person to make decisions for you if, someday, you can no longer speak for yourself. If you're looking for a living will or durable power of attorney for health care, you're in the right place. They are both types of health care directives.

If you're older or in ill health, you surely understand why these documents are important. But if you're younger—perhaps using this program to help prepare health care documents for a loved one—consider making documents for yourself now, even if you don't think it's necessary.

While it's true that the elderly and the seriously ill should make health care directives to smooth the way for decision making at the end of life, we tend to avoid another, disturbing truth: Younger, healthy adults should also have health care directives, because an incapacitating accident or unexpected illness can occur at any time. In fact, if you look at the painful stories that make headlines (see "You Have the Legal Right to Direct Your Own Care," below), you'll quickly notice that the bitterest family fights over end-of-life health care don't happen when a patient is very old or has a long illness. The worst disputes arise when tragedy strikes a younger adult who never clearly expressed any wishes about medical treatment.

You Have the Legal Right to Direct Your Own Care

Your right to direct your own health care is now well established. But that wasn't always the case. Just a few decades ago, heart-wrenching legal battles were fought to win permission to create a document stating that life-prolonging treatments should be terminated—or continued—at the end of life.

Landmark cases involving Karen Ann Quinlan and Nancy Cruzan—two young women who became brain damaged and unable to communicate their wishes—opened the way to laws supporting health care documents. Now, every state has a law that permits you to express your health care wishes and requires medical personnel to follow those wishes—or transfer you to the care of someone else who will do so.

Here, we walk you through the process of making your own customized health care directives. It won't take long to make your preferences known: You can most likely prepare your documents in less than an hour. That hour might save your family days, months or even years of confusion and grief.

What Happens If You Don't Make Documents

If you do not prepare health care documents, state law tells your doctors what to do. In some states, they may decide what kind of medical care you will receive. Most states, however, require doctors to consult your spouse, registered domestic partner or an immediate relative. The person entitled to make decisions on your behalf is called your "surrogate." A few states allow a "close friend" to act as surrogate. If there is a dispute about who should be your surrogate, it may have to be resolved in court.

Whether required by law or not, if there is a question about whether surgery or some other serious procedure is authorized, doctors will usually turn for guidance to a close relative—spouse, registered domestic partner, parent, child. Friends and unmarried partners, although they may be most familiar with your wishes for your medical treatment, are rarely consulted, or—worse still—are sometimes purposefully left out of the decision-making process.

Problems arise when loved ones and family members disagree about what treatment is proper and everyone takes sides, claiming they want what is best for the patient. Battles over medical care may even end up in court, especially now that some religious organizations finance lawsuits to block the removal of feeding tubes from permanently unconscious patients. In court, a judge, who usually has little medical knowledge and no familiarity with the patient, must decide the course of treatment. Such battles—which are costly, time-consuming and painful to those involved—are unnecessary if you have the care and foresight to prepare a formal document to express your wishes for your health care.

What You Can Do With This Program

This program allows you to create comprehensive health care documents that are valid for your state. With these documents, you can clearly express your preferences for medical care if you become unable to communicate your wishes. Specifically, you can:

- appoint a trusted person, called your "health care agent" in most states, to oversee your medical care if you become unable to speak for yourself
- name the doctor you'd like to supervise your care
- specify whether or not you want your life prolonged with medical treatments and procedures
- identify specific medical treatments and procedures that you want provided or withheld, and
- provide instructions for donating your organs, tissues or body after death.

You can also state any general wishes you have about your care, such as where you would like to be cared for (for example, in a particular hospice facility or at home, if possible) or any special directions that may affect your comfort or awareness (for instance, whether you would like to receive full doses of pain medication even if it makes you unaware of the presence of family and friends).

> **TIP**
>
> **Keep track of other health care information.** In addition to your health care directives, caregivers need other medical information as well. You can use our Information for Caregivers and Survivors form to help with this task. Among other details, the form includes the names of and contact information for your health care providers and information about your insurance coverage. This important information will be a great help to those who take care of you in the event of your incapacity. To find out more, go to My Documents and select Information for Caregivers and Survivors from the list.

The Basics of Health Care Directives

This section explains what you need to know about health care directives before you start making yours, including:

- the different types of health care directives you may need to make
- what your state's documents are called
- who is legally permitted to make health care directives
- how to help someone else make health care directives
- when the documents take effect, and
- how to make sure your documents cover all the issues that are important to you.

Types of Health Care Directives

A health care directive is any document in which you set out instructions or wishes for your medical care. Most states provide two basic documents for this purpose:

- A durable power of attorney for health care, in which you name someone you trust to oversee your health care and make medical decisions should you become unable to do so.
- A living will, in which you spell out any wishes about the types of care you do or do not wish to receive if you are unable to speak for yourself. Your doctors and the person you name as your agent in your durable power of attorney for health care must do their best to follow any instructions you leave.

The exact names of these documents vary from state to state, and some states combine the two into a single form, usually called an "advance health care directive." The table below shows how your state handles it.

What Your Documents Are Called

State	Number of Documents	Living Will	Durable Power of Attorney for Health Care
Alabama	1	Advance Directive for Health Care	
Alaska	1	Advance Health Care Directive	
Arizona	2	Living Will	Health Care Power of Attorney
Arkansas	2	Declaration	Durable Power of Attorney for Health Care
California	1	Advance Health Care Directive	
Colorado	2	Declaration as to Medical or Surgical Treatment	Medical Durable Power of Attorney
Connecticut	1 or 2	Document Concerning Health Care and Withholding or Withdrawal of Life Support Systems	Appointment of Health Care Representative
		If you name a health care agent and leave health care instructions, your wishes will be combined into a single form called Health Care Instructions and Appointment of Health Care Representative.	
Delaware	1	Advance Health Care Directive	
District of Columbia	2	Declaration	Durable Power of Attorney for Health Care
Florida	2	Living Will	Designation of Health Care Surrogate
Georgia	1	Advance Directive for Health Care	
Hawaii	1	Advance Health Care Directive	
Idaho	1	Living Will and Durable Power of Attorney for Health Care	
Illinois	1 or 2	Declaration	Durable Power of Attorney for Health Care
		If you name a health care agent and leave health care instructions, your wishes will be combined into a single Durable Power of Attorney for Health Care form.	

What Your Documents Are Called (continued)			
State	**Number of Documents**	**Living Will**	**Durable Power of Attorney for Health Care**
Indiana	2	Living Will Declaration	Durable Power of Attorney for Health Care and Appointment of Health Care Representative
Iowa	2	Declaration	Durable Power of Attorney for Health Care
Kansas	2	Declaration	Durable Power of Attorney for Health Care Decisions
Kentucky	1	Advance Directive	
Maine	1	Advance Health Care Directive	
Maryland	1	Advance Directive	
Massachusetts	2	Document Directing Health Care	Health Care Proxy
Michigan	2	Document Directing Health Care	Patient Advocate Designation
Minnesota	1	Health Care Directive	
Mississippi	1	Advance Health Care Directive	
Missouri	2	Declaration	Durable Power of Attorney for Health Care
Montana	2	Declaration	Durable Power of Attorney for Health Care
Nebraska	2	Declaration	Durable Power of Attorney for Health Care
Nevada	2	Declaration	Durable Power of Attorney for Health Care Decisions
New Hampshire	1	Advance Directive	
New Jersey	1 or 2	Instruction Directive	Proxy Directive
	If you name a health care agent and leave health care instructions, your wishes will be combined into a single form called a Combined Advance Directive for Health Care.		
New Mexico	1	Advance Health Care Directive	

What Your Documents Are Called (continued)

State	Number of Documents	Living Will	Durable Power of Attorney for Health Care
New York	2	Document Directing Health Care	Health Care Proxy
North Carolina	2	Advance Directive	Health Care Power of Attorney
North Dakota	1	Health Care Directive	
Ohio	2	Declaration	Durable Power of Attorney for Health Care
Oklahoma	1	Advance Directive for Health Care	
Oregon	1	Advance Directive	
Pennsylvania	2	Living Will	Health Care Power of Attorney
Rhode Island	2	Declaration	Durable Power of Attorney for Health Care
South Carolina	1 or 2	Declaration	Health Care Power of Attorney
	If you name a health care agent and leave health care instructions, your wishes will be combined into a single Health Care Power of Attorney form.		
South Dakota	2	Living Will Declaration	Durable Power of Attorney for Health Care
Tennessee	1	Advance Health Care Directive	
Texas	2	Directive to Physicians and Family or Surrogates	Medical Power of Attorney
Utah	1	Advance Health Care Directive	
Vermont	1	Advance Directive	
Virginia	1	Advance Medical Directive	
Washington	2	Health Care Directive	Durable Power of Attorney for Health Care
West Virginia	2	Living Will	Medical Power of Attorney
Wisconsin	2	Declaration to Physicians	Power of Attorney for Health Care
Wyoming	1	Advance Health Care Directive	

The Five Wishes Document: Does It Help or Hurt?

You may have heard of Five Wishes, an easy-to-prepare advance health care directive said to be legally valid in almost every state. While a single, straightforward health care document that would pass legal muster in all states is a good idea, it is not, unfortunately, an idea whose time has come.

The laws governing health care directives include plenty of state-specific provisions, including terms, definitions and procedures that state health care providers know and trust. The generic language in Five Wishes could create confusion, delays or—at worst—legal tussles, which is exactly what health care directives should seek to avoid.

While we don't recommend that you use Five Wishes as your official health care document, it can help you as you think through the issues involved in end-of-life care—and discuss them with your loved ones. You can view a free copy of the document or download a printable copy for a few dollars at the Aging with Dignity website: www.agingwithdignity.org.

Who Can Make Health Care Directives

To make a health care directive, you must be able to understand what the document means, what it contains and how it works. People with physical disabilities may make valid health care documents; they can direct another to sign for them if they are unable to do so. (See the next section for more information on helping others with documents.)

In most states, you must be 18 years old to make a valid document directing your health care. (In Alabama, you must be 19. In Nebraska, you must be 19 or married.)

Helping Someone Else Make Health Care Directives

If the person you want to help is of sound mind and wants to write down health care wishes, your job should not be difficult. You can use this program to explain the process, answer questions and help prepare and finalize the right documents.

But if you think someone who needs help will resist your efforts, you need to carefully consider the way you approach the subject.

Explaining why the documents are important. If you're concerned about a loved one who is becoming mentally or physically frail, you might begin by simply talking about the benefits of the documents. Some people may be moved by a request to plan ahead because it will relieve anxiety and pressure for you and other caretakers. Others may be more inclined to make health care documents if they understand that doing so is the best way for them to stay in control and get the kind of medical care they want. (You can emphasize that whomever they name to make decisions for them must follow their instructions in every possible way.)

Helping someone who is becoming forgetful or absentminded. Of course, when you talk with someone who's struggling with increasing mental frailty, you will have to be sensitive to feelings about deteriorating mental abilities. Frustration, shame or a sense of loss may well make your loved one more resistant to your help. You may want to underscore that planning is a good thing for anybody—including the young and healthy—just in case it's necessary someday.

Ultimately, however, you should never try to force someone to follow a certain course because you think it's best. If you strong-arm someone whose mental abilities are waning, and the documents you make are later challenged in court, you could find yourself in a lot of legal trouble.

Signing for someone with physical disabilities. You could also get into big trouble if you fake signatures on any legal documents. Even if the person you're helping asks you to sign his or her name, don't do it.

Someone who is physically unable to sign health care documents can direct you to sign them, but you must carefully follow the instructions in "Making It Legal," below.

When Your Documents Take Effect

Your health care documents will take effect only if someday you are so ill or injured that you cannot make and express health care decisions. Generally, this means that:

- You can't understand the nature and consequences of the health care options available to you (including significant benefits, risks and alternatives), and
- You are unable to communicate your own wishes for care, either orally, in writing or through gestures.

If there is some question about your ability to understand your treatment choices or communicate clearly, your doctor (with the input of your health care agent or close relatives) will decide whether it is time for your health care directives to become operative.

Of course, in order for any of this to happen, medical personnel must know about your documents. In most instances, you can ensure that your directives become part of your medical record when you are admitted to a hospital or other care facility. But your need for care could arise unexpectedly or while you are away from home, so it's a good idea to give copies of your documents to several people. (See "Making and Distributing Copies," below.)

What Your Documents Can Cover

Each state may say what makes a health care document legal. Many states list what you can include in your documents and define specific medical terms—and all states set out rules for having your document witnessed or notarized.

If your state law demands a specific form or precise language, the health care documents you produce with this program will contain it. However, in some instances, your documents may go beyond what is addressed by your state law. For example, your state's law may be silent on whether individuals can direct their own health care if they become permanently unconscious, or your state's law may specifically restrict you from removing life support if you are pregnant, or your state's form may not provide a place for you to address your wishes about donating your organs after death. However, if you want to address these issues when using this program, you may do so.

The U.S. Supreme Court has ruled that the U.S. Constitution guarantees your right to direct your own health care. A state law that restricts your rights contradicts this ruling. The Court also ruled that if an individual has left "clear and convincing evidence" of medical wishes, those wishes should be followed. By far the best way to make your wishes known is to leave detailed written instructions.

If your choices are contrary to what your state law allows, your health care directive will state that your instructions should be respected anyway and followed in keeping with your constitutional right to direct your own health care.

On the off chance that anyone later challenges your health care directive in a court because it goes beyond your state's law, there is an additional legal failsafe. Your document contains a paragraph that allows the rest of your health care directive to be enforced as written even if any one of the directions you leave is found to be legally invalid.

Hospitals May Have Their Own Rules

While your legal right to direct your own health care is well established, hospitals and other health care institutions (such as nursing homes) have their own policies and practices for providing care at the end of life. Many give great weight to a patient's wishes, but others have strong positions of their own.

For example, Catholic hospitals and care facilities, under the direction of the United States Conference of Catholic Bishops, may require that all patients receive artificially administered food and water at the end of life, even if a patient has a valid health care directive saying that's not what he or she wants. Patients in these facilities will have to accept treatment or be transferred to another facility that will respect their wishes.

It may be worthwhile to familiarize yourself with the policies of the facilities you are likely to use. That way, you and your health care representative will know where to go for care in an emergency. And if you're making plans for long-term care, you can do so with your eyes open to the rules of your treatment providers.

Entering Your Personal Information

To begin making your health care documents, we ask you to provide some basic identifying information about yourself. (We assume here that you are making documents for yourself. If that is not the case, enter the information for the person you are helping.)

Your State

You are asked to specify the state of your legal residence, sometimes called a domicile. This is the state where you make your home now and for the indefinite future. This information is essential, because the program produces health care directives that are geared to the laws of the state you select. (If you travel to another state, your document will be honored in that state as long as it meets the requirements of the state where you live.)

If you divide up the year living in two or more states, you may not be sure which state is your legal residence. To decide, choose the state where you are the most rooted—that is, the state in which you:

- are registered to vote
- register your car
- own valuable property—especially property with a title document, such as a house
- have checking, savings and investment accounts, or
- maintain a business.

> ! CAUTION
>
> **Don't make documents for more than one state.** If you regularly spend time in more than one state, you might be tempted to make health care documents for each—but you shouldn't. The reason is simple: Creating a new health care document almost always revokes an older one. In almost all cases, you cannot have two documents simultaneously in force. Besides, it is not necessary. As mentioned above, all states honor health care directives made in other states as long as they are valid in the state where they were made. You should make and sign your directive in the state in which you legally reside.

Your Name

Enter your name in the same form that you use on other formal documents, such as your driver's license or bank accounts. If you customarily use more than one name for official purposes, list all of them, separated by aka ("also known as").

There is room for you to list several names. But use your common sense. For purposes of your health care directive, your name is needed to identify you and to match you with your medical records. Be sure to include any names you have used on other medical documents such as prior hospital or doctor records.

Your Gender

Many states have restrictions or special considerations that may apply if a woman's health care directive takes effect while she is pregnant. If you are a woman, it may be necessary for you to answer a few more questions to address this possibility. (See "How Pregnancy May Affect Your Wishes," below.)

We also use information about your gender to make your documents and instructions grammatically elegant and accurate, avoiding the cumbersome use of "he or she" and "his or her."

Additional Information

A few states ask you to provide more biographical information, such as your address or birthdate. If your state does, we will ask you for the additional information, and your documents will contain it, too.

Naming Your Primary Physician

Next, you can name a doctor to serve as your primary physician. This is the doctor who will:

- oversee your medical care, and
- make legally significant determinations regarding your mental capacity and the state of your health, if necessary.

You will probably want to name a primary physician if you already have an established relationship with a doctor you trust and with whom you have discussed—or will discuss—your health care wishes. (See "Talking to Your Doctor," below.)

If you don't have an established relationship with a doctor, you can skip to the next part of the program.

What Your Primary Physician Does

Your primary physician may be required to make important decisions about your mental state and your overall health. For example, your health care documents will take effect if you ever lack the capacity to make health care decisions for yourself, and somebody may need to decide whether or not that time has come. The doctor you name will be responsible for making the determination.

In addition, your health care documents may set out instructions for end-of-life care in very specific situations—for instance, you may leave one set of instructions to take effect if you are permanently unconscious and another to govern your care if you are terminally ill. (You'll learn more about this in "Specifying Your Health Care Wishes," below.) Your primary physician will diagnose these conditions, putting your specific instructions into effect.

Choosing Your Primary Physician

If you have more than one doctor and you're not sure which one to pick, think about who would do the best job of supervising your overall care. This may be your family doctor or general practitioner, rather than a specialist.

If you're really on the fence, you can talk to each doctor you're considering. You may find that one of them seems more comfortable taking on the responsibility of managing your care or you might just get a better sense of whom to pick.

Another possibility is to name one doctor as your first choice and another as an alternate.

Choosing an Alternate

The program also asks you to name an alternate physician. Choose your alternate with the same care you use for your first pick. Keep in mind that this doctor may be responsible for making critical decisions about your care. If there isn't a second doctor you know and trust, skip this question.

Talking to Your Doctor

It's wise to talk to your doctor about your treatment preferences before you finalize your health care documents. Talking with your primary physician (and alternate, if any) is especially important because he or she will be in charge of other caregivers. Make sure your doctor understands your health care wishes and is willing to follow them. If you have questions or concerns about specific treatments, your doctor should be able to answer them. If you have other, more subjective concerns about a particular medical condition, such as the effects of certain treatments or how the condition is likely to affect you, discuss those, too.

Let your doctor know that you are completing a health care directive. If you will name an agent, be sure your doctor knows how to contact that person in an emergency. Better still, introduce your agent to your doctor if you have not already done so.

Naming Your Health Care Agent

This is one of the most important parts of the program. It's where you name the person who will work with your doctors to direct your health care and make treatment decisions for you if you are unable to do so. This person is usually called your "health care agent," though some states use a term such as "representative," "proxy" or "surrogate." Your health care documents will use the correct term for your state.

We strongly recommend that you appoint a health care agent—and at least one alternate—if you know someone you trust enough to take the job. The chances that your health care wishes will be enforced increase greatly if you name someone to supervise your care and speak for you if necessary.

And because life is unpredictable, there is no way your health care instructions can cover every possible health-related situation that might arise. Rapidly developing technology and new medical treatments underscore the need for flexible decision making. The best approach is to choose a trusted person who fully understands your feelings, beliefs and wishes.

If you absolutely cannot think of anyone you trust to oversee your medical care, you can skip this part of the program. It is better not to name anyone than to name someone who is not likely to strongly assert your wishes.

It's still a good idea to put your wishes for final health care in writing. Medical personnel are legally bound to follow your written wishes—or to find someone who will. If you do not name a health care agent, make an extra effort to discuss your wishes for medical care with a doctor or patient representative likely to be involved in providing that care.

What a Health Care Agent Does

If you become unable to direct your own health care, your agent will:

- supervise any treatment instructions you set out in your health care documents, and
- make decisions about any health care matters your documents do not cover.

Your health care power of attorney can give your agent very broad authority to direct your medical care. Or you can fine-tune your document by answering some questions about your agent's specific powers, discussed below.

To carry out your wishes and make decisions for you, your agent will always be allowed to:

- review your medical records
- grant releases to medical personnel so that they can perform necessary treatments

- go to court, if necessary to ensure your wishes are followed
- hire and fire medical personnel, and
- visit you in a hospital or other health care facility.

This should allow your agent to do everything needed to make sure your health care wishes are carried out—and if they are not, to get you transferred to another facility or to the care of another doctor who will enforce them.

Your Agent's Responsibility to You

You may be concerned that by naming a health care agent, you are giving up control of your own medical treatment—but you needn't worry. Your agent is legally required to follow your known wishes and to act in your best interest. If you leave written health care instructions, your agent is required to follow them, as are your doctors. On the other hand, if you want to leave certain treatment decisions entirely in the hands of your agent, you may do so.

The Health Insurance Portability and Accountability Act (HIPAA)

If you've recently visited a doctor, you know there's a law that requires patients to sign forms regarding medical privacy and the release of medical information. This federal law is called HIPAA, the Health Insurance Portability and Accountability Act. Some folks have worried that HIPAA requirements apply to your agent's powers under your health care documents, and that you must prepare special HIPAA release forms to give your agent the authority to take over your health care decisions for you. In fact, this is not the case. An agent is authorized to obtain the medical information necessary to put your document into effect and carry out your wishes.

The health care power of attorney you make with this program contains an explicit statement that your agent is allowed to act as your personal representative under HIPAA, authorized to receive full medical information about you. We took this extra step to avert any hassles for your agent.

Mental Health Care Decisions

Most states define health care to include mental health. To leave no confusion on the matter, our health care documents explicitly give your agent the power to make mental health decisions for you. This may include the power to discuss mental health treatments with your health care providers, to request or change medications or even to admit you to a mental health care facility if necessary. However, some states require special documents or authorization before they will allow a health care agent to authorize extreme treatments, such as shock therapy, or to commit someone under their care to a psychiatric facility. Because of these state restrictions, a mental health care directive may be quite useful for individuals with serious mental illness, including those in the early stages of Alzheimer's disease or who have Alzheimer's in their families.

If you have particular concerns about your mental health treatment, you can fill out a special medical health care directive, giving your agent the maximum authority allowed by your state's laws. The Bazelon Center for Mental Health Law, at www.bazelon.org, offers a detailed mental health care directive that allows you to express your preferences on a wide range of treatment issues, such as:

- medication preferences
- electroconvulsive therapy, and
- involuntary commitment to a mental health facility.

The directive is not easy to locate on the website, but it is worth the effort to find it. Try entering "directive" in the search box on the home page.

If you want to make a mental health care directive, you will need to determine whether you should prepare that document in addition to or instead of the health care documents this program creates. The answer depends on your personal circumstances and the state where you live. Whatever you do, take care not to prepare overlapping directives—that is, two directives covering the same issues. The risk of confusion would be too great.

Start your research at The Bazelon Center, and consult a good estate planning lawyer if you're not sure which documents are best for you.

The decisions your agent makes for you must always agree with what you direct in your health care documents and any other wishes you make known to him or her. If a situation arises in which your agent does not know your specific wishes, your agent must make the decision that he or she believes you would make if you were capable of doing so. (For possible state-specific exceptions, see "State-Specific Powers," later in this chapter.)

To ensure you get the care you want, one of the most important things to do is talk with your agent (and other loved ones) about your wishes. For tips on having this important conversation, see "Talking to Your Agent," below.

You may wonder what happens if your health care agent lets you down. If someone goes to court and proves that your agent is harming you by acting in ways that you would not want, a court could revoke your agent's authority. In this case, the first person to take over would be an alternate agent you've named in your power of attorney for health care. If you haven't named an alternate or if your alternate is not available, the court will appoint a guardian or conservator to make your health and personal care decisions. (See "Nominating a Guardian," below.)

Choosing Your Agent

The person you name as your health care agent should be someone you trust and someone with whom you feel confident discussing your wishes. Choose someone who respects your right to get the kind of medical care you want, even if he or she doesn't completely agree with your wishes.

You can choose your spouse or partner, a relative or a close friend. Keep in mind that your agent may have to assert your wishes in the face of medical personnel and family members who may be driven by their own beliefs and interests, rather than yours. If you foresee the possibility of conflict in enforcing your wishes, be sure to choose someone who is strong-willed and assertive.

CAUTION

How marriage or divorce may affect your document. The document you create with this program revokes the appointment of your spouse or registered domestic partner if you file for divorce or legally separate. If this happens, you should prepare a new document or know that an alternate agent will step in to serve.

It's also a good idea to prepare a new health care document if you get married, unless your new spouse is already named as your health care agent. You are never required to name your spouse as your health care agent, but if you want to name someone else, be sure you do it in a document created after the date of your marriage. If you have an old document naming someone other than your spouse as your agent, some states will consider it automatically revoked when you marry.

Naming More Than One Agent: A Bad Idea

This program allows you to name just one person at a time to serve as your agent. We believe it's unwise to name two people to serve together, even if you know two people who are willing to take the job. There may be problems, brought on by passing time and human nature, with naming coagents. In the critical time during which your representatives will be overseeing your wishes, they could disagree or suffer a change of heart, rendering them ineffective as lobbyists on your behalf while they argue with each other.

If you know of two people you would like to name as your agents, choose one to serve first and name the other as your alternate.

While you need not name someone who lives in the same state as you do, proximity is one factor to consider. If you have a protracted illness, the person you name may be called upon to spend weeks or months near your bedside, making sure health care providers abide by your wishes for treatment.

Finally, if you have made—or are planning to make—a durable power of attorney for finances (see Chapter 14), you should think strongly about naming the same person to oversee both your finances and your health care. If you decide not to name the same person— perhaps because one has a much better head for business and the other is likely to be better at your bedside—keep in mind that your health care agent and your agent for finances may have to work very closely at times. (For example, your agent for finances will be responsible for paying your medical and insurance bills at your health care agent's direction.)

State Restrictions on Who Can Serve as Your Agent

A number of states have rules about who can serve as your agent. Attending physicians and other health care providers are commonly prohibited from serving. Some states presume that the motivations of such people may be clouded by self-interest. For example, a doctor may be motivated to provide every medical procedure available—to try every heroic or experimental treatment—even if that goes against a patient's wishes. On the other side, treatments may sometimes be withheld because of concerns about time or cost.

Before you select an agent, consult the list below for the specifics of your state's agent requirements and restrictions before you select an agent.

Choosing Alternate Agents

You may name one or two alternate agents. Your first alternate will serve only if your first choice becomes unavailable. Your second alternate will step in only if your primary agent and first alternate are unable or unwilling to act or cannot quickly be located.

Use the same principles to choose your alternates as you did when making your first pick: trustworthiness, dependability, assertiveness and availability.

Do not choose as an alternate someone who is disqualified by state law from serving in your state. (See the list below.)

State Law Restrictions on Agents

Alabama

Your health care proxy may not be:

- your treating health care provider
- an employee of your treating health care provider, unless the employee is related to you, or
- under the age of 19.

Alaska

Your health care agent may not be an owner, operator or employee of the health care institution at which you are receiving care, unless related to you by blood, marriage or adoption.

Arizona

Your health care agent must be at least 18 years old.

Arkansas

Your health care agent must be at least 18 years old.

California

Your health care agent may not be:

- your treating health care provider or an employee of your treating health care provider, unless the individual is your registered domestic partner or is related to you, or you and the employee both work for your treating health care provider
- an operator or employee of a community care facility, unless the individual is your registered domestic partner or is related to you, or you and the employee both work at the community care facility
- an operator or employee of a residential care facility for the elderly, unless the individual is your registered domestic partner or is related to you, or you and the employee both work at the residential care facility.

Colorado

Your health care agent must be at least 21 years old.

Connecticut

If, when you appoint your health care agent and attorney-in-fact for health care decisions, you are a patient or a resident of, or have applied

State Law Restrictions on Agents (continued)

for admission to, a hospital, residential care home, rest home with nursing supervision or chronic and convalescent nursing home, your health care agent and attorney-in-fact for health care decisions may not be:

- an operator, unless the operator is related to you by blood, marriage or adoption
- an administrator, unless the administrator is related to you by blood, marriage or adoption, or
- an employee, unless the employee is related to you by blood, marriage or adoption.

In any case, your health care agent and attorney-in-fact for health care decisions may not be:

- under the age of 18
- a witness to the document appointing him or her as your health care representative
- your attending physician, or
- an employee of a government agency which is financially responsible for your medical care—unless that person is related to you by blood, marriage or adoption.

Delaware

Your health care agent may not be an owner, operator or employee of a long-term health care institution where you are receiving care, unless he or she is related to you by blood, marriage or adoption.

District of Columbia

Your health care attorney-in-fact may not be your health care provider.

Florida

Your health care surrogate may not be a witness to the document naming your health care representative.

Georgia

Your health care agent may not be a physician or health care provider who is directly involved in your health care.

State Law Restrictions on Agents (continued)

Hawaii

Your health care agent may not be an owner, operator or employee of your treating health care provider, unless the person is related to you by blood, marriage or adoption.

Idaho

Your health care agent may not be:

- your treating health care provider
- an employee of your health care provider, unless the employee is related to you
- an operator of a community care facility, or
- an employee of an operator of a community care facility, unless the employee is related to you.

Illinois

Your health care agent may not be:

- your health care provider, or
- your attending physician.

Indiana

No restrictions on who may serve as your attorney-in-fact and health care representative.

Iowa

Your health care agent may not be:

- your health care provider, or
- an employee of your health care provider, unless these individuals are related to you by blood, marriage or adoption—limited to parents, children, siblings, grandchildren, grandparents, uncles, aunts, nephews, nieces and great-grandchildren.

Kansas

Your health care agent may not be:

- your treating health care provider
- an employee of your treating health care provider, or
- an employee, owner, a director or an officer of a health care facility.

These restrictions do not apply, however, if your agent is:

State Law Restrictions on Agents (continued)

- related to you by blood, marriage or adoption, or
- a member of the same community of people to which you belong who have vowed to lead a religious life and who conduct or assist in conducting religious services and actually and regularly engage in religious, charitable or educational activities or the performance of health care services.

Kentucky

Your health care surrogate may not be an employee, owner, a director or an officer of a health care facility where you are a resident or patient, unless they are:

- related to you more closely than first cousins, once removed, or
- a member of the same religious order.

Maine

Your health care agent may not be an owner, operator or employee of a residential long-term health care institution in which you are receiving care, unless he or she is related to you by blood, marriage or adoption.

Maryland

Your health care agent may not be an owner, operator or employee—or the spouse, parent, child or sibling of an owner, operator or employee—of a health care facility where you are receiving treatment unless he or she would qualify as your surrogate decision maker under Maryland law or is appointed before you receive, or contract to receive, health care from the facility.

Massachusetts

Your health care agent may not be an operator, administrator or employee of a facility where you are a patient or resident or have applied for admission, unless the operator, administrator or employee is related to you by blood, marriage or adoption.

Michigan

Your patient advocate must be at least 18 years old.

Minnesota

Your health care agent may not be your treating health care provider or an employee of your treating health care provider, unless he or she is related to you by blood, marriage, registered domestic partnership or adoption.

State Law Restrictions on Agents (continued)

Mississippi

Your health care agent may not be an owner, operator or employee of a residential long-term care facility where you are receiving treatment, unless related to you by blood, marriage or adoption.

Missouri

Your health care attorney-in-fact may not be:

- your attending physician
- an employee of your attending physician, or
- an owner, operator or employee of the health care facility where you live, unless:
  - you and your attorney-in-fact are related as parents, children, siblings, grandparent or grandchildren, or
  - you and your attorney-in-fact are members of the same community of people who have vowed to lead a religious life and who conduct or assist in conducting religious services and actually and regularly engage in religious, charitable or educational activities or the performance of health care services.

Montana

Your health care agent must be at least 18 years old.

Nebraska

Your health care attorney-in-fact may not be:

- under the age of 19, unless he or she is married
- a witness to your durable power of attorney for health care
- your attending physician
- an employee of your attending physician, unless the employee is related to you by blood, marriage or adoption
- a person unrelated to you by blood, marriage or adoption who is an owner, operator or employee of a health care provider of which you are a patient or resident, or
- a person unrelated to you by blood, marriage or adoption who is presently serving as a health care attorney-in-fact for ten or more people.

State Law Restrictions on Agents (continued)

Nevada

Unless he or she is your spouse, legal guardian or next of kin, your health agent may not be:

- your health care provider
- an employee of your health care provider
- an operator of a health care facility, or
- an employee of a health care facility.

New Hampshire

Your health care agent may not be:

- your health care provider
- an employee of your health care provider, unless the employee is related to you
- your residential care provider, or
- an employee of your residential care provider, unless the employee is related to you.

New Jersey

Your health care representative may not be:

- under the age of 18, or
- an operator, administrator or employee of a health care institution in which you are a patient or resident, unless the operator, administrator or employee is related to you by blood, marriage, domestic partnership or adoption or, in the case of a physician, is not your attending physician.

New Mexico

Your health care agent may not be an owner, operator or employee of a health care facility at which you are receiving care—unless related to you by blood, marriage or adoption.

New York

Your health care agent may not be:

- under the age of 18, unless he or she is the parent of a child, or married
- your attending physician
- presently appointed agent for ten or more other people, unless he or she is your spouse, child, parent, brother, sister or grandparent

State Law Restrictions on Agents (continued)

- an operator, administrator or employee of a hospital if, at the time of the appointment, you are a patient or resident of, or have applied for admission to, such hospital. This restriction shall not apply to:
  - an operator, administrator or employee of a hospital who is related to you by blood, marriage or adoption, or
  - a physician, who is not your attending physician, except that no physician affiliated with a mental hygiene facility or a psychiatric unit of a general hospital may serve as agent for you if you are living in or being treated by such facility or unit unless the physician is related to you by blood, marriage or adoption.

North Carolina

Your health care agent must be at least 18 years old.

North Dakota

Your health care agent may not be:

- your treating health care provider
- an employee of your treating health care provider, unless the employee is related to you
- an operator of a long-term care facility, or
- an employee of an operator of a long-term care facility, unless the employee is related to you.

Ohio

Your health care attorney-in-fact may not be:

- under the age of 18
- your attending physician
- an administrator of any nursing home in which you are receiving care
- an employee or agent of your attending physician, or
- an employee or agent of any health care facility in which you are being treated.

These restrictions do not apply, however, if your attorney-in-fact is 18 years of age or older and a member of the same religious order as you—or is related to you by blood, marriage or adoption.

Oklahoma

Your health care proxy must be at least 18 years old.

State Law Restrictions on Agents (continued)

Oregon

Your health care representative may not be:

- under the age of 18
- your attending physician or an employee of your attending physician, unless the physician or employee is related to you by blood, marriage or adoption, or
- an owner, operator or employee of a health care facility in which you are a patient or resident, unless related to you by blood, marriage or adoption—or appointed before you were admitted to the facility.

Pennsylvania

Your health care agent may not be:

- your attending physician or other health care provider, unless related to you by blood, marriage or adoption, or
- an owner, operator or employee of a health care provider from which you are receiving care, unless related to you by blood, marriage or adoption.

Rhode Island

Your health care agent may not be:

- your treating health care provider
- an employee of your treating health care provider, unless the employee is related to you
- an operator of a community care facility, or
- an employee of an operator of a community care facility, unless the employee is related to you.

South Carolina

Your health care agent may not be:

- under the age of 18
- your health care provider at the time you execute your health care power of attorney, unless he or she is related to you
- a spouse or an employee of your health care provider, unless he or she is related to you, or
- an employee of the nursing care facility where you live, unless he or she is related to you.

State Law Restrictions on Agents (continued)

South Dakota

No restrictions on who may serve as your health care agent.

Tennessee

Your health care agent may not be:

- your treating health care provider
- an employee of your treating health care provider, unless he or she is related to you by blood, marriage or adoption
- an operator of a health care institution
- an employee of an operator of a health care institution, unless he or she is related to you by blood, marriage or adoption, or
- your conservator, unless you are represented by an attorney who signs a specific statement—required by Tennessee Code § 34-6-203(c).

Texas

Your health care agent may not be:

- your health care provider
- an employee of your health care provider, unless the employee is related to you
- your residential care provider, or
- an employee of your residential care provider, unless the employee is related to you.

Utah

Your health care agent may not be:

- your health care provider, or
- an owner, operator or employee of the health care facility at which you are receiving care, unless related to you by blood, marriage or adoption.

Vermont

Your health care agent may not be:

- your health care provider, or
- an owner, operator, employee, agent or a contractor of a residential care facility, health care facility or correctional facility in which you reside, unless related to you by blood, marriage, civil union or adoption.

State Law Restrictions on Agents (continued)

Virginia

Your health care agent must be at least 18 years old.

Washington

Your health care agent may not be:

- your physician
- your physician's employee, or
- an owner, administrator or employee of the health care facility where you live or receive care.

These restrictions do not apply, however, if your representative is your spouse, adult child or sibling.

West Virginia

Your health care representative may not be:

- your treating health care provider
- an employee of your treating health care provider, unless he or she is related to you
- an operator of a health care facility serving you, or
- an employee of an operator of a health care facility, unless he or she is related to you.

Wisconsin

Your health care agent may not be:

- your health care provider or the spouse or employee of your health care provider unless he or she is related to you, or
- an employee or the spouse of an employee of the health care facility in which you live or are a patient, unless he or she is related to you.

Wyoming

Your health care agent may not be an owner, operator or employee of a residential or community care facility where you are receiving care, unless he or she is related to you by blood, marriage or adoption.

Granting Specific Powers to Your Agent

After you name your agent, the program will ask you some questions about granting specific powers to him or her. This section explains each of these powers.

Withdrawing Life-Prolonging Procedures

It is important to specify whether or not your agent may direct health care providers to withhold or withdraw life-prolonging procedures when you are close to death.

A life-prolonging procedure or treatment is one that would only prolong the process of dying or sustain a condition of permanent unconsciousness. In other words, the patient would die soon—or die without regaining meaningful consciousness—whether or not the treatment was administered.

It is generally agreed that cardiopulmonary resuscitation (CPR), dialysis, artificial respiration and complicated invasive surgery are life-prolonging procedures when performed on a terminally ill or permanently comatose patient. (For more information, see below.)

In most states, agents automatically have the power to withdraw life-prolonging procedures. In other states, if you wish to grant the power it must be specifically spelled out in your health care document.

To avoid any confusion, the document you make with this program will clearly state whether or not your agent has the power to withdraw life-prolonging procedures, knowing that to do so may result in your death. You will be instructed to sign or initial this specific clause to underscore that you knowingly granted or denied this power to your agent. Doing this ensures that your wishes will be honored in any state.

Note that giving your agent the power to make this decision is *not* the same as telling your agent what decision to make. Later in the program, you can leave specific instructions about whether or not you want to receive life-prolonging procedures—and when. Your agent is legally bound to follow your wishes. Here, you are just giving your agent power to direct your care on this matter. You should grant your agent this power if you know that you do not want some or all life-prolonging procedures when you are close to death.

Withdrawing Food and Water

If you are close to death and cannot communicate your wishes for health care, it is also likely that you will not be able to eat or drink normally. The medical solution to this is to provide you with food and water—as a mix of nutrients and fluids—through tubes inserted in a vein or into your stomach, depending on your condition. This is typically called "artificially administered nutrition and hydration," though your state may use a slightly different term.

Even though artificially administered food and water is often considered a life-prolonging procedure, it is critical that you state your wishes about this issue separately from other life-prolonging procedures. The withdrawal of food and water from terminally ill or permanently unconscious patients has proven to be a bitterly contested personal and political issue. The document you make with this program explicitly states your wishes on this matter so there is no chance of confusion about what you want. You should grant your agent this power if there are any circumstances under which you would not want to receive artificially administered food and water.

Authorizing Organ, Tissue or Body Donation

Using this program, you can give your agent the authority to carry out your wishes for organ, tissue or body donation after your death—or specify that your agent should not have this power.

In almost all cases, it's wise to give your agent the power to assert your wishes about anatomical gifts. If you want to be a donor, giving your agent clear authority to approve your donation will help to expedite the procedure. (Donations must be carried out quickly in order to succeed.) If you don't want to donate, your agent can ensure your wishes are carried out by speaking firmly on your behalf, even in the face of others who may disagree with your choice. And if you're not sure what you want, you can be assured that someone you trust will have the authority to make a decision based on the circumstances when the time comes.

If you give your agent this authority, a little later in the program you will have the opportunity to provide further instructions about anatomical gifts—or to assert that you do not want to be an organ donor, if that is your wish. (See "Stating Your Wishes for Organ Donation," below.) Your agent must try to follow any wishes you express.

If you don't grant your agent this authority and the question of whether or not to donate your organs arises after your death, your doctors will ask your next of kin to make the decision.

Authorizing an Autopsy

In some circumstances, such as a sudden or suspicious death, state law may require an autopsy. In these cases, a medical examiner does not need to get permission before proceeding.

In other situations, your loved ones or family members may request an autopsy—for example, if they have questions about the cause of your death or wish to advance society's medical knowledge about a little-understood disease, such as Alzheimer's. You can use the program to give or refuse consent to this type of autopsy, or you can give your agent the power to make the decision for you. Here is a little information about each choice.

Advantages of authorizing an autopsy. Your first option is to state that you authorize an autopsy after your death. This doesn't mean there will be an autopsy; it just allows your loved ones to get more information about your death if they feel they need it.

This type of information can provide comfort to grieving family members, but there is a practical reason for it as well: An autopsy may reveal conditions that could be inherited by other members of your family, giving them opportunities for early diagnosis and treatment.

When you may not want to authorize an autopsy. Your second option is to refuse consent to an autopsy after your death. You may want to avoid an autopsy for personal or practical reasons. For example, some people have religious concerns about the procedure. If that's true for you, you may want to discuss the issue with a clergy member or other spiritual adviser before making your decision.

The most common practical reason for refusing an autopsy is the cost. A complete autopsy can cost several thousand dollars and is usually not covered by insurance. Before you consent to an autopsy, you may want to investigate the costs and be sure your estate has money on hand to cover them.

In rare cases, grants are available to cover the cost of an autopsy. For example, in cases of Alzheimer's or dementia, the National Institutes of Health provides some autopsy services without charge to the family. In order to receive these benefits, however, you must be enrolled in a research program before your death.

Letting your agent decide. When you consider the pros and cons of consenting to an autopsy, you may find that the third option is best. It allows you to leave the matter in your agent's hands.

Whether or not an autopsy is helpful or prudent will depend on the circumstances of your death—many of which are unpredictable ahead of time. If you talk to your agent about your general feelings and wishes, he or she can make a decision when the time comes, taking into account all the circumstances.

Authorizing Disposition of Your Remains

Unless you specify otherwise, your closest family members will decide whether your body will be buried or cremated. This program offers three ways to express your wishes about this decision.

Directing your agent to follow existing wishes. If you want to write down your preferences for final arrangements, including burial or cremation, you can use our "final arrangements" letter for this purpose. It allows you to prepare a detailed document stating your preferences about burial, cremation and a funeral or memorial services. (See Chapter 16.) Once you have done this—or prepared a similar document—you can select the option that states you have already made arrangements that your agent should follow. You will then have the opportunity to describe the document or arrangements you've made, so that your agent and others can locate your papers and carry out your wishes when the time comes.

Letting your agent decide. If you choose this option, your agent will have the power to decide how your body should be handled after you die. You can either leave these matters entirely in the hands of your agent or, better for everyone involved, discuss your wishes with your agent and other loved ones.

Letting family decide. If there is some reason that you do not want to give your agent the authority to make decisions about burial or cremation, you can select the third option, which denies your agent this power. The practical result is that your closest family members will make decisions about your remains, following any wishes that you may have expressed.

If You Give Your Agent This Power: Special Signing Requirements

In some states, if you grant your agent the authority to make decisions about your burial or cremation, you must follow special directions when you finalize your document.

For example, if you live in Nevada, your durable power of attorney for health care decisions may be signed by two witnesses or notarized. Usually, the choice is yours. However, if you grant your agent the power to direct your final arrangements, you must have the document notarized—and witnesses are not necessary.

The program will provide the correct finalization instructions for your state, depending on the choices you make when you prepare your document. To learn whether your state has special requirements, see "State Witnessing and Notarizing Requirements," below.

State-Specific Powers

A handful of states ask you to make decisions about very specific powers you can grant to your agent. If you live in one of the states below, the program will guide you step by step through your choices. Here, we provide a brief overview of each power.

New Hampshire. You will be asked to decide whether, under certain circumstances, your agent may override your objections to treatment. New Hampshire, like most other states, requires your agent and medical providers to make an effort to inform you of any proposed medical treatments, or of any proposal to withdraw or withhold treatment from you. Usually, your caretakers may not provide or withhold treatments if you object, even if you are determined to be incapacitated and incapable of making informed health care choices.

In New Hampshire, however, you can state that your agent should carry out your treatment wishes when your health care providers have determined that you are no longer capable of making informed decisions—even if you verbally object to those treatments when the time comes. When you make your health care document, we ask you whether or not you want to give your agent this power.

You may want to grant this authority if you are concerned about being diagnosed with Alzheimer's disease or another form of severe dementia. Dementia may cause you to become argumentative and resist the reasoned treatment decisions that you made before you became ill.

This power can make it much easier for your agent to carry out your wishes if you ever become incapable of making rational decisions. But do think carefully before you add it to your document. It places an enormous amount of authority in your agent's hands. Before granting the power, be certain your agent is someone you completely trust to treat you well, and that he or she fully understands your wishes for care.

Utah. You will be asked to decide whether your agent can admit you to a nursing home. In most states, a health care agent automatically has the power to decide whether or not to admit you to a nursing home or other long-term care facility—whether for a short stay or a long one. In this state, however, you must specifically state whether or not you want your agent to have the power to admit you for anything other than a short-term stay for recuperation or rest. The program will ask you to express your wishes on this matter.

Granting this authority to your health care agent does not mean that you want or prefer to be admitted to a nursing home or residential care facility. As with other matters, your agent must follow your specific wishes. For example, if you would consent to be admitted to a nursing home only as a last resort, you can give your agent the power to admit you, but make sure he or she understands your feelings and preferences.

Keep in mind that if you do not grant this authority and your situation changes or deteriorates to the extent that your health care providers and agent agree that admitting you to a long-term care facility is best for you, your agent may be required to initiate court proceedings in order to get you the care you need.

Ultimately, the choice is deeply personal. The best you can do is make the choice that feels right to you now—and be sure to talk with your agent about your wishes.

Virginia. You will be asked to decide about four special powers:

- **Authorizing mental health treatment.** If you grant this power, your agent will be able to admit you to a health care facility for mental health treatment after a physician examines you and certifies that you need such care. Without this power, your agent will be required to ask a judge for permission to admit you. If you don't think you'll need mental health treatment, or if you'd rather have a court oversee your mental health care, you may not want to grant this power. But if you are concerned that you may require mental health treatment and you fully trust your agent to decide for you, granting this power could avoid a lot of time, expense and trouble.

- **Authorizing treatment over your objections.** This power is very similar to the power for New Hampshire agents described above. See that description for more information.

- **Continuing to serve over your objection.** This power states that, if you are incapable of making informed health care decisions, your agent may continue to represent you even if you protest your agent's authority at the time. If you don't grant this power, your agent's authority will be revoked upon your objection and your alternate agent will step in. If you haven't appointed an alternate or none of your alternates are available, Virginia law will determine who makes medical decisions for you.

- **Enrolling you in health care studies.** If you grant this power, your agent will have permission to enroll you in qualified health care studies. You can limit your participation to studies that may personally benefit you, or you may allow studies that may not help you personally, but might contribute to greater scientific knowledge and advances for patients in the future. As with any other health care choice, your agent will be required by law to act in your best

interests and avoid any decisions that conflict with your known
beliefs and values.

Wisconsin. You will be asked to decide whether your agent can admit
you to a nursing home. For more information, see the note for Utah,
above.

Talking to Your Agent

It may not be an easy conversation to start, but those who make the
effort to discuss the hard topic of what kind of medical care they want
at the end of life usually find the effort worth the price. You'll probably
want to begin by talking with your agent; then, if you can, discuss your
feelings with close family members and friends as well. If the topic seems
too difficult to broach, consider using a relevant news item, television
show or film as a catalyst for discussion.

There are three basic goals when talking with your agent:

- making sure the person you've picked is willing to take on the
  responsibility of acting on your behalf
- sharing your written directions and other wishes, and
- allowing your agent to ask questions so you are both clear on what
  you want.

During your discussion, your agent may ask about issues you
haven't considered. This is a great chance for each of you to clarify the
understanding between you so that you both can feel confident that
your agent will know what to do if he or she must represent you.

If you have a regular doctor, you may want to encourage your doctor
and your agent to meet and establish communication. If you are already
a patient in a medical facility, your agent will also want to get to know
the social worker or patient representative of the facility.

Why are these discussions so important? First, it gives you the
opportunity to let people know that you are preparing health care
documents, and why you feel strongly about doing so.

Second, it is impossible to foresee all of the circumstances or illnesses
that may arise and address them in your documents. Giving people a
clear understanding of your personal views and values can avoid future

disagreements as to how your written desires should be applied to specific circumstances.

In discussing your values, you may want to cover some or all of the following:

- your overall attitude toward life, including what gives you feelings of purpose and meaning and how you feel about your independence
- fears you may have about no longer being able to speak for yourself or make your own decisions
- any strong feelings you have about medical treatments that you do or do not wish to receive at the end of your life, including life support and feeding tubes
- what a phrase such as "death with dignity" or "no heroic measures" actually means to you
- anything you want others to know about the spiritual or religious part of your life and how it affects your feelings about serious illness and death
- what you might want for comfort and support when you are close to death (for example, to have certain people present, to be read to or to have music playing)
- your feelings about doctors and caregivers, in general, as well as any opinions about specific caregivers, and
- what you want after your death, including feelings about organ donation, an autopsy and final arrangements (for example, burial, cremation or memorial ceremonies).

Obviously, these conversations are not always easy to initiate or carry out, but they present all involved with an opportunity for greater peace of mind. Your loved ones will know your true wishes, and you may find that this is not only a chance to gain clarity and understanding, but also a bridge to closer relationships.

Nominating a Guardian

In most cases, your health care agent will be able to make all necessary health care and personal decisions for you, perhaps working with a financial agent you've named under a durable power of attorney for finances (this document is discussed in Chapter 14). However, although it's unlikely, there may come a time when a court must name someone to make personal decisions for you that go beyond the authority granted in your health care documents. If you need a great deal of help, this person, usually called a "guardian of the person" or "conservator of the person," may be granted the power to decide where you live, what you eat, the clothes you wear or what your daily activities will be.

You can use this program to nominate your agent to serve as guardian if it's ever necessary. Doing so strengthens your statement that you want your agent to speak for you in all matters relating to both your health and personal care.

In almost all cases, a court will appoint the person you nominate to be your conservator or guardian. The only time a court will override your nomination is if someone proves to the court that your choice is unlikely to act in your best interests. These types of disputes are very rare.

If your agent is unavailable. If you nominate your agent as your guardian or conservator and your agent is not willing or able to take the job if called on, your document will automatically nominate any alternate agents you have named, in the order designated.

If you don't nominate your agent. If you don't nominate your agent as guardian or conservator and a court must later appoint one, who gets the job depends on where you live. In some states, your health care agent is automatically nominated for the position. In others, priority is given to your spouse—or registered domestic partner in a few states—followed by close relatives in an order established by state law.

Nominating a guardian or conservator of your estate. While a guardian or conservator of your person is responsible for your personal comfort and care, a guardian or conservator of your estate is responsible for your finances. If you make a durable power of finances, you can nominate your financial agent to serve as the guardian or conservator of your estate if that ever becomes necessary. (Again, see Chapter 14 for more information about durable powers of attorney for finances.)

Specifying Your Health Care Wishes

After you have named (or declined to name) a health care agent, the program offers you the opportunity to express your wishes and feelings about medical treatment in as much detail as you choose. You have four basic options:

- leave all health care decisions in the hands of your agent, if you have named one
- make a general statement that you do not wish to receive life support when death is imminent
- make a general statement that you wish to be kept alive as long as possible, or
- specify different treatment wishes for different situations.

In this section, you will also have a chance to express any additional general wishes about end-of-life health care.

You Control Your Health Care If You Are Able

Most people know it is a good idea to write down their health care wishes. But some run smack into a psychological roadblock. They are worried that they may experience a change of heart or mind later—and that they will receive more or less medical care than they would want in a particular situation.

If this concerns you, it may help to keep the following in mind. First, the directions set out in your health care documents will be followed only if you someday become unable to communicate your wishes about your treatment. If, for example, you indicate in a health care directive that you do not wish to have water provided, health care providers will not deny you a glass of water as long as you are able to communicate your wishes for one—even through gestures.

Second, you can change or revoke your written health care wishes at any time. If you find that your document no longer accurately expresses your wishes for your medical care, you can easily create a new one to meet your needs. (See "Revoking Your Documents," below.)

Types of Medical Care: What You Should Know

Here, we briefly discuss some medical procedures that you should be familiar with before you provide directions about your care. Dry or off-putting as it may seem, it's a good idea to at least read quickly through the sections below to gain a basic understanding of:

- what the term "life-prolonging" means from a medical perspective
- what "artificially provided food and water" is and when it may be necessary, and
- what constitutes comfort or "palliative" care.

However, you will not need to deal with these definitions if you are already certain of any of the following:

- You want your agent to make all decisions for you.
- You want all procedures to be withheld.
- You want all procedures to be provided.

If any of these apply to you, you can skip directly to "If Your Wishes Are Simple," below.

Life-Prolonging Medical Care

When completing your health care instructions, we ask for your preferences about life-prolonging treatments or procedures. Many people need a little more information before answering these questions.

A life-prolonging procedure or treatment is one that would only prolong the process of dying or sustain a condition of permanent unconsciousness. In other words, the patient would die soon—or die without regaining meaningful consciousness—whether or not the treatment was administered. This section describes the most common life-prolonging treatments—a respirator, cardiopulmonary resuscitation (CPR), surgery and so on—in some detail.

Bear in mind that the types of medical procedures that are available will change over time. Technological advances mean that currently unfathomable procedures and treatments will become available and treatments that are now common will become obsolete. Also, the treatments that are available vary drastically depending on the sophistication of medical facilities.

Blood and blood products. Partial or full blood transfusions may be recommended to combat diseases that impair the blood system, to foster healing after a blood loss or to replenish blood lost through surgery, disease or injury.

Cardiopulmonary resuscitation. CPR is used when a person's heart or breathing has stopped. CPR includes applying physical pressure and using mouth-to-mouth resuscitation. Electrical shocks are also used if available. CPR is often accompanied by intravenous drugs used to normalize body systems. A final step in CPR is often attaching the patient to a respirator.

Diagnostic tests. Diagnostic tests are commonly used to evaluate urine, blood and other body fluids and to check on all bodily functions. Diagnostic tests can include X-rays and more sophisticated tests of brainwaves or other body systems. Some tests—including surgery—can be expensive, painful and invasive.

It Does Not Get More Personal Than This

For many people, the desire to direct what kind of medical care they want to receive is driven by a very specific event—watching a loved one die, having an unsatisfactory brush with the medical establishment or preparing for serious surgery.

Your ultimate decisions are likely to be influenced by factors such as your medical history, your knowledge of other people's experiences with life-prolonging medical procedures or your religious beliefs. If you are having great difficulty deciding about your preferences for medical care, take a few moments to figure out what's getting in your way. If you are unsure about the meaning or specifics of a particular medical treatment, turn to a doctor you trust for a more complete explanation. If the impediment is fear of sickness or death, talk over your feelings with family members and friends.

Dialysis. A dialysis machine is used to clean and add essential substances to the blood—through tubes placed in blood vessels or into the abdomen —when kidneys do not function properly. The entire cleansing process takes three or more hours and is performed on most dialysis patients two or three times a week. With portable dialysis machines, it is possible for some patients to have the procedure performed at home rather than in a hospital or other advanced care facility.

Drugs. The most common and most controversial drugs given to seriously ill or comatose patients are antibiotics—administered by mouth, through a feeding tube or by injection. Antibiotics are used to arrest and squelch infectious diseases. Patients in very weakened conditions may not respond even to massive doses of antibiotics.

Many health care providers argue that infectious diseases can actually be a benefit to those in advanced stages of an illness, since they may render a patient unconscious, and presumably not in pain, or help to speed up the dying process. Others contend that if an antibiotic can eliminate symptoms of an illness, it is almost always the proper medical treatment.

Drugs may also be used for pain. If, within your health care directive, you state that you do not want drugs to prolong your life, they will still be administered for pain control unless you specifically indicate that you do not want them.

Respirator. A mechanical respirator or ventilator assists or takes over breathing for a patient by pumping air in and out of the lungs. Patients are connected to respirators either by a tube that goes through the mouth and throat into the lung or attaches directly to the lung surgically.

Respirators are often used to stabilize patients who are suffering from an acute trauma or breathing crisis, and they are removed as soon as they are no longer needed. If a respirator has been attached to a person who is terminally ill or in a permanent coma, however, most doctors will resist removing the machinery unless there is clear written direction that this is what the patient would want.

Surgery. Surgical procedures, such as amputation, are often used to stem the spread of life-threatening infections or to keep vital organs functioning. Major surgery such as a heart bypass is also typically performed on patients who are terminally ill or comatose. You might want to consider the cost, time spent recovering from the invasive surgery and inevitability of death when deciding whether to include surgery in your final medical treatment.

Artificially Administered Food and Water

If you are close to death from a serious illness or permanently comatose, you may not be able to survive without the administration of food and water. Unless you indicate that treatment should be withheld, doctors will provide you with a mix of nutrients and fluids through tubes inserted in a vein, into your stomach through your nose or directly into your stomach through a surgical incision, depending on your condition.

Intravenous (IV) feeding, where fluids are introduced through a vein in an arm or a leg, is a short-term procedure. Tube feeding, however, can be carried on indefinitely.

Permanently unconscious patients can sometimes live for years with artificial feeding and hydration without regaining consciousness. If food and water are removed, death will occur in a relatively short time due to dehydration, rather than starvation. Such a course of action generally includes a plan of medication to keep the patient comfortable.

When you make your health care documents, you can choose whether you want artificially administered food and water withheld or provided. This decision is difficult for many people. Keep in mind that as long as you are able to communicate your wishes, by whatever means, you will not be denied food and water if you want it.

RESOURCE

Where to get more help. If you are not sure whether or not you would want to receive artificially administered food and water, you may wish to talk with your doctor or do some more research on your own. The following book is a good resource that may help you sort out your feelings about the issue: *Hard Choices for Loving People: CPR, Artificial Feeding, Comfort Care and the Patient With a Life-Threatening Illness*, by Hank Dunn (A & A Publishers).

This well-written resource features a good discussion of the issues surrounding artificial nutrition and hydration, exploring the various medical, religious and philosophical views on the subject. You can download the entire text of the book for free from www.hardchoices.com.

Palliative Care

If you want death to occur naturally—without life-prolonging intervention—it does not mean you must forgo treatment to alleviate pain or keep you comfortable. In fact, the health care directive you make with this program will state that you wish to receive any care that is necessary to keep you pain free, unless you specifically state otherwise.

This type of care, sometimes known as "comfort care," is now more commonly called "palliative care." Rather than focusing on a cure or prolonging life, palliative care emphasizes quality of life and dignity by helping a patient to remain comfortable and free from pain until life ends naturally.

Studies have shown that palliative care services are greatly appreciated by the family and friends of dying patients. Numerous organizations promote public awareness of palliative care options, and information about treatment options is widely available on the Internet. (See "Where to get more help," below.) However, despite the wide recognition of the benefits of palliative care, a major nationwide study in 2002 revealed that relatively few people get the palliative care they should. Most hospitals do not have integrated palliative care plans among their treatment options. Very few doctors understand it well, and it is still not emphasized in medical training. Almost a decade later, the benefits of palliative care are more widely known and accepted, but it still does not get the attention it deserves. As a result, many people die in hospital intensive care units, sometimes in severe pain, not knowing their suffering could have been greatly eased. You may wish to spend some time educating yourself about palliative care so that you can discuss your wishes with your health care agent and your treatment providers. When you complete your health care directive, you will have the opportunity to express any particular wishes you have about palliative care.

In an Emergency: DNR Orders and POLST Forms

In addition to the health care documents produced by this program, you may want to make a Do Not Resuscitate, or DNR, order. Some states are supplementing or replacing DNR orders with a similar form, often known as a POLST form. This sidebar discusses both documents.

DNR orders. A DNR order tells emergency medical personnel that you do not wish to be administered cardiopulmonary resuscitation (CPR). DNR orders are used both in hospitals and in situations where a person might require emergency care outside of the hospital.

You may want to consider a DNR order if you:

- have a terminal illness
- are at significant risk for cardiac or respiratory arrest, or
- have strong feelings against the use of CPR under any circumstances.

In most states, any adult may secure a DNR order. But a few states allow you to create an order only if you have been diagnosed with a terminal illness.

Because emergency response teams must act quickly in a medical crisis, they often do not have the time to determine whether you have a valid health care directive explaining treatments you want provided or withheld. If they do not know your wishes, they must provide you with all possible life-saving measures. But if emergency care providers see that you have a valid DNR order—which is often made apparent by an easily identifiable bracelet, anklet or necklace—they will not administer CPR.

If you ask to have CPR withheld, you will not be given:

- chest compression
- electric shock treatments to the chest
- tubes placed in the airway to assist breathing
- artificial ventilation, or
- cardiac drugs.

If you want a DNR order, or if you would like to find out more about DNR orders, talk with a doctor. In many states, a doctor's signature is required to make the DNR valid—he or she will often need to obtain and complete the necessary paperwork. If the doctor does not have the form or

In an Emergency:
DNR Orders and POLST Forms (continued)

other information you need, call the Health Department for your state and ask to speak with someone in the Division of Emergency Medical Services.

POLST forms. Many states are starting to use a form that is similar to a DNR order, but differs in a few important ways. The form is most often called Physician's Orders for Life Sustaining Treatment (POLST), though a few states use the term Clinician's Orders for Life Sustaining Treatment (COLST) or Medical Orders for Scope of Treatment (MOST). A POLST form may be used in addition to—or instead of—a DNR order.

Like a DNR order, a POLST form must be signed by a doctor and the form may be used in or out of a medical facility. A POLST is often prepared to ensure that different health care facilities and service providers (including EMS personnel) understand a patient's wishes. In many states, a POLST form is printed on bright paper so it will easily stand out in a patient's medical records.

Unlike a DNR order, a POLST form includes directions about life-sustaining measures—such as intubation, antibiotic use and feeding tubes—in addition to CPR. The POLST form helps to ensure that medical providers will understand your wishes at a glance, but it is *not* a substitute for a thorough and properly prepared Advance Directive.

When you enter a hospital, hospice or other health care facility, a member of the staff may ask whether you want to complete a POLST form. If not, you can ask for one.

If you obtain a DNR order or make a POLST form, discuss your decision with your family or other caretakers and tell them where your form is located. Even if you are wearing identification, such as a bracelet or necklace, keep your form in an obvious place. You might consider keeping it by your bedside, on the front of your refrigerator, in your wallet or in your suitcase if you are traveling. If your form is not apparent and immediately available, or if it has been altered in any way, CPR will most likely be performed.

> **RESOURCE**
>
> **Where to get more help.** The following resources can help you understand your options when it comes to palliative care:

Websites

- www.growthhouse.org. A nationwide clearinghouse of palliative care information and resources.
- www.pbs.org/wnet/onourownterms. On Our Own Terms is a website created in conjunction with a Bill Moyers/PBS documentary on end-of-life treatment. The site features interviews with professionals, patients and loved ones sharing insights and perspectives on making these difficult choices.

Books

- *Care at the Close of Life: Evidence and Experience*, by Stephen McPhee, Margaret A. Winker, Michael W. Rabow, Steven Z. Pantilat and Amy J. Markowitz (McGraw-Hill Professional)
- *Handbook for Mortals: Guidance for People Facing Serious Illness*, by Joanne Lynn, M.D., and Joan Harrold, M.D. (Oxford University Press)
- *Caring for Patients at the End of Life: Facing an Uncertain Future Together*, by Timothy E. Quill (Oxford University Press)
- *The Needs of the Dying: A Guide for Bringing Hope, Comfort, and Love to Life's Final Chapter*, by David Kessler (Harper Paperbacks).

If Your Wishes Are Simple

After you've familiarized yourself with the types of medical treatment that are typically administered at the end of life, it is time to express your own wishes. To begin, the program offers several ways for you to indicate your preferences if you don't want to delve into the specifics of different types of treatments. These are:

- leaving all decisions in the hands of your health care agent, if you've named one
- making a general statement that you do not want your life prolonged when you are close to death, or
- making a general statement that you want your life to be prolonged as long as possible, no matter what your condition.

Letting your agent make all treatment decisions. The first question you will be asked is whether you want to express specific wishes for medical treatment or whether you want your agent to make all decisions for you. If you specify your wishes for treatment, your agent will make decisions for you only on matters you do not specifically address.

Of course, the best way to be sure you'll get the medical care you want if you are someday unable to speak for yourself is to clearly state any preferences that you have. This is especially true if your choices could be considered in any way controversial. For instance, the withholding of artificially administered food and water (feeding tubes) has proved to be a culturally and politically contentious issue in recent years. If you know that you do not want to receive artificially administered food and water (feeding tubes) when you are close to death, it's wise to continue with the program so you can make that wish explicit.

However, if illness or exhaustion have left you feeling that it is too much to formulate and express specific wishes—or if the most important thing to you is simply to name a trusted agent who can act for you— you can leave all decision-making authority in the hands of your agent. If you do, the program won't ask for more information about your treatment wishes, and you can quickly finish up your documents.

On the other hand, if you indicate that you want to specify your wishes for medical treatment, you will first be given the opportunity to make one of the two simple statements below about your wishes.

Asking that your life not be prolonged when you are close to death. If you choose this option, your document will specify that you do not want to receive life-prolonging treatments when you are close to death from any of the conditions defined by your state's law. Usually, this means that your life will not be artificially prolonged if you are close to death from a terminal condition or are diagnosed as being permanently unconscious. (If you want more information about these specific medical conditions, see the next section.)

You will also be asked to specifically state whether or not you want to receive artificially administered food and water if you are in any of these conditions.

If you make this choice, you will still receive palliative care—that is, treatment to keep you comfortable—unless you specifically state that you do not want it.

Asking for all life-prolonging measures. This option is the opposite of the one just above. If you choose it, your document will state that you want your life to be prolonged for as long as possible within the limits of generally accepted health care standards. This includes receiving artificially administered food and water when you are close to death from a terminal condition or permanently unconscious.

If You Want to Specify Care for Different Situations

Despite rapid technological advances in medicine, much about the end of life remains uncharted. For example, medical experts disagree over whether comatose patients can feel pain and over whether some treatments are universally effective.

People who have strong feelings about what medical care they want to receive are usually guided by personal experience rather than extensive medical knowledge. For example, if you have watched a parent suffer a prolonged death while attached to a respirator, you may opt not to have a respirator as part of your medical care. If a friend who was diagnosed as terminally ill was much improved by a newly developed antibiotic, you may demand that drugs be administered to you, no matter what the medical prognosis.

To accommodate such wishes, while balancing the unknowns of medicine, some flexibility is built into health care documents. You can specify that you should receive different kinds of medical care under certain conditions defined by your state's law. In most states, this means you can leave specific instructions for the care you want when you are permanently unconscious and when you are diagnosed to be close to death from a terminal condition. In a few states, other conditions are covered as well.

For example, medical personnel usually give those diagnosed to be terminally ill a short time to live—less than six months or so. Some people feel that the best medical care under such a prognosis would be to have as much pain and suffering alleviated as possible through drugs and IVs, without any heroic medical maneuvers, such as invasive surgery or painful diagnostic tests.

However, patients often prove doctors wrong. Some people who are expected to die of a terminal illness within a few months stabilize or improve and live on for many years. If you opt to direct that no life-prolonging treatments be provided, you gamble that your condition will not improve—a gamble you must weigh against the chances you will beat the odds.

Permanently unconscious patients can be kept alive for many years with some mechanical assistance to keep breathing, circulation and other vital bodily functions operating. While chances are statistically miniscule that these patients will ever regain consciousness, in these cases, there is a chance that the diagnoses were incorrect in the first place.

There is no general rule to offer on this topic. You must be guided by your own very personal definitions of quality of life. Some people direct that all possible medical treatments be administered to them if they become permanently unconscious, just in case a medical cure becomes available. Others feel strongly that life without consciousness would completely lack meaning—and direct that all medical procedures, including food and water, be discontinued. Still others walk the middle ground, opting to be kept alive by feeding tubes, but not by other life-sustaining measures.

If you are having a difficult time making this choice, you may get good guidance by discussing the matter with a doctor or other experienced health care worker you trust. Internet resources also discuss the medical, spiritual and philosophical aspects of this decision.

If you want to direct that you receive different types of treatment in different situations, the following information will help you understand and evaluate the various conditions for which you can leave directions.

Where to Go for More Help

The growing awareness of health care directives is coupled with a growing number of resources you can turn to if you need help completing your directive or have specific questions about it.

A local senior center may be a good place to go for help. Many of them have trained health care staff on hand who are willing to discuss health care options.

The patient representative or social worker at a local hospital may also be a good person to contact for help. And if you have a regular physician, by all means discuss your concerns with him or her.

Local special groups and clinics may help you fill out your directive—particularly hospice or other organizations set up to meet the needs of the severely ill, such as AIDS or cancer groups. Check your telephone book for a local listing—or call one of the group's hotlines for more information or a possible referral. In addition, www.growthhouse.org has an extensive listing of local resources.

There are also a number of seminars offered. Beware of groups that offer such seminars for a hefty fee, however. Hospitals and senior centers often provide them free of charge.

Close to Death From a Terminal Condition

Generally, a terminal condition is any disease or injury from which doctors believe there is no chance of recovery and from which death is likely to occur within a short time—such as the final stages of cancer.

State laws on health care directives define terminal condition slightly differently, but commonly refer to it as "incurable" or "hopeless." Many state laws explain in addition that a patient who is terminally ill will die unless artificially supported through life-sustaining procedures.

Most states require that one or two physicians verify that the patient has a terminal condition before health care instructions will go into effect. In some states, this verification must be in writing.

Permanently Unconscious

Permanent unconsciousness may be caused by various medical conditions, head traumas or other body injuries.

While permanently unconscious people appear to go through sleep cycles and to respond to some noises and physical stimulation, medical experts disagree about whether a permanently unconscious person is capable of experiencing pain or discomfort. Most permanently unconscious people do not require mechanical assistance with breathing or circulation but must be provided food and water—usually through tubes inserted in the veins or stomach—if the condition persists.

Generally, people who lose consciousness either recover it within a short time (often a matter of hours, days or sometimes weeks) or enter a permanent coma or a persistent vegetative state in which it is extremely unlikely that they will ever regain consciousness. Medical personnel usually declare that a person who remains in a persistent vegetative state for many months without change has passed into a terminal condition.

Once unconsciousness is diagnosed as permanent, the chances of recovery are statistically extremely low. But medical technology (respirators and tube feeding and hydration) can typically keep an unconscious person alive indefinitely—48 years in one case. Consequently, the only way to allow a permanently unconscious person to die naturally may be to discontinue tube feeding and hydration.

To complicate matters, the external symptoms of permanent uncon-sciousness are somewhat subjective and can be misdiagnosed or the subject of dispute. The highly publicized case of Terri Schiavo involved a Florida woman kept alive by feeding tubes for more than ten years. While most medical experts declared her to be unconscious of her surroundings, at least one doctor offered the opinion that her responses to stimuli were not just reflexive, but were, in fact, evidence that she was conscious of her environment. (After her death, an autopsy showed that she had massive and irreversible brain damage and was indeed in a persistent vegetative state.)

Other factors, such as overmedication, can cause an unresponsive, unconscious condition that may abate once the treatment is halted or changed. To guard against misdiagnosis, many states require two physicians, at least one of whom is an expert on such conditions, to declare a patient permanently unconscious before any stated wishes are carried out.

In cases such as these, the person you appoint as your health care agent can play a crucial role, to make sure that diagnoses are not made in haste or that second opinions can be sought if there is reason to doubt the initial diagnosis.

Other Medical Conditions

A few states define a condition where death may not be imminent but the medical condition is nonetheless irreversible. If your state's official form addresses a condition like this, we allow you to choose the kind of treatment you want.

Special Conditions: State-by-State	
If you live in one of the following states, you will be asked about the additional condition or conditions listed here. As you prepare your document, the program defines these conditions to help you make your decisions about care.	
Florida	End-Stage Condition
Illinois	Incurable or Irreversible Condition
Maryland	End-Stage Condition
North Carolina	Advanced Dementia
Oklahoma	End-Stage Condition
Oregon	Advanced Progressive Illness
Pennsylvania	End-Stage Medical Condition
Tennessee	End-Stage Condition
Texas	Irreversible Condition

If the Burdens of Treatments Outweigh the Benefits

In addition to addressing your care in the specific conditions outlined above, you will also have the opportunity to give your agent or other surrogate decision maker the power to withhold or withdraw medical treatments if he or she determines that they are not in your best interest. (This option is not allowed in Oregon, which requires a health care form that covers only certain conditions.)

This broad, catch-all instruction will be offered to you only if you have stated that you do not wish to receive life-prolonging treatment or artificially administered food and water in all other conditions. It lets your decision maker evaluate your situation and direct that treatments be withheld in situations that may go beyond those conditions defined by your state's law. One good example of this is late-stage Alzheimer's disease, which can fall outside the definitions of both "terminal condition" and "permanent unconsciousness."

If you grant this power, a clause like the following will appear in your document:

If I have expressed, in this document or in any other manner, a clear wish regarding a specific treatment or condition, I want that wish to be followed. In all other situations, I direct that my life not be prolonged and that life-prolonging procedures not be provided or continued, in accordance with what my agent determines to be my best interest. In determining my best interest, my agent shall weigh the burdens of treatment against the expected benefits, considering my personal values to the extent known to my agent.

Your known wishes carry much weight in determining what is in your "best interest." In some states, they are conclusive—that is, the law says that a patient's wish is, by definition, the patient's "best interest." In other states, your doctor has some say in determining your best interest when it comes to medical decisions. Regardless of the law in your state, including this provision in your document should shorten the debate by putting clear authority in the hands of your appointed decision maker.

> ### Who Makes the Decision?
>
> If you appoint a health care agent, he or she will be making the determination of whether or not a particular treatment is in your best interest. If you do not appoint a health care agent, you can still include this power in your document. The decision will be placed in the hands of whomever the law appoints as your surrogate decision maker—usually a spouse, registered domestic partner or other close family member.

Do understand that if you grant this power, you are giving your decision maker considerable authority to decide what's best for you. Be sure to talk with your agent, if you have named one, and other loved ones about any specific benefits or burdens that matter to you. For example, would the burden of having to leave your home and spend the rest of your days in a hospital be so significant that you would not wish to receive life-prolonging treatment?

You can also include any strong feelings and preferences for your treatment when you are asked to provide additional instructions or wishes for your health care, in the next part of the program.

Expressing Other Wishes for Your Care

For some people, health care directives—no matter how detailed about things like respirators and surgery—do not reach the heart of their concerns: spiritual matters, money available for care, dying with dignity, quality of life or the well-being of those who care for them.

If you have such concerns, you should discuss them with your health care agent if you have named one—but you can also include them in your written health care instructions. We ask you whether you would like to describe, in your own words, your feelings on any of the following topics:

- the location of your care
- palliative care
- limits or exceptions for pain relief
- personal or religious values, and
- any additional wishes.

This section provides you with a little more information about each option.

> ! CAUTION
>
> **State your wishes carefully to avoid confusion.** You don't want your health care instructions to be confusing to those charged with carrying them out. Be sure that any wishes you specify here do not conflict with other directions you have given.

Location of Care

If where you receive care in the final months, weeks or days of your life is very important to you, you have many ways to set out your wishes. You may state a specific location that you would prefer, such as "at home" or at a particular hospital or hospice facility. Or, you may want to make a more general statement of your preferences, such as any location that lets you be with loved ones at all times.

On the other hand, you may wish to make clear that the location of your care is not as important as getting the treatment you desire. Perhaps you feel that if getting the care you want means being in the intensive care unit of a hospital, you would want to be there. You can state that whatever it takes to prolong your life is more important than where your care is administered.

Location of care may also arise as an issue surrounding diseases such as Alzheimer's or other types of severe dementia. If you have preferences regarding nursing homes or other long-term care options, you may say so.

When specifying wishes for the location of your care, be mindful of creating possible inconsistencies with other health care instructions you have given. For example, if you've expressed a wish for continuation of life-prolonging treatments during a terminal illness, and you've also expressed a preference to receive care at home, make clear which factor is more important. That is, are you willing to forgo some care in order to remain at home, or does the availability of life-sustaining treatment trump your concern about location?

Most important, don't forget to discuss your feelings and wishes with your doctor, your health care agent (if you have named one) and other loved ones.

Palliative Care

Whether or not you want to forgo treatments designed to prolong your life, your health care directive will state that you wish to receive treatment to keep you comfortable and alleviate pain. As discussed above, this type of care is commonly called comfort care or palliative care. Such care attempts not only to provide physical comfort, but also tends to emotional and spiritual needs as well.

If you wish, you can use your document to express any additional or specific wishes you have regarding the way comfort care should be administered. For example, if you prefer a particular course of treatment for pain, including specific medications, you can describe that here.

In addition, you can use this section to describe any wishes or arrangements you have made for hospice or other end-of-life comfort care, and you can set out specific feelings about what would help you remain comfortable at the end of your life. Perhaps you'd like some particular music played or to have favorite stories, poems or passages read aloud during your final days, when you may be too weak to speak for yourself. This kind of wish is appropriate for this section as well as a discussion with your doctor and loved ones.

Pain Relief Exceptions

Unless you specify otherwise, your health care document authorizes your doctors to provide you with as much medication as they deem necessary to keep you pain free. If for any reason you do not want this, you may state your wishes in this section.

For example, you may wish to specify that you do not want particular types of pain drugs. Or, you may state that you do not want so much pain medication that it compromises your ability to remain alert and aware of your loved ones.

Personal or Religious Values

At the end of life, health care issues inevitably arise that are not covered by specific directions. When that happens, a statement of your overall philosophy or religious beliefs on matters of medical treatment and dying can help your care providers make decisions on your behalf.

This can be a difficult subject to address, but you may want to consider topics such as:

- your overall goals for your health care
- any fears that you have
- your spiritual or religious beliefs or traditions
- your beliefs about when life would no longer be worth living, and
- your thoughts about how your medical condition may affect your family—personally, practically, financially or otherwise.

Certainly, you should not feel obligated to write a treatise on these matters in your health care directive. If you have any particularly strong feelings, however, they are worth noting. You should also make a particular point to discuss these issues with your health care agent, if you have named one, and other loved ones.

Any Other Wishes or Statements

Finally, we provide a place where you can write out any other feelings or preferences for your health care. You may use this section to write whatever you like, being careful not to create conflicts with any instructions you've already given. In addition, you will want to be sure you've thoroughly discussed your other wishes with your health care agent or other caretakers.

How Pregnancy May Affect Your Wishes

There is one limited situation in which your specific directions about health care might be challenged or ignored: if you are pregnant. Many states' laws say that doctors may not withdraw or withhold life support from a pregnant woman—or that such treatment may not be withheld if the fetus can be brought to term.

These state restrictions have rankled many supporters of women's rights and are legally suspect under U.S. Supreme Court rulings that the Constitution protects women's right to choose whether or not to bear children.

For this reason, if you might become pregnant, this program asks you to say whether you want your health care directions to be:

- given no effect if you are pregnant, or
- carried out as written.

If you specify that your health care directives be given no effect, your health care providers will have the discretion to decide what care is appropriate. They are most likely to administer whatever life-prolonging procedures are available—particularly if the fetus is at least four or five months old and potentially viable and unharmed.

If you choose that your health care directions be carried out as written if you are pregnant, beware that you may meet some resistance from the medical establishment. This is particularly true if you have directed that life-prolonging treatment, food and water or palliative care should be withheld. And you are more apt to run into resistance the more advanced your pregnancy becomes. If you are into the second trimester—fourth through sixth months—doctors are likely to administer all medical care they deem necessary to keep you and the fetus alive.

By the third trimester, it may be practically impossible to overcome a state's proscription against withholding life-prolonging medical care.

If you have strong feelings about overcoming your state's strictures— that is, you live in a state that renders your directive completely ineffective if you are pregnant, but you wish to have it enforced—it is important for you to discuss your wishes and alert your health care agent to lobby on your behalf. It would also be wise to write a brief explanation of your thoughts on this specific issue in the "other wishes" section of your health care directive. (See "Expressing Other Wishes for Your Care," above.)

State Laws on Pregnancy and Health Care Directives

No Effect: The law in your state does not allow your document directing health care to take effect when you are pregnant.

To Term: The law in your state will not allow your document directing health care to take effect if you are pregnant and your doctors believe the fetus could be brought to term while you are receiving life-sustaining treatment.

No Statute: Your state does not have any law about prohibiting withdrawal of life support if you are pregnant.

Alabama	No Effect
Alaska	To Term
Arizona	You may state whether or not you want your health care directions to be carried out if you are pregnant and it is possible for the fetus to develop to the point of live birth.
Arkansas	To Term
California	No Statute
Colorado	To Term
Connecticut	No Effect
Delaware	To Term
District of Columbia	No Statute
Florida	Life-prolonging procedures will be provided unless you have expressly stated that your health care surrogate may authorize that life-prolonging procedures may be withheld if you are pregnant, or if your health care surrogate obtains court approval for withholding life-prolonging procedures.
Georgia	Life-sustaining procedures will be provided unless the fetus could not develop to the point of live birth and you expressly state that you want your health care instructions carried out.
Hawaii	No Statute
Idaho	No Effect
Illinois	To Term

State Laws on Pregnancy and Health Care Directives (continued)

Indiana	No Effect
Iowa	To Term
Kansas	No Effect
Kentucky	No Effect
Maine	No Statute
Maryland	You may indicate whether or not you want your health care directions carried out in the event of your pregnancy.
Massachusetts	No Statute
Michigan	If you are pregnant, your health care representative cannot make any medical decision to withhold or withdraw treatment that would result in your death.
Minnesota	You may indicate whether or not you want your health care directives to be carried out in the event of your pregnancy.
Mississippi	No Statute
Missouri	No Effect
Montana	To Term
Nebraska	To Term
Nevada	To Term
New Hampshire	Life-sustaining treatment will be provided unless your doctors conclude that such treatment will not permit the fetus to develop to the point of live birth, or that such treatment will cause you physical harm or prolong severe pain that cannot be alleviated by medication.
New Jersey	You may indicate whether or not you want your health care directions to be carried out in the event of pregnancy.
New Mexico	No Statute
New York	No Statute
North Carolina	No Statute

State Laws on Pregnancy and Health Care Directives (continued)	
North Dakota	Life-sustaining procedures will be provided unless those procedures will not permit the fetus to develop to the point of live birth, or your doctor concludes that prolonging your life would cause you physical harm or severe pain, or would prolong severe pain that cannot be alleviated by medication.
Ohio	To Term
Oklahoma	You may indicate whether or not you want your health care directions carried out in the event of pregnancy.
Oregon	No Statute
Pennsylvania	Life-sustaining procedures will be provided unless your doctors conclude that the fetus could not develop to the point of live birth with continued application of those life-sustaining procedures, or prolonging your life would be physically harmful to you or cause you pain that could not be alleviated by medication.
Rhode Island	No Effect
South Carolina	No Effect
South Dakota	Life-sustaining procedures will be provided unless your doctors conclude that the fetus could not develop to the point of live birth with continued application of those life-sustaining procedures, or that prolonging your life would cause you physical harm or prolong severe pain that cannot be alleviated by medication.
Tennessee	No Statute
Texas	No Effect
Utah	No Effect
Vermont	You may indicate whether or not you want your health care directions carried out in the event of pregnancy.
Virginia	No Statute
Washington	No Effect
West Virginia	No Statute
Wisconsin	No Effect
Wyoming	No Statute

Stating Your Wishes for Organ Donation

Before finalizing your health care documents, you can express your wishes on one more matter: donating your organs, tissues or body after death.

If you already know whether or not you want to be an organ donor—or have already made arrangements to donate your organs or body—simply follow the instructions on the screen to indicate your wishes or plans. (Skip to "Making Your Wishes Known," below, for help.) If you are not yet certain whether you want to be a donor, the following information may help you make your decision.

The Need for Donated Organs

Although the number of organ donations has been steadily and slowly rising, the need for organs still far exceeds the number of organs donated. Nearly 100,000 people are currently waiting for lifesaving organ transplant surgery. Based on current rates of donation, one in three of them will die before receiving a transplant.

Religious Views and Concerns

Most major religions support organ donation. Reverence for life is the basis for almost all religious traditions, and organ donation is viewed as a lifesaving act of compassion and generosity. Donated organs must be removed immediately after death, however, and some religions strongly believe that a deceased person's body should remain undisturbed for a number of days. For the practitioner of a religion that holds both of these views—such as many types of Buddhism—a dilemma may arise. On one hand, it is beneficial and compassionate to donate organs, while on the other, it may violate the body. If you are uncertain about the right choice for you, it may be helpful to discuss the issue with your religious or spiritual adviser.

For a brief statement of different religions' views on organ donation, visit www.transweb.org.

Costs of Organ Donation

It will not cost your family anything if you want to donate your organs. The recipient pays the expenses, usually through insurance.

The Organ Donation Procedure

Before an organ is removed from a donor, doctors who are not involved in the procedure must certify that the patient is deceased. The body is then kept on a respirator to keep blood flowing through the organ until it can be removed and given to a waiting recipient. All of this usually takes about 24 hours.

Donation does not disfigure the body and does not interfere with having a funeral, even an open-casket service.

Making Your Wishes Known

Your health care directive is a good place to state your wishes regarding organ donation. Using this program you can choose from the following four options.

Indicate that you have already made arrangements or signed a document expressing your donation wishes. If you choose this option, you will be asked to briefly describe the arrangements you have made or the document you have signed, including its location.

Leave specific instructions about organ, tissue or body donation in your health care document. If you have not made arrangements to donate your organs but you know that you want to be a donor, you can add specific instructions directly to your health care directive. If you choose this option, you may state whether you want to donate any needed organs or body parts, or only specific ones that you name. You will also be able to indicate the purposes for which your donation must be used, including transplant, therapy, research, education or any necessary purpose that is allowed by law.

Indicate that you do not want to donate your organs. If you choose this option, your health care document will clearly state that you don't want to be a donor.

Leave the decision to your agent. If you named a health care agent, you can let him or her make organ donation decisions. If you choose this option, it will be helpful to discuss your feelings with, and offer some guidance to, your agent.

Other Ways to Make Your Wishes Clear

If you want to be a donor, there are a few more steps you can take to be sure your wishes are carried out. First, if your state offers a donor card—for example, a card or sticker that accompanies your driver's license—it's a good idea to obtain it and fill it out. It can alert others to your wishes in the event of an accident, when your health care documents may not be immediately available.

Second, many states now have donor registries, where you can sign up to donate any usable organs or tissues at your death. These registries, which are run by the state or by a nonprofit organization, provide computerized, confidential lists to authorized medical personnel 24 hours a day. You can check the Internet to see whether a donation registry is available in your state.

Finally, and most important, you should discuss your views about organ donation with your health care agent, close relatives and friends. Even if you've put your wishes in your health care directive and filled out a separate donor card, it's possible that an objection by a close family member could defeat your wishes after death. The best thing you can do is let those close to you know that you feel strongly about donating your organs.

Making It Legal

When you arrive at this part of the program, know that you have finished with the hard parts of making your health care directives. You have overcome the lure of procrastination to assert your right to keep control over your own health care.

However, you still must comply with a few technical requirements before your documents will be legally valid and binding. Very detailed, state-specific instructions will print out with your documents. But here's a brief overview of what you must do.

Signing Your Documents

Every state requires that you sign your documents—or direct another person to sign them for you.

But do not sign them immediately. You must sign your documents in the presence of witnesses or a notary public—sometimes both, depending on state law. That way, there is at least one other person who can attest that you were of sound mind and of legal age when you made the documents.

Signing for Someone Else

If you are helping someone else prepare health care documents and that person is too ill or weak to sign them, you or another person may sign the documents at his or her direction. The document will print with a special place for you to add the signer's name and signature.

The person making the document and the signer should appear together in front of the witnesses and/or notary public (see below), so that someone can observe the signing and confirm, if it is ever necessary, that it is what the document maker wanted and directed.

Having Your Documents Witnessed and Notarized

In most states, witnesses must sign your documents. In some states, you may have your documents notarized instead of witnessed. In others, you will be required to have both witnesses and a notary sign your document. Each state's rule is listed below. Note that a few states have different requirements for the document directing your health care and the document naming your agent.

Witnessing

Many states require that two witnesses see you sign your health care documents and that they verify in writing that you appeared to be of sound mind and signed the documents without anyone else influencing your decision.

Each state also has rules about who may serve as your witnesses. In many states, for example, a spouse, another close relative or any person who would inherit property from you is not allowed to act as a witness for the document directing health care. And many states prohibit your attending physician from being a witness. The goal of these laws is to be sure your witnesses do not have a personal or professional interest in your health care and, therefore, a conflict of interest.

If your state has restrictions on who may serve as witnesses to your health care documents, those restrictions are listed below and will also be noted on your documents, just before the witness signature lines.

Notarization

A notary public is an individual who is authorized by the state to verify signatures on documents. It shouldn't be difficult to find a notary. Many are listed in the yellow pages. Many hospitals also have a notary on staff.

Depending on your circumstances, you may take your document to the notary, or the notary may come to you. The notary will watch you sign the document and may then sign the notary language on the form or fill in a separate form and attach it to your document.

Be prepared to show the notary some identification and to pay a small fee for the services. If you are a patient in a hospital, the service may be free of charge.

The table below, as well as the instructions accompanying your documents, will tell you whether your state requires that your documents be notarized and whether there are any restrictions on who may serve as the notary.

Glossary of Witnessing Terms

When you read the requirements for witnesses in your state, you may find some unfamiliar words. Here are brief definitions of some terms that commonly occur.

Beneficiary. Any person who is entitled to inherit property from a deceased person.

Beneficiary of a will. Any person or organization named in a will to receive property, either as a first choice or if the first choice as beneficiary does not survive the person making the will.

Claim against the estate. Any right that a person has to receive property from a person's estate. This may arise under a will or living trust, from a contract or because of a legal liability that the deceased owes to the person.

Devisee. Any person who either is entitled to inherit property from a person under state law or who has been named to inherit property in a will or living trust.

Heir at law. Any person who qualifies to inherit property from a person under state law. Usually, heirs at law are spouses, children, parents, brothers and sisters. However, if none of these people exist, an heir at law might be a niece, a nephew or even a distant cousin.

Inherit by operation of law. When a person dies owning property that has not been left by a will or by some other legal device such as a living trust, the property will be distributed according to the laws of the state where the person died—that is, by operation of law. These laws—commonly referred to as the "laws of intestate succession"—usually give property first to a spouse and children and then to parents, brothers and sisters.

Presumptive heir. Someone who would inherit property under state law unless a child was later born to the current owner of the property the presumptive heir expects to receive.

State Witnessing and Notarizing Requirements

Alabama

Advance Directive for Health Care

Two witnesses are required. Neither of your witnesses may be:

- under the age of 19
- your health care proxy
- the person who signed your advance directive for you, if you were unable to sign it yourself
- related to you by blood, marriage or adoption
- entitled to any portion of your estate by operation of law or under your will, or
- directly financially responsible for your medical care.

Alaska

Advance Health Care Directive

Must either be signed by two adult witnesses or notarized.

If you choose to have the document witnessed, neither of your witnesses may be:

- your health care agent
- your health care provider
- an employee of your health care provider, or
- an employee of the health care institution or health care facility where you are receiving health care.

In addition, at least one of your witnesses must not be related to you by blood, marriage or adoption—and must not be entitled to any part of your estate under a will or codicil (amendment to a will).

Arizona

Living Will

Health Care Power of Attorney

Both documents must be signed by at least one witness or notarized.

If you choose to have the document witnessed, you may choose to have one or two witnesses. If you choose to have one witness, your witness may not be:

State Witnessing and Notarizing Requirements (continued)

- any person involved in providing your health care
- related to you by blood, marriage or adoption, or
- entitled to any part of your estate by operation of law or under your will.

If you have two witnesses, your witnesses do not need to meet the last two requirements on the list above.

If you choose to have your document notarized, the notary may not be:

- your health care agent, or
- any person involved in providing your health care.

Arkansas

Declaration

Durable Power of Attorney for Health Care

Both documents must be signed by two witnesses who are at least 18 years old.

California

Advance Directive for Health Care

Must either be signed by two witnesses or notarized.

If you choose to have the document witnessed, neither of your witnesses may be:

- your health care agent
- your health care provider
- an employee of your health care provider
- the operator of a community care facility
- an employee of a community care facility
- the operator of a residential care facility for the elderly, or
- an employee of a residential care facility for the elderly.

In addition, one of your witnesses must not be related to you by blood, marriage or adoption—and must not be entitled to any part of your estate by operation of law or under your will.

Finally, if you are in a skilled nursing facility, the document must also be witnessed by a patient advocate or ombudsman. (This requirement applies whether the document is witnessed or notarized.)

State Witnessing and Notarizing Requirements (continued)

Colorado

Declaration as to Medical or Surgical Treatment

Medical Durable Power of Attorney

Both documents must be signed by two witnesses and may also be notarized.

If you choose to have the document witnessed, neither of your witnesses may be:

- a physician
- an employee of your attending physician
- an employee of a health care facility where you are a patient
- a person with a claim against your estate, or
- a person entitled to any part of your estate by operation of law or under your will.

In addition, if you are a patient or resident of a health care facility, the witnesses cannot be patients of that facility.

Connecticut

Health Care Instructions and Appointment of Health Care Agent and Attorney-in-Fact for Health Care Decisions

Must be signed by two witnesses.

Although the law does not restrict who can serve as a witness, we suggest that your witnesses be at least 18 years old and the person named to serve as your health care agent and your attorney-in-fact for health care decisions not act as a witness. You and your witnesses may also sign in front of a notary public, but you are not required to do so.

Document Concerning Withholding or Withdrawal of Life Support Systems

Must be signed by two witnesses. Although the law does not restrict who can serve as a witness, we suggest that your witnesses be at least 18 years old and the person named to serve as your health care agent and your attorney-in-fact for health care decisions not act as a witness.

Appointment of Health Care Agent and Attorney-in-Fact for Health Care

Must be signed by two witnesses. Although the law does not restrict who can serve as a witness, we suggest that your witnesses be at least 18 years old and the person named to serve as your health care agent and your attorney-in-fact for health care decisions not act as a witness.

State Witnessing and Notarizing Requirements (continued)

Delaware

Advance Health Care Directive

The document must be signed by two witnesses. Neither of your witnesses may be:

- under the age of 18
- related to you by blood, marriage or adoption
- an owner, operator or employee of a residential long-term health care institution in which you are a resident
- a person directly financially responsible for your medical care
- a person with a claim against any portion of your estate, or
- a person entitled to any portion of your estate by operation of law or under your will.

If you are a resident of a sanitarium, rest home, nursing home, boarding home or related institution, one of the witnesses must be, at the time you sign the Advance Health Care Directive, a patient advocate or ombudsman designated by the Division of Services for Aging and Adults with Physical Disabilities or the Public Guardian.

District of Columbia

Declaration

Must be signed by two witnesses. Neither of your witnesses may be:

- under the age of 18
- related to you by blood, marriage or domestic partnership
- your attending physician
- an employee of your attending physician
- an employee of a health care facility where you are a patient
- the person who signed your declaration for you, if you were unable to sign it yourself
- a person entitled to any part of your estate by operation of law or under your will, or
- a person directly financially responsible for your medical care.

If you are a patient in a skilled care facility, one witness must be a patient advocate or ombudsman.

State Witnessing and Notarizing Requirements (continued)

Durable Power of Attorney for Health Care

Must be signed by two witnesses. Neither of your witnesses may be:

- under the age of 18
- your health care attorney-in-fact
- your health care provider, or
- an employee of your health care provider.

In addition, one of your witnesses must not be related to you by blood, marriage or adoption and must not be entitled to any part of your estate by operation of law or under your will.

Florida

Living Will

Must be signed by two witnesses, one of whom must not be your spouse or related to you by blood.

Designation of Health Care Surrogate

Must be signed by two witnesses, both of whom must be at least 18 years old. Neither witness may be your health care surrogate. In addition, one of your witnesses must not be your spouse or a blood relative.

Georgia

Advance Directive for Health Care

Must be signed by two witnesses. Neither of your witnesses may be:

- under the age of 18
- your health care agent
- a person who is directly involved in your health care, or
- a person who will knowingly inherit anything from you or knowingly gain a financial benefit from your death.

In addition, only one of your witnesses may be an employee, agent or medical staff member of the hospital, skilled nursing facility, hospice or other health care facility in which you are receiving health care. (This witness is still prohibited from being directly involved in your health care.)

State Witnessing and Notarizing Requirements (continued)

Hawaii

Advance Health Care Directive

Must be signed by two witnesses or notarized. If you choose to have the document witnessed, neither of your witnesses may be:

- your health care agent
- a health care provider, or
- an employee of a health care provider facility.

In addition, at least one of your witnesses must not be related to you by blood, marriage or adoption—and must not be entitled to any part of your estate by operation of law or under your will.

Idaho

Living Will and Durable Power of Attorney for Health Care

Idaho law does not require that your documents be witnessed or notarized. However, witnesses are recommended to avoid concerns that the document was forged, that you were forced to sign it or that it does not represent your wishes. If you choose to have your documents witnessed, we suggest that your witnesses be at least 18 years old and that your health care agent not act as a witness.

Illinois

Declaration

Must be signed by two witnesses. Neither of your witnesses may be:

- under the age of 18
- the person who signed your declaration for you, if you were unable to sign it yourself
- a person entitled to any part of your estate by operation of law or under your will, or
- a person directly financially responsible for your medical care.

Durable Power of Attorney for Health Care

Must be signed by one witness. Your witness may not be:

- your attending physician or mental health care provider, or a relative of the physician or provider
- an owner, operator or relative of an owner or operator of a health care facility in which you are a patient or resident (this includes

State Witnessing and Notarizing Requirements (continued)

directors or executive officers of an operator that is a corporate entity, but not other employees of the operator)

- a parent, sibling or descendant, or the spouse of a parent, sibling or descendant, of either you or your agent or alternate agent, regardless of whether the relationship is by blood, marriage or adoption, or
- your agent or alternate agent for health care.

Indiana

Living Will Declaration

Must be signed by two witnesses. Neither of your witnesses may be:

- under the age of 18
- your parent, spouse or child
- a person entitled to any part of your estate
- a person directly financially responsible for your medical care, or
- the person who signed your declaration for you, if you were unable to sign it yourself.

Durable Power of Attorney for Health Care and Appointment of Health Care Representative

Must be notarized.

Iowa

Declaration

Durable Power of Attorney for Health Care

Both documents must follow the same requirements:

Must be signed by two witnesses or notarized.

If you choose to have the document witnessed, neither of your witnesses may be:

- under the age of 18
- your health care agent
- your health care provider, or
- an employee of your health care provider.

In addition, one of your witnesses must not be related to you by blood, marriage or adoption within the third degree of consanguinity (parents, children, siblings, grandchildren, grandparents, uncles, aunts, nephews, nieces and great-grandchildren).

State Witnessing and Notarizing Requirements (continued)

Kansas

Declaration

Must be signed by two witnesses or notarized. Neither of your witnesses may be:

- under the age of 18
- the person who signed your declaration for you, if you were unable to sign it yourself
- related to you by blood or marriage
- entitled to any part of your estate by operation of law or under your will, or
- directly financially responsible for your health care.

Durable Power of Attorney for Health Care Decisions

Must be signed by two witnesses or notarized.

If you choose to have the document witnessed, neither of your witnesses may be:

- under the age of 18
- your agent for health care decisions
- related to you by blood, marriage or adoption
- entitled to any part of your estate by operation of law or under your will, or
- directly financially responsible for your health care.

Kentucky

Advance Directive

Must be signed by two witnesses or notarized. Neither of your witnesses nor the notary may be:

- related to you by blood
- your beneficiary by operation of Kentucky law
- your attending physician
- an employee of a health care facility where you are a patient, unless the employee serves as a notary public, or
- directly financially responsible for your health care.

State Witnessing and Notarizing Requirements (continued)

Maine

Advance Health Care Directive

The document must be signed by two witnesses. Although the law does not restrict who can serve as a witness, we suggest that your witnesses be at least 18 years old and that your health care agent not act as a witness.

Maryland

Advance Directive

The document must be signed by two witnesses. The person you name as your health care agent cannot serve as a witness. In addition, at least one of your witnesses must be a person who is not entitled to any portion of your estate, and who is not entitled to any financial benefit by reason of your death.

Massachusetts

Document Directing Health Care

Health Care Proxy

Both documents must be signed by two witnesses. Neither of your witnesses may be:

- under the age of 18, or
- your health care agent.

Michigan

Document Directing Health Care

Must be signed by two witnesses. Although the law does not restrict who can serve as a witness, we suggest that your witnesses be at least 18 years old and that your patient advocate not act as a witness.

Patient Advocate Designation

Must be signed by two witnesses. Neither of your witnesses may be:

- under the age of 18
- your spouse, parent, child, grandchild or sibling
- your patient advocate
- your physician
- an employee of your life or health insurance provider
- an employee of a health care facility where you are a patient
- an employee of a home for the aged where you live, or

State Witnessing and Notarizing Requirements (continued)

- entitled to any portion of your estate by operation of law or under your will.

Minnesota

Health Care Directive

Must be signed by two witnesses or notarized. Neither your witnesses nor the notary may be your health care agent.

If you choose to have the document witnessed, at least one of the witnesses may not be a health care provider or an employee of a provider directly attending to you.

If you choose to have the document notarized, the notary may not be your health care agent.

Mississippi

Advance Health Care Directive

Must be signed by two witnesses or notarized.

If you choose to have the document witnessed, neither of your witnesses may be:

- under the age of 18
- your health care agent
- a health care provider, or
- an employee of a health care provider or facility.

In addition, one witness must not be related to you by blood, marriage or adoption and must not be entitled to any part of your estate by operation of law or under your will.

Missouri

Declaration

Must be signed by two witnesses. Neither of your witnesses may be:

- under the age of 18, or
- the person who signed your declaration for you, if you were unable to sign it yourself.

Durable Power of Attorney for Health Care

If you grant your agent power to direct your burial or cremation, your document must be signed in front of two witnesses and notarized. If you do not grant this power, only the notary is necessary.

State Witnessing and Notarizing Requirements (continued)

Montana

Declaration

Durable Power of Attorney for Health Care

Both documents must be signed by two witnesses. Although the law does not restrict who can serve as a witness, we suggest that your witnesses be at least 18 years old and that your health care agent not act as a witness.

Nebraska

Declaration

Must be signed by two witnesses or notarized. If you choose to have the document witnessed, neither of your witnesses may be:

- under the age of 18, or
- an employee of your life or health insurance provider.

In addition, one witness may not be a director or employee of your treating health care provider.

Durable Power of Attorney for Health Care

If you grant your agent power to direct your burial or cremation, your document must be signed by two witnesses and notarized. Neither of your witnesses may be:

- your attorney-in-fact for health care decisions
- your attending physician
- your spouse, parent, child, grandchild or sibling
- your presumptive heir or known devisee, or
- an employee of your life or health insurance provider.

In addition, one of your witnesses must not be an administrator or employee of your health care provider.

If you do not grant your agent the power to direct your burial or cremation, you may choose to have your document signed by two witnesses (subject to the requirements above) or notarized.

Nevada

Declaration

Must be signed by two witnesses. Although the law does not restrict who can serve as a witness, we suggest that your witnesses be at least 18 years old and that your attorney-in-fact for health care decisions not act as a witness.

State Witnessing and Notarizing Requirements (continued)

Durable Power of Attorney for Health Care Decisions

If you grant your agent power to direct your burial or cremation, your document must be notarized. If you do not grant this power, you may choose to have your document signed by two witnesses or notarized. If you choose to have the document witnessed, neither of your witnesses may be:

- under the age of 18
- your attorney-in-fact for health care decisions
- a health care provider
- an employee of a health care provider
- the operator of a health care facility, or
- an employee of the operator of a health care facility.

In addition, one of your witnesses must not be related to you by blood, marriage or adoption and must not be entitled to any part of your estate by operation of law or under your will.

New Hampshire

Advance Directive

Must be signed by two witnesses or notarized. If you choose to have the document witnessed, neither of your witnesses may be:

- under the age of 18
- your health care agent
- your attending physician or advanced registered nurse practitioner (ARNP) or a person acting under the direction or control of the attending physician or ARNP
- your spouse, or
- entitled to any part of your estate by operation of law or under your will.

In addition, no more than one witness may be a health or residential care provider or such provider's employee.

New Jersey

Combined Advance Directive for Health Care

Instruction Directive

Proxy Directive

Any document must be signed by two witnesses or notarized.

State Witnessing and Notarizing Requirements (continued)

If you choose to have the document witnessed, neither of your witnesses may be:

- under the age of 18, or
- your health care representative.

New Mexico

Advance Health Care Directive

The law does not require that your advance directive be witnessed. However, witnesses are recommended to avoid concerns that the document might be forged, that you were forced to sign it or that it does not genuinely represent your wishes. If you choose to have your document witnessed, we suggest that your witnesses be at least 18 years old.

New York

Document Directing Health Care

Health Care Proxy

Both must be signed by two witnesses. Neither of your witnesses may be:

- under the age of 18
- your health care agent, or
- the person who signed the declaration for you, if you were unable to sign it for yourself.

If you reside in a mental health facility, your witnesses must meet additional requirements. Ask your mental health care provider for more information.

North Carolina

Advance Directive

Must be signed by two witnesses and notarized. Neither of your witnesses may be:

- related to you by blood or marriage
- your attending physician or mental health treatment provider
- a licensed health care provider who is (1) an employee of your attending physician or mental health treatment provider, (2) an employee of the health facility in which you are a patient or (3) an employee of a nursing home or any adult care home where you reside

State Witnessing and Notarizing Requirements (continued)

- a person entitled to any part of your estate by operation of law or under your will, or
- a person with a claim against you or your estate.

Health Care Power of Attorney

Must be signed by two witnesses and notarized. Neither of your witnesses may be:

- under the age of 18
- related to you by blood or marriage
- your attending physician or mental health treatment provider
- a licensed health care provider who is (1) an employee of your attending physician or mental health treatment provider, (2) an employee of the health facility in which you are a patient or (3) an employee of a nursing home or any adult care home where you reside.
- a person entitled to any part of your estate by operation of law or under your will, or
- a person with a claim against you or your estate.

North Dakota

Health Care Directive

Must be signed by two witnesses or notarized. Neither the witnesses or the notary may be:

- under the age of 18
- your spouse or another person related to you by blood, marriage or adoption
- your health care agent
- a person entitled to any part of your estate upon your death, or
- a person with a claim against your estate.

In addition, at least one witness must not be a health care or long-term care provider providing you with direct care or an employee of the health care or long-term care provider providing you with direct care. (This restriction does not apply to the notary.)

State Witnessing and Notarizing Requirements (continued)

Ohio

Declaration

Must be signed by two witnesses or notarized. If you choose to have the document witnessed, neither of your witnesses may be:

- under the age of 18
- related to you by blood, marriage or adoption
- your attending physician
- an administrator of a nursing home where you receive care, or
- the person who signed your declaration, if you were unable to sign it yourself.

Durable Power of Attorney for Health Care

Must be signed by two witnesses or notarized. If you choose to have the document witnessed, neither of your witnesses may be:

- under the age of 18
- related to you by blood, marriage or adoption
- your attorney-in-fact
- your attending physician, or
- an administrator of a nursing home where you receive care.

Oklahoma

Advance Directive for Health Care

If you grant your agent power to direct your burial or cremation, your document must be signed in front of two witnesses and notarized. If you do not grant this power, only the witnesses are necessary. Neither of your witnesses may be:

- under the age of 18
- related to you by blood, marriage or adoption, or
- a person who might inherit from you.

Oregon

Advance Directive

Must be signed by two witnesses.

Neither of your witnesses may be:

- your health care representative, or
- your attending physician.

State Witnessing and Notarizing Requirements (continued)

One witness may not be:
- related to you by blood, marriage or adoption
- an owner, operator or employee of a health care facility where you are a resident, or
- a person entitled to any part of your estate upon your death.

Pennsylvania

Declaration

Durable Power of Attorney for Health Care

Both documents must be signed by two witnesses. Neither of your witnesses may be:
- under the age of 18, or
- the person who signed your declaration for you, if you were unable to sign it yourself.

Rhode Island

Declaration

Must be signed by two witnesses. Your witnesses may not be related to you by blood or marriage.

Durable Power of Attorney for Health Care

If you grant your agent power to direct your burial or cremation, your document must be notarized. If you do not grant this power, you may choose to have your document signed by two witnesses or notarized.

If your document will be notarized, the notary may not be:
- related to you by blood, marriage or adoption, or
- entitled to any part of your estate by operation of law or under your will.

If you choose to have the document witnessed, neither of your witnesses may be:
- under the age of 18
- your health care agent
- a health care provider
- an employee of a health care provider
- the operator of a community care facility, or
- an employee of an operator of a community care facility.

State Witnessing and Notarizing Requirements (continued)

In addition, one of your witnesses must not be related to you by blood, marriage or adoption and must not be entitled to any part of your estate by operation of law or under your will.

South Carolina

Declaration

Must be signed by two witnesses and notarized. Neither of your witnesses may be:

- related to you by blood, marriage or adoption
- your attending physician
- an employee of your attending physician
- a person directly financially responsible for your medical care
- a person entitled to any part of your estate by operation of law or under your will
- a beneficiary of your life insurance policy, or
- a person who has a claim against your estate.

No more than one of your witnesses may be an employee of a health care facility where you are a patient. If you are in a hospital or nursing care facility when you sign your declaration, at least one of your witnesses must be an ombudsman designated by the state.

Health Care Power of Attorney

Must be signed by two witnesses and notarized. Neither of your witnesses may be:

- your health care agent
- your attending physician
- an employee of your attending physician
- related to you by blood, marriage or adoption
- directly financially responsible for your medical care
- the beneficiary of an insurance policy on your life
- a person with a claim against your estate at the time you sign your document, or
- a person entitled to any portion of your estate by operation of law or under your will.

State Witnessing and Notarizing Requirements (continued)

In addition, only one witness may be an employee of a health facility in which you are a patient.

South Dakota

Living Will Declaration

Must be signed by two witnesses, both of whom are at least 18 years old, and may also be notarized, although notarization is optional.

Durable Power of Attorney for Health Care

Must be signed by two witnesses, both of whom are at least 18 years old.

Tennessee

Advance Health Care Directive

Must be signed by two witnesses or a notary. If you choose to have your document witnessed, both witnesses must be competent adults and neither may be your health care agent. In addition, at least one of your witnesses must not be related to you by blood, marriage or adoption—and must not be entitled to any part of your estate by operation of law or under your will.

Texas

Directive to Physicians and Family or Surrogates

Must be signed by two witnesses. Your witnesses must be at least 18 years old. In addition, at least one of your witnesses may not be:

- your health care agent
- related to you by blood or marriage
- your attending physician
- an employee of your attending physician
- an employee of a health care facility in which you are a patient if the employee is providing direct care to you or is an officer, director, partner or business office employee of the health care facility or of any parent organization of the health care facility, or
- a person who is entitled to or has a claim against any part of your estate after your death.

Medical Power of Attorney

If you grant your agent power to direct your burial or cremation, your document must be signed by two witnesses and notarized. Your witnesses

State Witnessing and Notarizing Requirements (continued)

must be at least 18 years old. In addition, at least one of your witnesses may not be:

- your health care agent
- related to you by blood or marriage
- your attending physician
- an employee of your attending physician
- an employee of a health care facility in which you are a patient if the employee is providing direct care to you or is an officer, director, partner or business office employee of the health care facility or of any parent organization of the health care facility, or
- a person who is entitled to or has a claim against any part of your estate after your death.

If you do not grant your agent power to direct your burial or cremation, you may choose to have your document signed by two witnesses (subject to the requirements, above) *or* notarized.

Utah

Advance Health Care Directive

Must be signed by one witness. Your witness may not be:

- under the age of 18
- your health care agent
- related to you by blood or marriage
- a health care provider who is providing care to you
- an administrator at a health care facility where you are receiving care
- a person directly financially responsible for your medical care
- a beneficiary of a life insurance policy, trust, qualified plan, pay-on-death account or transfer-on-death deed that is held, owned, made or established by you or on your behalf
- entitled to benefit financially upon your death
- entitled to a right to, or interest in, any of your real or personal property upon your death, or
- the person who signed your document for you, if you were unable to sign it yourself.

If you grant your agent power to direct your burial or cremation, your document must be signed in front of two witnesses.

State Witnessing and Notarizing Requirements (continued)

Vermont

Advance Directive

Must be signed by two witnesses. Neither witness may be:

- under the age of 18
- your health care agent, or
- your spouse, reciprocal beneficiary, parent, adult sibling, adult child or adult grandchild.

In addition, if you are a patient in a hospital, nursing home or residential care facility, a designated person must sign the document after explaining it to you. Ask a patient representative for help with this requirement.

Virginia

Advance Medical Directive

If you grant your agent power to direct your burial or cremation, your document must be signed in front of two witnesses and notarized—and your health care agent must sign the part of the document that grants the power.

If you do not grant your agent power to direct your burial or cremation, only the witnesses are necessary.

Your witnesses must be over the age of 18. In addition, we suggest that your health care agent not act as a witness.

Washington

Health Care Directive

Must be signed by two witnesses. Neither of your witnesses may be:

- related to you by blood or marriage
- your attending physician
- an employee of your attending physician
- an employee of a health care facility where you are a patient
- a person entitled to any part of your estate by operation of law or under your will, or
- a person with a claim against your estate.

State Witnessing and Notarizing Requirements (continued)

Durable Power of Attorney for Health Care

Must be signed by two witnesses. Although the law does not restrict who can serve as a witness, we suggest that your witnesses be at least 18 years old and that your health care agent not act as a witness.

West Virginia

Living Will

Medical Power of Attorney

Both documents must meet the same requirements:

Must be signed by two witnesses and notarized.

Neither of your witnesses may be:

- under the age of 18
- your health care representative or successor representative
- the person who signed your document, if you were unable to sign it yourself
- related to you by blood or marriage
- your attending physician
- a person directly financially responsible for your medical care, or
- a person entitled to any part of your estate by operation of law or under your will.

Wisconsin

Declaration to Physicians

Must be signed by two witnesses. Neither of your witnesses may be:

- related to you by blood, marriage or adoption
- your domestic partner
- your health care provider
- an employee of your health care provider, other than a chaplain or a social worker
- an employee of an inpatient health care facility where you are a patient, other than a chaplain or a social worker
- a person directly financially responsible for your medical care
- a person who has a claim against your estate, or
- a person entitled to any part of your estate by operation of law or under your will.

State Witnessing and Notarizing Requirements (continued)

Power of Attorney for Health Care

Must be signed by two witnesses. Neither of your witnesses may be:

- under the age of 18
- your health care agent
- related to you by blood, marriage or adoption
- your domestic partner
- your health care provider
- an employee of your health care provider, other than a chaplain or a social worker
- an employee of an inpatient health care facility where you are a patient, other than a chaplain or a social worker
- a person directly financially responsible for your medical care, or
- a person with a claim against your estate.

Wyoming

Advance Health Care Directive

Must be signed by two witnesses or notarized. If you choose to have the document witnessed, both witnesses must be competent adults who know you personally. In addition, neither of your witnesses may be:

- your health care agent
- a treating health care provider
- an employee of a treating health care provider
- the operator of a community care facility
- an employee of an operator of a community care facility
- the operator of a residential care facility, or
- an employee of an operator of a residential care facility.

Making and Distributing Copies

Ideally, you should make an effort to make your wishes for your future health care widely known. Keep the originals of your health care documents and, at a minimum, give copies to your agent, if you named one, and to the doctors or medical facility most likely to be treating you. Also consider giving copies to:

- any physician with whom you now consult regularly
- the office of the hospital or other care facility in which you are likely to receive treatment
- the patient representative of your HMO or insurance plan
- immediate family members—spouse, children, siblings, and
- trusted friends.

Some people are hesitant to discuss the particulars of their medical care with other people, feeling that it is an intensely private issue. However, in the case of health care directives, you must weigh your desire for privacy against the need for the documents to be effective. Your carefully reasoned medical directive will simply be wasted words unless you make sure it gets into the hands of the people who need to know about it.

Keeping Your Documents Up to Date

Review your health care documents occasionally—at least every few years—to make sure they still accurately reflect your wishes for your medical care. Advances in technology and changes in health prompt many people to change their minds about the kind of health care they want.

In addition, you should consider making new documents if:

- You move to another state.
- You get married. You should prepare new health care documents if you get married, unless your new spouse is already named as your health care agent. You are never required to name your spouse as your health care agent, but if you want to name someone

else, be sure you do it in a document created after the date of your marriage. If you have an old document naming someone other than your spouse as your agent, some states will consider it automatically revoked when you marry.

- You get divorced. If you divorce or separate, revoke your health care documents and make new ones. In most cases, your former spouse's authority as agent terminates automatically if you file for divorce, but you should still create a new document to make your wishes clear.
- You made a health care directive many years ago, because your state's law controlling them has probably changed substantially.
- The agent you named to supervise your wishes becomes unable to do so.

Revoking Your Documents

If you have a change of heart and want to revoke or cancel your health care documents, you can do so at any time.

If you want to revoke the appointment of your health care agent (or an alternate agent), most states require that you either deliver a written notice to your agent and health care providers or personally inform your primary physician that you no longer want your agent to serve. You may revoke other health care choices simply by informing or demonstrating to your health care providers and others who know about your wishes that you want to revoke them.

But the best practice is to revoke any document in writing—if you are well enough to do so. You should also tear up the original document and ask anyone who has a copy to return it to you to be destroyed. The program will print a revocation form that you can keep for later use, if you need it.

As a practical matter, even if you prepare a written revocation, it is important to tell everyone who knows about your document that you have revoked it.

A New Document Trumps an Old One

If there is more than one health care directive, and there is any discrepancy between the two, the statements in the most recent one win. Technically, there is no need to formally revoke an earlier document. However, confusion may arise if an old document still exists—for example, if it covers issues on which the newer document is silent. For this reason, you should do all you can to make sure your old document is clearly revoked and destroyed. And of course you should make sure that your new document is properly finalized, that you give it to your doctor and your health care agent and that it is placed in your medical records.

Final Arrangements

M ost people avoid the subject of death—and are especially uncomfortable thinking about their own mortality. You, too, may be tempted to leave the details of your final arrangements to those who survive you. But there are two good reasons not to do this: care and cost.

Making Final Arrangements in Advance

Anyone who has lost a loved one knows how agonizing it can be to plan an appropriate commemoration. And most people have attended funerals or memorial services that seem uniquely unsuited to the person who has died.

Letting your survivors know whether you'd like to be buried or cremated, and what kind of ceremonies you envision, saves them the pain of making such decisions at a difficult time. Many family members and friends also find that an open discussion is a great relief—especially if death is likely to occur soon.

Planning some of these details in advance and doing wise comparison shopping can also save money. For many people, after buying a home and car, after-death goods and services are the most expensive things they ever pay for.

Without some direction, your survivors may choose the most expensive goods and services available, to assuage their own feelings of grief or obligation or perhaps due to pressure from funeral industry providers. The best way to prevent this from happening is to write down your preferences. You can use this program to do just that, creating a final arrangements document to point the way for your loved ones.

A Will Is Not the Way

Despite what many people think, a will is a poor place to express your death and burial preferences. It probably won't be located and read until several weeks after you die—too late to help your family. It's better to write up a separate document such as the one you can prepare with this program.

(!) **CAUTION**

Get organized for your family. Making a final arrangements document won't do any good unless your loved ones can find it when the time comes. Here are two suggestions for making sure your wishes aren't overlooked:

- Use Quicken WillMaker Plus to make an Information for Caregivers and Survivors form. It provides the location of all your important paperwork, including your final arrangements document. This form also lets you document other essential information, such as financial accounts and medical information. To learn more, go to the "My Documents" screen and select "Information for Caregivers and Survivors" from the list.
- Turn to *Get It Together*, by Melanie Cullen with Shae Irving (Nolo). This comprehensive workbook walks you step by step through the process of gathering and organizing all your important records and personal information. You can order a customized binder to neatly store your work.

The Legal Effect of Your Document

Your final arrangements document provides valuable guidance for your family members. It will tell them what kind of body disposition and services you want and direct them to any sources you've set aside for payment. As long as your wishes are reasonable and financially feasible, they should be carried out as you intend.

If relationships among your loved ones are amicable, this should be all you need. You can talk with those who will be most likely to carry out your wishes and give them a copy of your instructions—or be sure they know where to find them when the time comes.

If a dispute arises among your loved ones—for example, between your partner or spouse and other relatives—funeral industry personnel are usually bound to follow any written instructions you left. The greatest sticking points arise when the deceased person has not provided in advance for payment of the arrangements. (See "Paying for Final Arrangements," at the end of this chapter.) Court battles over preferences for body or funeral ceremonies almost never arise, primarily because of the lack of time and the costs of litigation.

Most disputes arise where more than one person is in charge—say you have three children—and they disagree over a fundamental decision, such as whether your body should be buried or cremated. Such disputes can be avoided if you are willing to put your wishes in writing.

If You're Worried About Family Fights

If you are concerned that your family may not agree with your final wishes—or if you expect them to argue with each other after your death—you can add legal force to your document by combining it with a health care directive.

It may not be possible to make your wishes ironclad. (State laws on the subject vary widely, and many are unclear or full of loopholes.) But a health care directive can help, primarily by allowing you to appoint someone to be sure your postdeath preferences are carried out.

The primary function of a health care directive is to set out wishes for medical treatment in an emergency or at the end of life. And one of the most important parts of making a health care directive is naming your health care agent—that is, the person who will oversee your medical care and make treatment decisions for you if you are unable to do so yourself. You can also give your health care agent the power to carry out your wishes for the disposition of your body and other final arrangements. (Using this program, you can make a health care directive that specifically includes this power.)

To provide guidance for your agent, you can simply attach your final arrangements document to your health care directive. After your death, if family members object to your wishes or squabble with each other about what's best, your health care agent is legally authorized to step in to ensure that you get what you wanted.

See Chapter 15 for more information on health care directives.

Expressing Your Wishes for Organ Donation

There are many ways to express your wishes for organ or body donation. You may have already indicated, on your driver's license or in another document, that you want to be a donor. You can also use your health care directive to state whether or not you wish to be a donor. Taken together, your health care directive and final arrangements document will act as a comprehensive guide to your end-of-life wishes.

If You Have Already Made Some Final Arrangements

If you have already made arrangements for burial or cremation, you may wonder whether it is necessary to make a final arrangements document. It is probably wise to do so. The program gives you the opportunity to describe any existing arrangements, and it may also direct your attention to issues that you have not yet addressed. The result is a comprehensive document that provides essential directions for your survivors.

What Happens If There Is No Document

If you die without leaving written instructions about your preferences, state law determines who has the right to control how your remains will be disposed. In most states, the right—and the responsibility to pay—rests with the following people, in order:

- spouse or registered domestic partner
- child or children
- parent or parents
- next of kin, or
- a court-appointed public administrator.

Getting Started

Before you jump into the details of your final arrangements document, you may want to spend some time thinking about the big picture. It may be easier to answer specific questions once you have a general sense of what you want.

How to approach this is up to you. You may find it helpful to talk with family or friends about end-of-life issues, reflecting on what appeals to you—and what doesn't. Perhaps you have participated in after-death events that you have particularly liked, or where you have felt noticeably uncomfortable. All these things can help to point the way.

If you want to do some additional research, you might browse the Funeral Consumers Alliance website at www.funerals.org. This nonprofit organization's "Frequently Asked Questions" page is a good place to begin exploring your options.

When you're ready, this program invites you to put the details in writing. We'll guide you through a number of topics, one at a time:
- burial or cremation
- mortuary or cremation facility
- embalming
- casket or urn
- pallbearers
- transportation to burial site
- headstone, monument or burial marker
- epitaph
- funeral or memorial ceremonies
- obituary, and
- financial plans.

You need answer only the questions you want to. While it helps to be as specific as possible, your final arrangements document can be as brief or as extensive as you wish. If there is an issue you don't care to address, simply skip it. If you like, you can always come back to the program later, either to change your answers or create a more detailed document.

If You Are an Organ Donor

You should state your preference for burial or cremation even if you have arranged to donate some organs or your entire body. (See Chapter 15 for more about organ donation.) Keep in mind that if one or more of your organs is donated, the rest of your body must be disposed of or buried. And even if you have arranged to have your entire body donated, there is the possibility the donation might not be accepted for some reason. And, finally, after the medical institution has finished using the body for teaching or research in one or two years, it must be disposed of or buried.

Burial or Cremation

One of the most important questions we will ask you is whether you want your body to be buried or cremated.

If your body will be buried, you can state your preferences for a burial site. If you choose cremation, you will be asked whether you want your ashes to be scattered, buried or interred or kept with a loved one.

Body Burial

While more people are choosing cremation than in the past, most bodies in the United States are buried. Depending on your wishes, your body may be buried immediately after death or several days later, after a funeral or other memorial service.

The Burial Process

A body may be buried in the ground, generally in a cemetery plot, or aboveground in the chamber of a mausoleum or family crypt. Typically, burial includes placing the body in a casket. However, if you want your body to be buried immediately, a casket may not be necessary. (Although required by many individual cemeteries, a casket is not a legal requirement for burials in the United States.)

Burial Costs

Burial can be expensive. The national average cost for a traditional funeral, with burial and headstone or monument, is about $10,000. Depending upon the costs of products, services and ceremonies, burial can cost several times as much as cremation.

How Much Does Burial Cost?	
Product or Service	**Cost Estimate**
Immediate burial, without embalming or casket	$4,500
In-ground cemetery plot	$4,000 or more
Labor charge for interment in a cemetery plot	$500 to $2,500
Casket	$500 to $20,000
Grave liner or in-ground vault, required by many cemeteries (but not by law) to help maintain a level, unshifting landscape	$500 to $10,000
Aboveground crypt	$1,500 or more
Mortuary services, including transfer of remains, embalming, visitation, funeral, funeral booklet or cards, preparing an obituary and ordering the death certificate	$5,000 or more—plus cost of casket, flowers, burial plot, interment and headstone or burial marker

Leaving Instructions

If you have decided where you wish to be buried, record that information. If you have already purchased a burial site and any other related products or services, describe your arrangements—and attach any related documents (for example, your contract with the cemetery) to your final arrangements document when you print it out.

If you haven't bought a burial site, but you know where you'd like to be buried, you can state your preference. There is no guarantee that it will be available when you die, but your survivors will know what you had in mind.

Cremation

The number of people who choose to be cremated is steadily increasing. For some, the relatively low cost makes this choice an easy one. But there are many other reasons why someone might prefer to be cremated—for example, you may want to have your ashes scattered or kept by a loved one at home.

Religious Concerns

Many religions accept cremation. Only Islam, the Baha'i faith and the Jewish Orthodox faith oppose cremation outright. The Catholic Church has significantly relaxed its views about cremation. If you are thinking of choosing cremation and have religious concerns, speak with your spiritual adviser.

The Cremation Process

Cremation is the burning of a body at extreme heat, resulting in a fine residue of ash and bone. The cremated remains (sometimes called "cremains," though we'll call them "ashes" here) may be buried, scattered or kept in an urn. A temporary casket is required to contain the body during cremation. Cremation caskets are generally made of unfinished wood, cardboard, pressboard or canvas. The cremation facility supplies the temporary casket.

Complete cremation arrangements usually include local transportation of the body to the cremation facility, visitation with the body prior to cremation, a temporary container for remains, cremation, a memorial service, preparation of an obituary, ordering the death certificate and the scattering or other disposition of the ashes.

Cremation Costs

As with burial, cost may play a part in your decision. Here are some cost estimates.

How Much Does Cremation Cost?	
Product or Service	**Cost Estimate**
Cremation	$800 to $1,800
Cremation with scattering at sea	$1,200 to $2,400
Niche in columbarium	$850 to $6,000, averaging about $3,000

What to Do With Cremated Remains

If you choose to have your body cremated, we will ask what you'd like your survivors to do with your ashes. You can state that you'd like your ashes to be:

- scattered over land or water
- buried
- stored above ground, or
- kept with family or friends.

After you make your initial selection, we'll ask you to provide more details about your wishes. If you want to divide your ashes among two or more of these options, select the one that feels most important to you. When you provide details, you can state exactly what you'd like your survivors to do, including how you want your ashes to be divided.

Scattering or Burying Ashes

If you choose to have your ashes scattered or buried, you should be aware of state or local laws that may affect your wishes.

Check state rules about scattering ashes. Some people wish to have their ashes scattered over some area that has special significance for them— such as a garden, a lookout point or the ocean.

Laws and restrictions on the scattering of ashes vary from state to state. To find out your state's laws, check with a local cremation facility or your state's health department (see "Finding your state's laws," below).

Scattering Services

Most people opt to have family members or friends scatter their ashes in private, in their own time and style. However, there are companies that arrange to transport and scatter cremated remains over land or sea. If you decide to hire one of these services in advance, make sure you understand its pricing structures. Also, attach a copy of any written agreement to your final arrangements document.

Check state and local laws about burying ashes. Ashes can be buried in the ground. Local zoning ordinances may restrict where the burial may take place—such as that they must be buried a specified distance from a residence.

If you wish to have a family member or friend bury your ashes, it is a good idea to first check local zoning ordinances to see whether burial is permitted on the site you have chosen. Ashes can also be buried in a cemetery, either in a special urn garden or in a plot. It is not necessary to place the ashes in an urn before burial, although some places may require a plot liner to prevent the earth from sinking over time.

RESOURCE

Finding your state's laws. You can find information about your state's laws and common practices by contacting the state health department or related agency that governs cemetery and funeral activities. To easily locate this department online, start at the state website: www.[xx].gov, substituting the state's postal abbreviation for "xx." You should then find a listing for the office you need.

TIP

Cashing in your crowns. If you want your dental work to be extracted prior to burial or cremation, metals can be redeemed for cash. (You can also cash in on replaced dental work during your life.) Garfield Refining Company buys dental metals—gold or semiprecious crowns, bridges and inlays. For more information, visit Garfield online at www.garfieldrefining.com.

Going Green

Burials and cremations can be hard on the environment. Embalming chemicals, metal caskets, concrete burial vaults and cremation facility emissions take a surprising toll. If you want to make plans that minimize environmental effects, here are some options.

Choose a green cemetery. The Green Burial Council can help you find providers that avoid toxins, use biodegradable materials and even help to preserve open space. Visit www.greenburialcouncil.org for more information.

Say no to embalming. Embalming fluid contains toxic chemicals—including up to three gallons of formaldehyde—that can seep into soil and groundwater. Embalming rarely serves a legitimate purpose and is almost never required. See "Embalming," below.

Ask for a biodegradable container. You can use a simple wood casket, cardboard box or shroud for burial. There are also biodegradable urns for ashes that will be buried. See "Caskets and Urns," below.

Avoid vaults. Vaults are large containers, usually made from reinforced concrete, that are placed in the ground before a burial. They're not required by law, but many cemeteries demand them because they make it easier to maintain the landscape. The result is that, every year, more than 1.5 million tons of reinforced concrete are buried along with caskets and bodies.

You can look for a cemetery that doesn't require vaults. In a few states, you can even refuse a vault on religious grounds. You may be required to pay an extra fee for grave maintenance.

Cremation conservation. Cremation uses the fewest resources, but it's not entirely clean. It burns fossil fuels and carries the risk of mercury pollution from incinerated fillings. Newer cremation facilities are more efficient, using about half the fuel. If you have amalgam fillings in your teeth, you can ask that they be removed before cremation.

Mortuaries and Cremation Facilities

From an economic standpoint, choosing the institution to handle your burial or cremation is one of the most important decisions you can make. If you consider this issue now, you'll have to think about your options, shop around if necessary—and then make recommendations to your survivors. That said, you may also want to give your loved ones some leeway. Circumstances may change significantly by the time of your death—for example, you may move or an institution may go out of business. Your survivors may need some flexibility when it comes time to carry out your plans.

A good mortuary is equipped to handle many of the details related to disposing of a person's remains. These include:

- collecting the body from the place of death
- storing it until burial or cremation
- making arrangements for burial or cremation
- conducting funeral ceremonies
- preparing the body for burial or cremation, and
- arranging to have the body transported for burial or cremation.

The mortuary can also help with administrative details, such as preparing an obituary and ordering copies of the death certificate.

If you wish to be cremated, the cremation facility may also be able to provide these services for you.

When you make your final arrangements document, you can suggest the mortuary and/or cremation facility you'd like your survivors to use. If you want your family to handle the disposition of your remains without involving a mortuary or cremation facility (this is rare, but it can be done), you may say so.

Below, you'll find more information on choosing the right facility—or taking a more independent approach.

Choosing a Facility

It is important that you find the mortuary or cremation facility that best meets your needs in terms of style, proximity and cost. Comparison shopping is fairly easy, because mortuaries and cremation facilities must by law give price lists to consumers who visit their facilities—and must disclose prices and other information to those who ask for it over the phone.

You can compare prices and services at local facilities before you make your choice. You may also consider joining a funeral consumer group, or memorial society, to make the task easier. These nonprofit groups can help you locate a mortuary and make other decisions and plans. For a small membership fee, you will receive information about local service providers, including costs. You can also take advantage of the society's discounted rates for funeral products and services.

To locate a group in your area, contact the Funeral Consumers Alliance (FCA) at www.funerals.org or 800-765-0107. For help locating and evaluating cremation facilities, you may want to contact the Cremation Association of North America at www.cremationassociation.org or 312-245-1077.

Making Independent Plans

There is a trend in America for people to care for their own dead, minimizing or even eliminating the involvement of funeral industry personnel. This could mean everything from preparing the body to burying it or transporting it to the cremation facility.

Most states do allow individuals to act completely on their own. But there are rules about how people may proceed. For example, most states have laws that regulate the depth of a site for a body burial. A few states throw up roadblocks to acting independently, requiring that a funeral director handle the disposition of a deceased person.

If you are considering directing that a family member or friend handle your disposition independently, the following resources can help you make your plans:

- The Funeral Consumers Alliance website, www.funerals.org, offers extensive resources to help you make your own plans.
- *Caring for the Dead: Your Final Act of Love,* by Lisa Carlson (Upper Access Press). This book will help you understand how to take

care of a body and what laws may apply. It includes a state-by-state guide to funeral and burial practices, as well as directories of cremation facilities and nonprofit funeral consumer groups.

- *Coming to Rest: A Guide to Caring for Our Own Dead*, by Richard Spiegel and Julie Wiskind (Dovetail). This guide covers details from washing the body and arranging ceremonies to complying with legal requirements and completing paperwork.

If you want to research your state's laws and common practices, see "Finding your state's laws," above.

Embalming

When making your final arrangements document, you will be asked whether or not you want your body to be embalmed. Embalming is a process in which the blood is drained and replacement fluids are pumped into the body to temporarily retard its disintegration. While it has now become a common procedure, embalming is rarely necessary; refrigeration serves the same purpose.

Originally considered a barbaric and pagan ritual, embalming first gained popularity during the Civil War, when bodies of the war dead were transported over long distances. When the war ended, embalming was promoted (mostly by those who performed the service) as a hygienic means of briefly preserving a body.

When Embalming Is Required

There is a popular misconception that embalming is always required by law after death. In fact, it is legally required only in some states and only in a few instances, such as:

- when a body will be transported by plane or train from one country or state to another
- where there is a relatively long time—usually a week or more—between the death and burial or cremation, and
- in some cases, where the death occurred because of a communicable disease.

If Your Body Is Not Embalmed

If you choose not to be embalmed, your body will be refrigerated until the time of burial. If you choose, you can still have a funeral or other service with an open casket.

The only effect of not being embalmed will be that if you opt to be buried, your body will begin to decompose within days instead of weeks.

Embalming Costs

The cost of embalming averages about $500, depending on your location and on the individual setting the rate. Refrigeration is usually less costly, involving a daily charge of $50 to $80. Some facilities provide refrigeration free of charge.

Caskets and Urns

Whether you choose to be buried or cremated, you will have the option to state your wishes for a casket or an urn. You may want both—for example, if you'd like a temporary casket for a funeral before your cremation and an urn for your ashes afterward.

Choosing your own casket or urn may seem like more than you want to think about right now, but there's a very practical reason to consider your preferences and make them known: Doing so may save your survivors thousands of dollars.

First, caskets and urns carry the biggest mark-up of all funeral goods and services. Second, grieving survivors aren't always capable of making sound decisions. This is a setup for overspending. Your loved ones may choose something elaborate and costly, not knowing that you would have been satisfied with simple arrangements.

On the other hand, if you want something ornate and you can afford it, now's your chance to make your wishes known.

Caskets

For immediate burial, a simple container or pine box is all that is necessary. But you may prefer to have a casket—and the cemetery you've chosen may require it. If there will be a service before burial with your body present, the type of container is entirely up to you. You may want something luxurious, something economical, or, if the viewing or service will be at home or in another private place, you may not feel the need for any type of container at all.

If your remains will be cremated but you first want to have a funeral or memorial service with your body present in a casket, your survivors may simply rent one. This is not as odd as it may sound; it is done quite frequently. A rental casket has a disposable liner.

Caskets are usually made from wood, metal, fiberglass or plastic and are available in a wide range of finishes, colors and styles. For example, the fittings or hinges may be finished in gold or silver, with a shine or antique finish. The inside of the casket is usually lined with cloth, which is also available in different fabrics and colors. The closure may be simple, or it may be fitted with a gasket or protective sealer—providing short-term protection from the elements—but at significant additional cost.

A casket may cost anywhere from $500 to $20,000 or more, averaging about $2,500. Casket rentals run about $600, on average. You may want to shop around and compare prices. Under federal law, a funeral home cannot charge you a fee if you provide your own casket, whether homemade or purchased from an outside source.

Urns

If your remains will be cremated and scattered, the cremation facility will provide a temporary container, and you won't need an urn. If you want your survivors to place your ashes in a columbarium or grave or to keep them at home, they will need a container of some sort.

Cremation urns are available in a wide range of materials and styles, from bronze book replicas to colorful porcelain vases. Attractive biodegradable urns are available for burial at sea. If your remains will be divided, smaller "keepsake" containers are available to hold just a portion of them.

If the cremated remains will be interred or buried, the columbarium or cemetery may impose restrictions on the size, shape or type of urn that you may use.

Cremation urns start at about $35 for simple wooden boxes and can run as high as $5,000 to $10,000 for materials such as gilded porcelain.

Shopping for Caskets and Urns

For more information, and to compare prices on caskets and urns, you can turn to the following resources:

- CasketXpress (www.casketxpress.com) and UrnXpress (www.urnxpress.com) allow you to browse a wide range of styles.
- The Funeral Consumers Alliance (www.funerals.org or 800-765-0107) provides information to help you get a fair deal on a casket or an urn. The organization can also help you locate independent casketmakers or artisans if you are interested in a low-cost or specialized container.

Pallbearers

In some funeral ceremonies, the casket is carried to and from the place where the ceremony is held—and sometimes again carried from a vehicle to a burial site. The covering traditionally draped over a casket is called a pall, and the people who carry the casket are called pallbearers.

If you envision a ceremony in which your casket will be carried, you can name the people you would wish to serve as pallbearers. Close friends and relatives are common choices. While women were not historically named as pallbearers, there is no logical reason to exclude them.

Your choices need only be physically able to lift and carry. And factor in that some people's psychological makeup may make them better or worse choices for the job.

The number of pallbearers usually ranges from four to eight, but you can name as many or as few as you wish. If you know of no one to nominate—or know just a couple of people you want to name—a mortuary should be able to provide people to help.

Transportation to Burial Site

You may have a preference about the type of vehicle that will carry your body to the burial site or cremation facility, usually after a funeral ceremony. This might be a horse-drawn carriage, a favorite antique car or a stretch limousine.

If you have selected a mortuary to handle some of your arrangements, it may have only one type of vehicle available. If the vehicle customarily provided is not what you would want for yourself, check to be sure the mortuary will allow you to provide your own—and be sure that it will not add its transportation charge to your costs. If this is an important issue to you, check with the mortuary you selected earlier and, if its arrangements about transportation are not satisfactory, shop for another mortuary.

Headstones, Monuments and Burial Markers

Headstones and monuments are upright grave markers (picture the traditional, rounded tombstone), generally used with in-ground burials in a cemetery. In contrast, burial markers are flat and flush to the ground or other surface (picture a plaque), and may be used with an in-ground burial or affixed to a vault above the ground. Burial markers are often used in mausoleums, columbariums and family crypts. Also, because of space constraints and maintenance considerations, many cemeteries now prefer burial markers for graves in the ground.

Headstones, monuments and burial markers come in an almost endless array of shapes and sizes, from the common tombstone to elaborate sculptures and designs. For example, a headstone or burial marker might be embossed with flowers, figures or a photograph. It might bear the logo of a fraternal organization or a military insignia. New "green" cemeteries may use simple stones or just a planting of wildflowers to mark a burial site. Designs are limited only by the constraints of cemetery policy, the craft of the builder and your budget. (An Internet search for "burial monument" or "grave marker" will turn up numerous providers to help you compare styles and prices.)

Traditional headstones and monuments are most often made from marble or granite. Both stones come in a variety of colors and shades. With granite, the darkest shades provide the best long-term resistance to erosion. Burial markers are usually made from stone or from various metals—such as steel, bronze or copper.

Headstones and burial markers start at about $400 and run into the thousands. An individual mausoleum or crypt costs about $20,000, and a family mausoleum (containing eight to ten caskets) can run as much as $2 million.

Epitaphs

Perhaps the most entertaining aspect of making final arrangements is choosing the words that you wish to appear on your burial marker. These words are known as your epitaph. Your epitaph can be extremely simple, stating only the years you were born and died—or it can reflect your personality by including a witty saying, favorite phrase or poem.

Famous Epitaphs

I am ready to meet my Maker. Whether my Maker is prepared for the great ordeal of meeting me is another matter.

—Winston Churchill

Cast a cold eye
On life, on death
Horseman, pass by!

—W.B. Yeats

3.14159265358979323846264338327950288...

—Ludolph van Ceulen computed π (pi) to 35 digits

Here lies one whose name was writ in water.

—John Keats

She did it the hard way.

—Bette Davis

The best is yet to come.

—Francis Albert Sinatra

That's all folks!

—Mel Blanc

Ceremonies

Death often involves at least one ceremony and sometimes more. To sort out the details for yourself and your survivors, you might find it helpful to consider the types of services that can occur at the following times:

- before burial or cremation
- at the time of burial or when ashes are scattered or interred, or
- after burial or cremation.

You may want a ceremony at each of these times—or at none of them. When you make your final arrangements document, you can leave instructions for each type of ceremony. If you don't want any services, the program allows you to say so. Or, if you have no preferences, you can indicate that and leave these decisions to your loved ones.

Ceremonies Before Burial or Cremation

Most people want at least one ceremony or gathering to be held before their remains are buried or cremated, even if it is a simple one. A wake or funeral is a way for your friends and family members to say goodbye to you, to comfort one another and to grieve.

That said, there may be good reasons why this type of ceremony is not right for you. You may live far from most of your friends and family members, meaning they would have to drop everything and attend the ceremony at great personal cost. In these circumstances, many people opt not to have a large funeral but instead prefer a memorial ceremony— usually held days or weeks after the burial—that more people can attend. (You may of course request a small gathering before your burial or cremation, followed later by a larger memorial ceremony.)

If you do want one or more ceremonies to be held before your body is buried or cremated, it's a good idea to write down your wishes. The more details you arrange while you are alive, the fewer decisions will be left for your survivors at a time when decisions are likely to be hard for them to make.

Here is basic information about common types of services before burial or cremation, to help you make your plans.

Viewing, Visitation or Wake

A viewing, visitation or wake is an opportunity for family and friends to view your body or to sit with you after you've died. For many, it is a quiet, meditative time. For others, it will be a time to gather with family and friends for remembering and honoring your life.

A viewing or visitation is commonly held in the viewing room of a funeral home or mortuary. However, you may wish to have it in another place, such as your home, a community hall or a church. It all depends on your wishes and the options available to you.

Traditionally, a wake is a gathering characterized by both sadness and gaiety—a celebration of the life that has passed and a send-off to whatever comes next. A wake is often held in the home of the deceased person, but many mortuaries now offer their facilities and services for one- or two-day wakes. A wake can be an important part of the grieving process, giving family and friends an opportunity to come together and comfort each other.

If you want a viewing, visitation or wake, you may wish to consider:

- where and when the gathering should be held
- who should be invited
- whether you will have a casket and, if so, whether it should be open or closed, and
- whether you want music, readings, certain types of food or drink, or other details for the gathering. (For wakes, there is of course no limit to the number of details you could specify. Some people have directed their loved ones to wear bright-colored clothing, bring their favorite pets or read a favorite poem.)

Funeral

A traditional funeral is a brief ceremony, most often held in a funeral home chapel or a church. The body is usually present, either in an open or a closed casket. Beyond that, there are no absolutes or requirements about what constitutes a funeral. If the deceased person adhered to a particular religion, funerals often include a brief mass, blessing or prayer service.

In some traditions, only family members attend the funeral, while friends and the general public are invited to attend other scheduled ceremonies. In other locales and traditions, this is reversed, and the funeral is the less private event.

Some concerns you may wish to address when planning a funeral are:

- where the ceremony should be held
- who should be invited
- whether clergy should be invited to lead the ceremony or participate in it and specific names of clergy you would like

- any music you would like played, along with the names of the musicians or singers you would like to perform it
- preferences for a eulogy or other readings, and the name of the person or people you would like to speak
- whether you want your body present at the ceremony or a picture displayed instead, and
- whether you want to suggest that friends donate to a certain organization instead of sending flowers.

If you'd like family and friends to gather at a reception after your funeral, you may specify that as well. Aside from where the reception should be held, you may want to consider the following details:

- who should be invited
- what kind of food and beverages should be served, and
- whether you want to request specific music, activities or entertainment for the gathering.

Burial, Interment or Scattering Ceremonies

In addition to or instead of holding a ceremony before burial, it is common to hold a brief ceremony at the burial site at which a religious leader, relative or close friend says a few prayers or words of farewell. This type of ceremony may also be appropriate after cremation, at the time your ashes are scattered or interred.

If this is something you want, and you have an idea of who should be there, who should speak and what they should say, describe those details.

Ceremonies After Burial or Cremation

Ceremonies after burial or cremation may range from a reception immediately following a burial or the scattering of ashes to a memorial ceremony held days, weeks or even months after death. Memorial ceremonies may be held anywhere—a mortuary, a religious building, a home, outside or even a restaurant.

Memorial ceremonies are more often the choice of those who wish to have an economic, simple commemoration. While funeral directors, grief counselors or clergy members may be involved in memorial ceremonies, they are not the people to consult for objective advice. Many will advocate that traditional funerals—often more costly and less personalized—are most effective in helping survivors through the mourning process. The truth is that most survivors are likely to take the greatest comfort in attending a ceremony that reflects the wishes and personality of the deceased person.

The details you may want to consider for a reception or memorial ceremony after burial or cremation are largely the same as those for wakes or funerals. For lists to jog your thinking, see "Ceremonies Before Burial or Cremation," above.

Your Obituary

An obituary is a notice printed in a newspaper or other publication after your death. It informs people that you have died and provides some biographical information about you. In addition, the obituary may specify the time and place of your funeral or memorial service and include other details, such as wishes for donations to be made in your name.

In the past, newspapers published two types of notices: death notices, which were paid notices supplied by the family, and obituaries, which were statements written by a newspaper's editorial department. Nowadays, the distinction has blurred for many newspapers and both paid and nonpaid statements are often grouped together. We refer to both types of notices as "obituaries."

If you are well-known in the community or the field in which you work, a newspaper or other publication will likely publish a detailed obituary or even an article about your life, and there won't be a fee associated with that. Otherwise, the length of your obituary depends on the local newspaper's obituary policy and fees, your budget and how much you wish to say.

Where Will Your Obituary Be Published?

Think about the places where your obituary might be published—newspapers, newsletters, magazines or online.

You might want to recommend to your survivors that specific publications run your obituary. For example, you might suggest that your obituary be published in newspapers in the various communities where you have lived and worked. If you work for a company or an organization that publishes a newsletter, provide the contact information for the newsletter. If you are well-known, you may want to recommend specific magazines or other publications that would be interested in publishing an article about your life.

More families are using online obituaries to give word about a loved one's death. Posting an obituary online greatly increases the number of people who are able to view it. And viewers are often able to post comments to the obituary—a unique way for your loved ones to read loving words about you from friends and family across the country or around the globe.

A newspaper usually posts an electronic version of an obituary on its website when you pay to have it printed in the paper, sometimes for an extra fee. Many funeral homes also provide online obituary services to their clients. Or, families can pay to post an obituary on a private memorial website, such as www.legacy.com.

Making the Choice

When you make your final arrangements document, you can state that:

- you have already written an obituary that you would like your survivors to publish
- you have not written an obituary, but would like to leave some guidelines for your survivors
- you do not want your survivors to publish an obituary, or
- you have no preferences for the publication of your obituary.

If you anticipate that your family will publish only a brief death notice, you may want to indicate that you have no preference and leave the decisions to them. But if you know that any source—be it a newspaper, website, organizational newsletter or church bulletin—will want to publish information about you after your death, it will help your survivors to know what these sources are and what you do or don't want your obituary to say.

Leaving Instructions

If you prefer to draft your own obituary, we will ask you to state where it is located, so your survivors can easily find it when they need it.

If you don't want to draft a full obituary, you can provide some guidance about what you'd like your survivors to include in your obituary and where they should publish it.

When deciding what to include, you may want to consider the following topics:

- where and when you were born
- family information, including the names of your spouse or partner, children, grandchildren, parents and siblings
- where you went to school
- information about your work
- military service
- community or recreational organizations
- awards or achievements
- special interests or hobbies
- whether or not you want people to send flowers in your name
- whether or not you want people to make donations to a particular charity or organization in your name, and
- anything else you'd like others to know or remember about you.

You may also want to select a photograph to include with your obituary. Your instructions can state which photograph you prefer and where your survivors can find it.

Following are a few sample obituaries to help you draft your own obituary or leave instructions for your survivors. For more examples, look at your newspaper or its website. This should give you many ideas for structuring your obituary.

> **EXAMPLE 1:** Paul Ralph Dillon, 67, 12 Sunset Lane, Mill Valley, died Thursday, October 5, in San Francisco. Funeral services will be at 10 a.m. Saturday at Grace Cathedral Episcopal Church in San Francisco.

> **EXAMPLE 2:** Paul Ralph Dillon, 67, 12 Sunset Lane, Mill Valley, died Thursday, October 5, in San Francisco. A native of Springfield, Massachusetts, and a graduate of the Stanford Law School, Mr. Dillon worked as a patent attorney and was a founding partner of Dillon & Winkler, a San Francisco patent law firm. He is survived by his wife, Margaret Evans-Dillon of Mill Valley and two sons, Mark Dillon of Los Angeles and James Dillon of Sacramento. Services will be at 10 a.m. Saturday at Grace Cathedral Episcopal Church in San Francisco.

> **EXAMPLE 3:** Margaret Evans-Dillon, 71, 12 Sunset Lane, Mill Valley, died Friday, January 11, in Mill Valley. A native of Pleasanton, Ms. Evans-Dillon was an ardent supporter of environmental causes in Marin County and one of the founders of the Marin Environmental Education Program, a series of programs that integrate environmental concerns into local class studies. In 1998, Ms. Evans-Dillon created Mill Valley Waterkeepers to preserve Mill Valley's watershed and plant and animal life. Ms. Evans-Dillon also served on the Board of the Marin Agricultural Land Trust.
>
> Ms. Evans-Dillon was the daughter of Grace and Woodward Evans of Pleasanton. Her father, Woodward Evans, served as city manager and city attorney for Pleasanton. Ms. Evans-Dillon attended San Francisco State University and received paralegal certification from the University of San Francisco. She worked for twelve years as a paralegal in San Francisco, specializing in patent

and copyright law, before marrying Paul Dillon in 1973. Paul Dillon passed away in 1989.

She is survived by two sons, Mark Dillon of Los Angeles and James Dillon of Sacramento. Services are at 12 noon Sunday at St. Anselm Church in Ross. In lieu of flowers, memorial contributions can be sent to the Marin Agricultural Land Trust, P.O. Box 809, Point Reyes Station, CA 94956.

Guarding Sensitive Information

Unfortunately, obituaries have become popular sources of information for identity thieves. You may want to use caution when supplying details for a death notice. Instead of providing a full birthdate, you might give just the month and year—for example, March 1927. For married women, you may choose to omit the maiden name, a common bit of information used to gain access to financial and other critical accounts.

Paying for Final Arrangements

Whatever arrangements you make, you have two main options for covering costs. You can:

- pay everything up front (in a lump sum or installments), or
- decide what you want and leave enough money for your survivors to pay the bills.

If you don't do any of these things, and your estate doesn't have enough money to cover the costs, your survivors will have to pay for any final expenses.

Paying in Advance

If you want to pay in advance, either all at once or under a payment plan, be sure you're dealing with a reputable provider of goods and services, and document your arrangements very clearly.

There are reasons to be cautious about paying up front. Though there are a number of legal controls on how the funeral industry can handle and invest funds earmarked for future services, there have been many reported instances of mismanaged and stolen funds. A great many other abuses go unreported by family members too embarrassed or grief stricken to complain.

In addition, when mortuaries go out of business, customers who have prepaid may be left without a refund and without recourse. Also, many individuals who move during their lifetimes discover that their prepayment funds are nonrefundable—or that there is a substantial financial penalty for withdrawing or transferring them. In addition, money paid now may not cover inflated costs of the future, meaning that survivors will be left to cover what's left.

Setting Aside Funds

A safe, simple and flexible option is to set aside funds that your survivors can use to cover the costs of your final plans.

After making your plans and estimating the cost, you can tuck away that sum (perhaps adding a bit to cover inflation or unexpected expenses) in a money market or other accessible fund. Tell the bank or financial institution that you want to set up a payable-on-death account. You can designate a beneficiary—a good choice might be the executor of your will or successor trustee of your living trust—who can claim the money immediately upon your death. The beneficiary will have no legal obligation to use these funds for your final arrangements, so make sure that person understands what the funds are for and that you trust him or her to do as you ask.

Leaving Instructions

We ask you to write out your financial plans in a few sentences. You'll also want to make sure your survivors have immediate access to any of the documents they'll need to carry out your arrangements, such as a prepayment contract or bank account information.

What to Do With Your Finished Document

After you have printed, dated and signed your final arrangements document, you may need to take a few more steps to ensure it works as you intend.

If you have paperwork to keep with your document, such as receipts or contracts, gather everything together. Attach the papers to your final arrangements document or create a binder or folder where you can store everything in the same place.

If you'll use your final arrangements document in conjunction with a health care directive (as discussed at the beginning of this chapter), you should attach your final arrangements document to the directive.

Store your documents where your loved ones can readily find them. You may want to make photocopies for people who should be aware of your wishes, and tell them where to find the originals, if necessary. It's a good idea to keep a list of folks to whom you've given copies, in case you need to retrieve them later.

Changing or Revoking Your Document

You can change or cancel your document at any time. There is no formal way to do this, so simply tear up the original. If you've given copies to others, be sure to get those copies back so you can destroy them, too. Then make a new document that reflects your current wishes.

If You Need More Help

Y ou probably won't need a lawyer's help to make a will or any of the other Quicken WillMaker Plus documents. But you may come up with questions about your particular situation that should be answered by an expert. This is especially likely if you have a very large estate, must plan for an incapacitated minor or have to deal with the assets of a good-sized small business. We highlight these and other "red flags" throughout the manual and program.

Learning More

If you've read most of this manual and started making your own will or other document, you may know more about wills than a fair number of lawyers do. If you have questions that these materials don't address, you may want to consult some other self-help books or websites before you consult a pricey expert. It's often worth the money to pay a good lawyer for advice about your specific situation; it's rarely worth it to pay by the hour for education. Reading some background information before hiring a lawyer is usually the best approach.

Here are some Nolo books that provide more in-depth information about estate planning:

- *Plan Your Estate,* by Denis Clifford. This book explains how to draw up a complete estate plan making use of a will, living trust and other devices. It introduces more complex estate planning strategies, including various types of tax-saving trusts for the very wealthy.

- *8 Ways to Avoid Probate,* by Mary Randolph. If you're interested in learning more about some of the probate-avoidance techniques discussed in this manual, check out this book.

- *Make Your Own Living Trust,* by Denis Clifford. This bestselling book with CD-ROM shows you how to make the right living trust for your situation. Find it at www.nolo.com or through your favorite bookseller.

- *Estate Planning for Blended Families: Providing for Your Spouse & Children in a Second Marriage,* by Richard E. Barnes. This is the first book written for parents who want to provide both for their current spouse and for their children from their current and prior marriages. It will help you identify your goals and put strategies in place to meet them.

- *Prenuptial Agreements: How to Write a Fair & Lasting Contract,* by Katherine E. Stoner and Shae Irving. Estate planning is often an important component of writing a prenuptial agreement. If you're planning to be married and considering a written agreement, this book will walk you through the process, including lots of guidance to help you communicate and negotiate a plan that will please both of you.

- *Special Needs Trusts: Protect Your Child's Financial Future,* by Stephen Elias and Kevin Urbatsch. This book will help you understand and draft a trust to protect a disabled child. Even if you decide to have a lawyer draw up or finalize the trust, you will be armed with the information you need to get the best possible help.

- *The Executor's Guide: Settling a Loved One's Estate or Trust,* by Mary Randolph. This is an invaluable handbook for anyone asked to serve as an executor. It can also help you prepare your estate for your own executor, to make the job as easy as possible.

Nolo Blogs

Nolo's experts are now blogging about day-to-day legal issues that affect your life. For useful, and often entertaining, information about wills, trusts and other estate planning issues, visit Nolo's Everyday Estate Planning Blog at blog.nolo.com/estateplanning.

What Kind of Expert Do You Need?

If you have questions, the first thing to decide is what type of expert you should seek. Questions about estate taxes may be better (and less expensively) answered by an experienced accountant than a lawyer. Or if you're wondering what type of life insurance to buy, you may be better off talking to a financial planner.

Consult a lawyer if you have specific questions about a provision of your will. Also see a lawyer if you want to get into more sophisticated estate planning—for instance, if you want to establish a charitable trust or a detailed plan to avoid estate taxes.

Different Ways to Get Advice From a Lawyer

Although many consumers (and some lawyers) don't know it yet, the way lawyers and their customers structure their relationships is changing fast. Lawyers used to insist on taking responsibility (and fees) for creating an entire estate plan. But, in what has become a very competitive market, many lawyers now offer piecemeal services, tailored to just what a customer wants.

This means you no longer have to walk into a lawyer's office, turn over your legal problems and wait for an answer—and a bill. Instead, you can often buy what you need, whether it's a bit of advice, a single estate planning document, a review of a document you've prepared with this program or regular coaching as you handle a probate court proceeding on your own.

If you adopt this approach, you and the lawyer should sign an agreement that clearly sets out your roles and states that the lawyer is not acting in a traditional role, but instead giving you limited services or representation. Without this type of agreement, lawyers fear that dissatisfied clients might later hold them responsible for more than they actually agreed to take on. The agreement should make things clear to you too, so you know what to expect from the lawyer. (For more, see "Working With a Lawyer," below.)

Finding a Lawyer

Finding a competent lawyer who charges a reasonable fee and respects your efforts to prepare your own estate planning documents may not be easy. First of all, you'll want to find a lawyer who specializes in estate planning. Most general practice lawyers are simply not sufficiently educated in this field to competently address complicated problems. Here are some other ways to look for help.

Personal Recommendations

The best way to find a lawyer is to get a recommendation from someone you trust. So ask your relatives and friends—especially those you know who have substantial assets and have likely made an estate plan. You may also want to ask those who run their own businesses. They are likely to have a relationship with a lawyer, and if that lawyer doesn't handle estate planning, he or she probably knows someone who does.

Finally, you might check with people you know in any social or other organization in which you are involved. Senior citizens' centers and other groups that advise and assist older people may have a list of local lawyers who specialize in wills and estate planning and are well regarded.

Group Legal Plans

Some unions, employers and consumer action organizations offer group legal plans to their members or employees, who can obtain legal assistance free or for low rates. If you are a member of such a plan, check with it first. Your problem may be covered free of charge. If it is, and you are satisfied that the lawyer you are referred to is knowledgeable in estate planning, this route is probably a good choice.

Some plans, however, give you only a slight reduction in a lawyer's fee. In that case, you may be referred to a lawyer whose main virtue is the willingness to reduce fees in exchange for a high volume of referrals. Chances are you can find a better lawyer outside the plan and negotiate a similar fee.

Attorney Directories

A lawyer directory will give you the names of attorneys who practice in your area. You will probably find several who specialize in estate planning and will give you an initial consultation for a low fee.

Following are two directories that may help you. Be sure to take the time to check out the credentials and experience of any lawyer who is listed.

Nolo's Lawyer Directory. Nolo offers a directory at www.nolo.com that provides a detailed profile for each attorney with information to help you select the right lawyer for you. Attorneys use their profiles to describe their experience, education and fees and also to tell you something about their general approach to practicing law. (For example, each lawyer states whether he or she is willing to review documents or coach clients who are doing their own legal work.) Nolo has confirmed that every listed attorney has a valid license and is in good standing with his or her local bar association.

West's Legal Directory. This directory lists most lawyers in the United States—more than 700,000 of them. You can look for a lawyer by location and legal practice category; there's a good chance you'll find more than one estate planning lawyer in your area. You can find the directory at lawyers.findlaw.com or in your local law library.

Attorney Referral Services

Your local county bar may have an attorney referral service, which differs from a directory in that a referral service will gather some information about your legal needs and match you with attorneys who might be a good fit for you. Usually you'll get only a few names of attorneys to consider, chosen for you by the knowledgeable people running the referral service, rather than having an entire directory to choose from on your own.

Working With a Lawyer

Before you talk to a lawyer, decide what kind of help you really need. Do you want someone to advise you on a complete estate plan or just to review the documents you prepare to make sure they look all right? If you don't clearly tell the lawyer what you want, you may find yourself agreeing to turn over all your estate planning work.

One good strategy is to do some background research and write down your questions as specifically as you can. If the lawyer doesn't give you clear, concise answers, try someone else. If the lawyer acts wise but says little except to ask that the problem be placed in his or her hands— with a substantial fee, of course—watch out. You're either dealing with someone who doesn't know the answer and won't admit it (common) or someone who finds it impossible to let go of the "me expert, you plebeian" philosophy (even more common).

Lawyer fees usually range from $100 to $350 or more per hour. But price is not always related to quality. It depends on the area of the country you live in, but, generally, fees of $150 to $250 per hour are reasonable in urban areas. In rural areas and smaller cities, $100 to $150 is more like it. The fee of an experienced specialist may be 10% to 30% higher than that of a general practitioner, but the specialist will probably produce results more efficiently and save you money in the long run.

Be sure you settle your fee arrangement—preferably in writing—at the start of your relationship. In addition to the hourly fee, you should get a clear, written commitment from the lawyer about how many hours your problem should take to handle.

RESOURCE

For more information about working with lawyers and holding down legal fees, visit www.nolo.com/legal-encyclopedia/lawyer or Nolo's Lawyer Directory at www.nolo.com/lawyers/tips.html.

Doing Your Own Legal Research

There is often a viable alternative to hiring a lawyer to resolve legal questions that affect your estate planning documents: You can do your own legal research. Doing your own legal research can provide some real benefits if you are willing to learn how to do it. Not only will you save some money, you will gain a sense of mastery over an area of law, generating confidence that will stand you in good stead should you have other legal problems.

Fortunately, researching wills and related estate planning issues is an area generally well suited to doing your own legal research. Most problems do not involve massive research or abstruse legal questions. Often, you need only check the statutes of your state to find one particular provision.

RESOURCE

Nolo's website, www.nolo.com, offers a section on estate planning that covers a range of topics including living trusts and estate and gift taxes. You can also find links to state and federal statutes at www.nolo.com/legal-research.

If you would like an in-depth resource, try *Legal Research: How to Find & Understand the Law*, by Stephen Elias and the Editors of Nolo (Nolo), which gives detailed instructions and examples explaining how to conduct legal research.

Finding Statutes in a Law Library

You can always find state statutes at a law library or, usually, at the main branch of a public library. Depending on the state, statutes are compiled in books called statutes, revised statutes, annotated statutes, codes or compiled laws. For example, the Vermont statutes are found in a series called *Vermont Statutes Annotated*, while Michigan's laws are found in two separate sets of books: *Michigan Statutes* or an alternate series called *Michigan Compiled Laws*. (The term "annotated" means that the statutes are accompanied by information about their history and court decisions that have interpreted them.) The reference librarian can point you toward the books you need.

After you've found the books, check the index for provisions dealing with the specific subject that concerns you—for example, wills. Generally, you will find what you want in the volume of statutes dealing with your state's basic civil or probate laws. Statutes are numbered sequentially, so once you get the correct number in the index, it will be easy to find the statute you need.

Once you find a law in the statute books, it's important to look at the update pamphlet in the back of the book (called the "pocket part") to make sure your statute hasn't changed or been repealed. Pocket parts are published only once per year, so brand-new laws often have not yet made it to the pocket part. Law libraries subscribe to services and periodicals that update the statute books on a more frequent basis than the pocket parts. You can ask a law librarian to help you find the materials you need.

Finally, you may find summaries of relevant court cases immediately following the statute. (These are the annotations mentioned just above.) If so, you'll want to skim them. If a summary looks like it might help answer your question, read the full court case cited there. (Ask the librarian for help finding the case, or turn to the legal research resource listed above.)

Finding Statutes Online

All states have made their statutes available on the Internet. You can find them by visiting the legal research area of Nolo's website at www.nolo. com/legal-research. Choose your state to search or browse the statutes.

In addition, almost every state maintains its own website for pending and recently enacted legislation. If you hear about a proposed or new law and you want to look it up, you can use your state's website to find not only the most current version of a bill, but also its history. To find your state's website, open your browser and type in www.state. [your state's postal code].us. Your state's postal code is the two-letter abbreviation you use for mailing addresses. For example, NY is the postal code for New York, so to find New York's state website, type www.state.ny.us. When you open your state's home page, look for links under "government." All states have separate links to their legislatures, and they offer many different ways to look up bills and laws. You can also find any state's legislature through the National Conference of State Legislatures at www.ncsl.org.

Users' Manual Table of Contents

Appendixes

Getting the Most Out of Quicken WillMaker Plus

Welcome to Quicken WillMaker Plus 2012. Quicken WillMaker Plus makes it easy for you and your immediate family to create wills, health care directives, powers of attorney and other legal documents for planning your estate and handling personal and financial matters.

You don't need legal training or estate planning experience to create documents with Quicken WillMaker Plus. The onscreen interviews provide easy-to-understand guidance every step of the way. And if you need more help than you see onscreen, the two product manuals are just a click away:

- This Users' Manual explains how to use the program.
- The Legal Manual provides legal and practical answers to help you create specific documents.

You can view electronic versions of both manuals at any time from within Quicken WillMaker Plus. Many screens have links that take you directly to the sections of the manuals that relate to the question you're answering.

This part of the Users' Manual gives you a preview of how the program works, along with some tips for using it to your best advantage.

How Quicken WillMaker Plus Works

Two points are key to understanding Quicken WillMaker Plus:

- The program interviews you and uses your answers to create documents.
- Much of the document creation work happens invisibly, behind the scenes.

Interviews at Your Own Pace

Each document you can create with Quicken WillMaker Plus has its own interview. You click through the questions and answer them at your own pace.

When you finish an interview, the program combines your answers with the appropriate legal language and displays the completed document for you to review.

Unlike some other programs, you don't type directly into Quicken WillMaker Plus documents or edit their language. This safeguard ensures that the documents use the exact language needed to make them legally valid. When you need to make changes to a document, you go back to the appropriate sections of the document interview and change your answers there.

Because Quicken WillMaker Plus customizes later interview questions based on the answers you give to earlier ones, a changed answer may affect the rest of your interview—so, after you make a change to a document, you may be asked to go back and review some (or all) of the interview questions you've already answered.

You can produce any document in Quicken WillMaker Plus in one sitting, but there's no point in rushing. Relax and take your time—after all, Quicken WillMaker Plus doesn't charge by the hour. Read the "Helpful Information" section of the screen and consider it thoughtfully. You can always stop a document interview and come back later; it's easy to pick up exactly where you left off.

When you're satisfied with your document, print and sign it, following the signing instructions that we provide for every document. These instructions tell you how to finalize your document and make it legal; for instance, signing your will in front of two witnesses or having a power of attorney notarized.

Looking Behind the Scenes

Part of what makes Quicken WillMaker Plus easy to use is the work the program does behind the scenes, without your noticing. For example, when you type in a person's name, the program automatically creates an entry for that person in My Contacts, where contact information is stored for reuse.

While you can get along fine without knowing most of what Quicken WillMaker Plus is doing behind the scenes, learning a little about what's happening in the background can help you use the program more efficiently and effectively. This manual's "Behind the Scenes" features alert you to actions the program is taking and tell you how they may affect you. Look for the "Behind the Scenes" icon shown below:

Read these notes to become a power user of Quicken WillMaker Plus.

Not Just Wills: Create Health Care Directives, Powers of Attorney and More

You can create many types of legal documents with Quicken WillMaker Plus:

- estate planning documents (such as wills, health care directives and durable powers of attorney for finances)
- executor documents (such as letters to creditors, financial institutions and others)
- home and family documents (such as house-sitting instructions and agreements for taking care of children, elders or pets), and
- personal finance documents (such as bills of sale and promissory notes).

Getting Started

I t's easy to start using Quicken WillMaker Plus. Typically, you'll need to:

1. Install Quicken WillMaker Plus.

2. Start the program.

3. Update your version of the program.

4. Register your copy of the program.

5. Get oriented to the screen elements.

6. Begin creating documents.

Steps 3 through 5 are optional, but we strongly recommend that you go through them all—especially Step 3, which ensures that you are using the most up-to-date version of the program.

This part of the manual takes you through all of the above steps except creating documents; you'll read about that in Part 3.

Making Sure Your System Meets the Requirements

Before you install Quicken WillMaker Plus, check that your system meets these minimum requirements:

- **Computer.** Pentium 400 MHz
- **Operating System.** Windows *XP SP2/Vista/7*
- **Memory.** 512 MB
- **Hard Disk Space.** 54 MB for WillMaker Plus (plus up to 500 MB for Microsoft .NET 2.0 SP2, if not already installed)
- **Monitor.** 800 x 600 (1024 x 768 recommended; 16-bit color)
- **CD-ROM Drive.** 2x speed
- **Internet Connection.** 56 Kbps modem required to access online features
- **Printer.** Any printer supported by Windows *XP SP2/Vista/7*
- **Software.** Microsoft *Internet Explorer* 6.0 or higher; Adobe *Reader*.

Installing Quicken WillMaker Plus

You install Quicken WillMaker Plus by running the installer. Here's how:

1. Insert the Quicken WillMaker Plus disc into your CD-ROM drive to launch the automatic setup program.

2. Follow the instructions that appear onscreen to complete installation. If you're prompted to restart your computer after installation, do so.

Jump-Starting the Setup Program

When you insert the Quicken WillMaker Plus Installation CD into your CD-ROM drive, setup should launch automatically. If it doesn't, here's what to do:
- Double-click the icon of your CD-ROM drive.
- Double-click the Setup file.
- Follow the instructions that appear on the screen.

Starting Quicken WillMaker Plus

You can start the program in either of the following ways:
- by double-clicking the Quicken WillMaker Plus icon on your desktop (if you chose this option during installation), or
- by choosing (from the Windows taskbar) **Start > Programs** (or **All Programs**) **> Quicken WillMaker Plus 2012** (folder) **> Quicken WillMaker Plus 2012** (program).

If you used an older version of Quicken WillMaker or Quicken Lawyer to create a file with a .pfl extension on your computer, you're asked if you'd like to open it after installation. Click **Yes** if you want your old documents to show up in My Documents when you get to it, or click **No** to work with a brand-new file.

> ⓘ **CAUTION**
> **Quicken WillMaker Plus 2012 may not convert all of your documents.** Be aware that some documents from earlier versions of the program can't be opened—and some may require you to review and update your interviews. The program will convert as many of your documents as possible, but sometimes extensive legal updates require us to significantly change the format of a particular document.

The first time you use the program, you won't go straight to My Documents. Instead, you'll encounter an introductory screen with a tutorial video.

If you like, you can come back to the tutorial later by choosing **Help > Quicken WillMaker Tutorial**.

Registering Your Copy of the Program

Registering your copy of Quicken WillMaker Plus gives you access to a variety of services and benefits, including technical support. We recommend that you register the first time you use the program.

To register your copy do one of the following:

- From the "Registration" screen, click **Register Now.**
- From anyplace else in the program, choose **Online > Online Registration**.

Then, follow the directions on the online registration page.

Updating Your Version of the Program

We regularly update Quicken WillMaker Plus to accommodate changing laws or fix problems our users report. To make sure you're running the latest version, use Web Update, a feature that downloads and installs any revisions we've made to the program.

Run Web Update the first time you use the program and as often as possible thereafter—either automatically at program startup (the default preference for the program) or manually at intervals you choose.

Enabling and Disabling Automatic Updates

By default, Quicken WillMaker Plus checks for newer versions every time you start up the program (as long as you have an open Internet connection). If it detects a newer version, you're prompted to download and install the newer files (which may take a few minutes). The program will then restart.

If you'd rather not have these checks done automatically, you can turn off this feature by changing the default preference. If you decide to change this preference—we recommend that you don't—be sure to run Web Update manually at regular intervals.

To change the automatic update preference:

1. Choose **Edit > Preferences**.

2. Click the checkbox next to **Automatically check for updates when the program starts** to mark it with a ✔—or to clear the ✔ from the box if it's already checked. If the checkbox is empty, the program will check for updates only when you run Web Update manually.

Quicken WillMaker Preferences

☑ Automatically save changes

☑ Automatically complete names

Quicken WillMaker will automatically fill in a name field with the name of the person that matches the letters as you type them in.

☑ Automatically fill in related fields

Quicken WillMaker will automatically fill in fields associated with the person or business you have named (such as Address, Phone Numbers, etc.).

☑ Automatically check spelling

Quicken WillMaker will automatically check spelling in long text entry fields.

☑ Automatically check for updates when the program starts

Quicken WillMaker will automatically check for Web Updates when it starts up and you are connected to the Internet.

☐ Show onscreen Guide text in a larger font size

Backup Files

Quicken WillMaker will save backups of your WillMaker file to this directory:

C:\Users\PJenkins\Documents\Nolo Documents Backup\

Browse...   Restore Default

OK

Cancel

Defaults

Running Web Update Manually

To run Web Update manually, choose **Online** > **Web Update**. Follow the directions that appear onscreen.

> 💡 TIP
>
> **If you have Internet connection problems.** If you're having trouble connecting to the Internet from within Quicken WillMaker Plus, open your Web browser as you normally would from outside the program, then return to the program and try again. If problems persist, see "Handling Web Update Problems" in Part 7.

Quitting and Restarting Quicken WillMaker Plus

You can quit Quicken WillMaker Plus by doing any of the following:
- Choose **File** > **Exit**.
- Click the close box (marked with an "X") in the upper right-hand corner of the program.
- Press ALT+F4.

Any changes you've made to your documents since the last time you saved your data are automatically saved when you quit. By default, the **Automatically save changes** feature is turned on. If you've turned **Automatically save changes** off (in **Edit** > **Preferences**) the program prompts you to save your changes when you quit. For more information on saving your data, see "Saving Your WillMaker File" in Part 5.

You can restart the program just as you started it the first time, either from the Windows taskbar or by double-clicking the program's icon on your desktop. If you completed the program's introduction before you quit, you'll go directly to My Documents. My Documents is your main jumping-off point for creating your essential estate planning documents (or for working with documents you've already created)—and you'll find out all about it in Part 3.

Creating Documents

Creating documents with Quicken WillMaker Plus is simple: You select the type of document you want to create and answer the interview questions for that document. When you've finished the interview, the program generates the document for you, with all the legal niceties in place.

This part of the Users' Manual orients you to My Documents (where you choose a document to work on) and describes how to start, proceed through and complete document interviews.

Starting Your Document

Quicken WillMaker Plus has two screens where you'll find a list of documents: the My Documents screen and the All Documents screen.

The first time you use the program, the My Documents screen will list the five Essential Documents that are the core estate planning documents we suggest you create. These five are:

- Will
- Health Care Directive (Living Will & Power of Attorney)
- Durable Power of Attorney for Finances
- Final Arrangements
- Information for Caregivers and Survivors

On the All Documents screen, you'll find all of the documents included in Quicken WillMaker Plus, listed by category. Once you've started a document other than the Essential Documents, it will also appear on the My Documents screen, in the Additional Documents section at the bottom.

Starting a Document

To start any document, click the **Start** button.

For each Essential Document on the My Documents screen, a button is always present, labeled **Start**, **Resume** or **Open**, depending on what stage you are at with the document.

To start a second Essential Document, click the **New** button, which is found to the right of "My Documents" at the top left of the screen.

To start a document from the All Documents screen:

1. Click on the + next to the category name to see the complete list.

2. Hover your mouse over the document title.

3. Click the **Start** button that appears.

Deleting a Document

Once you've started a document, when you hover over its title on the My Documents screen, an **X** will appear to the right of the **Resume/Open** button. Clicking the **X** will delete the document you created (a pop-up will ask you to confirm that you want to). The document template will remain. If it's one of your Additional Documents listed on the My Documents screen, you'll still be able to create a new version from the All Documents screen. The five titles listed under Essential Documents cannot be deleted.

Creating an Identical Will for a Spouse or Partner

> **SKIP AHEAD**
> **If you haven't created a will and aren't married or partnered.** You can skip this section if you haven't yet created a will and aren't married or in a domestic partnership.

Some couples may want to create identical wills in which all the provisions—such as beneficiaries, alternate beneficiaries and children's guardians—are the same, except that the spouses' or partners' names are reversed. For example, if you make a will and name your spouse or partner as your executor, the identical will for your spouse or partner will name you as your spouse's or partner's executor.

Couples are not required to create identical wills. But for those who want to do so, Quicken WillMaker Plus offers a feature specifically for this purpose.

> **TIP**
>
> **Work on the will interview together.** Because the first spouse or partner to write a will is, in effect, creating the will for both of you, we suggest that the two of you complete the will interview together, discussing and agreeing to all decisions and choices.

When you have completed a will for one spouse or partner, here's how to duplicate it for the other:

1. Go to the "Congratulations" screen for the will of the first spouse or partner. (See "Completing Your Interview.")

2. Click **Duplicate for Spouse**.

3. Read an advisory dialog box and click **OK**. You will go to the My Documents screen where the duplicated will appears under your spouse/partner's name.

4. Click the **Resume** button next to it.

5. Read an advisory dialog box and click **OK**.

6. The checklist for the duplicated will appears. Note that none of the parts on this checklist are checked, even though this will contains the information carried over from the first will; these parts will be checked when you have reviewed the information.

7. For each part in the checklist, click through all interview screens to make sure the second spouse or partner agrees with the choices the first one has made. You can change the information in this will, but keep in mind that these changes will not be reflected in the will of the first will-writing spouse or partner.

8. When you've reviewed all screens, you can preview and print the completed will as described in Part 4.

Proceeding Through a Document Interview

Once you start the interview for the document you selected, all you have to do is click through the screens and supply the information needed.

This section of the manual shows you how to navigate through an interview using the various data entry formats you may encounter along the way. Each document in Quicken WillMaker Plus has its own set of interview screens, but they all use the same basic process and formats.

Read each interview question carefully and consult the program's help resources ("Helpful Information" onscreen, the Legal Manual and this Users' Manual) to help you decide on your answers. (For more information about help resources and how to access them, see Part 7, "Troubleshooting.")

Moving Forward

To move to the next screen in an interview, use any of the following methods:

- Click **Next**.
- Choose **Navigate > Next**.
- Press ALT+RIGHT ARROW.
- Use the TAB key to move the keyboard focus to the **Next** button, then press the ENTER key or the SPACEBAR. (The keyboard focus is on a button when a dotted outline surrounds the button.)

If the information requested on the current screen is optional, you can go on to the next screen without supplying the information. However, if the information is required, the program won't let you move to the next screen without answering.

If you're not sure how to answer, we suggest you quit the interview and return to it later; when you return, the interview will pick up where you left off. Or you can give a placeholder answer and move on—but, if you do so, you may need to come back and change several answers later, because later parts of the interview may be determined by your placeholder answer.

Moving Backward

To go back to the previous screen in an interview, use any of the following methods:

- Click **Back**.
- Choose **Navigate > Back**.
- Press ALT+LEFT ARROW.
- Use the TAB key to move the keyboard focus to the **Back** button, then press the ENTER key or the SPACEBAR. (The keyboard focus is on a button when a dotted outline surrounds the button.)

> **CAUTION**
>
> **Don't lose data when you backtrack.** Quicken WillMaker Plus may not record what you've entered on the current screen until you move to the next screen. If you enter or change an answer and then try to go back to the previous screen, the program will warn you if your answer or change won't be saved. To save your answer before backtracking, first click **Next** to move one screen forward, then back up to previous screens.

If you are working on a document that has a checklist, you have an additional method for going backward: Use the checklist to reopen sections of the interview you've already completed. To find out more about checklists, see "Using Checklists for Interview Management," below.

Revising Answers You've Entered

Because Quicken WillMaker Plus sometimes chooses interview questions based on your answers to earlier questions, revising one answer may affect everything that comes after it. So, after you go back to revise a recent answer (using any of the methods described in "Moving Backward," above), you'll need to continue going forward, one screen at a time, making any necessary corrections. If the document has a checklist, use the checklist to reopen the section of the interview that contains the answer you want to change; then click forward through that entire section, making changes as needed. (See "Using Checklists for Interview Management," below.)

Tips for Entering Names

Because a name used in one part of a document interview may appear again in that document (or in others), Quicken WillMaker Plus keeps track of all the names you enter and stores them in My Contacts.

Using this list, the program checks your answers for logical inconsistencies and alerts you if a name entered in one place can't be used there based on answers you've given earlier.

To enable Quicken WillMaker Plus to perform its error checking correctly and keep your contact list as accurate as possible, follow these tips when entering names:

- Use full names, first name first.
- Be consistent: Use the same exact name for a person or an organization throughout the document interview. If you use a full name in one answer and a nickname in another, the program will assume they are different and add both to My Contacts.
- Carefully check the spelling of all names before you leave a screen. The program assumes different spellings are different people and adds both names to My Contacts.
- If the program fills in a name automatically after you've typed in a few characters (guessing that it is a name from My Contacts), check that it truly is the name you want to enter. If it isn't, continue typing the correct name. (To turn off the "automatic completion" feature, choose **Edit > Preferences**.)
- Enter only one name per line. To begin a new line for an additional name, follow the onscreen instructions.
- Whenever possible, use My Contacts to paste in names that you've entered previously.

If you discover you entered a name incorrectly and want to change it, select the name from the list at the left in My Contacts, edit and save; the program will make the correction in all documents where the name occurs. To find out more about working with My Contacts, see Part 6.

Using Checklists for Interview Management

SKIP AHEAD

Not all documents use checklists. You can skip this section *unless* you are creating one of the following estate planning documents:

- Will
- Final Arrangements Document
- Health Care Directive
- Durable Power of Attorney for Finances or
- Information for Caregivers and Survivors.

Only these documents use checklists in their interviews; all others have shorter interviews, so the checklist format isn't necessary.

When you start each of these estate planning documents in Quicken WillMaker Plus, the first screen is the interview checklist. This checklist provides an overview of the parts of the interview.

The checklist helps to keep track of which parts of an interview you've completed and simplifies the process of going back to change an answer.

Rather than stepping through the whole interview, you can go directly to the part you want to change.

Understanding Check Marks and Dimmed List Items

The check marks on a checklist show which parts of the interview you have completed. Dots show items in progress. Dimmed items are unavailable for you to work on.

List items are dimmed to prevent you from:

- working on interview parts out of order, or
- working on interview parts that aren't relevant to your situation.

Quicken WillMaker Plus determines which parts of an interview don't apply to you based on the answers you've given to previous questions. For example, in the will interview, if you say in "2. Your Family— Children and Grandchildren" that you don't have kids, then "4. Property Management" is dimmed because it's not relevant to your situation.

Working on Document Parts

In most documents that have checklists, you must go through the interview parts in order. However, you can return to previously completed parts (parts with check marks) in any order.

The one exception to the above rule is the Information for Caregivers and Survivors form. After completing the introductory part of this document, you can work on the remaining parts in any order you wish.

To work on a document part listed in the checklist, hover over and select the part you want to work on. The first screen in the selected part of the interview appears. If you select Preview and Print, you may go through a dialog. Then, you will go to a screen where you can preview and print or export your document. (For more information about performing these tasks, see Part 4.)

Stopping and Restarting Your Interview

You can stop an interview in progress at any time, either by quitting the program or by navigating to another part of the program.

Answering Interview Questions

A Quicken WillMaker Plus interview may ask you to supply information in any or all of the following ways:

- typing into text entry boxes
- using icons to select names and dates
- adding items to list boxes
- choosing radio button options
- choosing checkbox options
- selecting from pick lists, or
- selecting from drop-down lists.

As you proceed through an interview, keep in mind that the program doesn't save the information you enter on a given screen until you move forward to the next one.

 BEHIND THE SCENES

Some questions are answered automatically. On some interview screens, you may find answers already filled in with information, such as the address or phone number for a person or an organization. Quicken WillMaker Plus finds this information in My Contacts and automatically inserts it for you. If you revise automatically inserted information on the interview screen, it will also be revised in My Contacts and in all documents that use this information.

CAUTION

Watch out for automatic ENTER-key navigation. On most interview screens, pressing the ENTER key triggers the default navigation button, which is usually the **Next** button. So, if you are in the habit of pressing ENTER after you type in an answer, you may find yourself jumping to the next screen unintentionally. While typing in data, the only time you need to press ENTER is to start a new line in a text box that allows multiple items. (Pressing ENTER at other times will probably send you to the next screen.)

Saving Your Data

Because Quicken WillMaker Plus automatically saves the information you provide on an interview screen when you move on to the next one (unless you've turned off the **Automatically save changes** feature in the program preferences), you generally don't need to worry about saving data. The program saves all of your documents and contact information in your WillMaker File. (WillMaker Files are explained in Part 5.)

If you have turned off the **Automatically save changes** feature in the program preferences, you'll need to save data manually at frequent intervals. The program asks if you want to save changes whenever you quit.

To save data manually:

• Choose **File > Save**.

To change your preference for the **Automatically save changes** feature:

1. Choose **Edit > Preferences** to open the **Preferences** dialog box.

2. Click the checkbox next to **Automatically save changes** to turn this feature on if it's off (or off if it's on). A check mark (✔) indicates the option is on.

We strongly recommend you leave this feature on. For more information on saving and backing up your data, see Part 5.

Completing Your Interview

When you've completed all the interview screens for a document, the program has all the information it needs to assemble and print your document. The next step takes you to the "Print Review" screen, which lets you view, print, revise or export your document. This screen appears automatically when you complete the interview—unless the interview for your document uses a checklist, in which case you need to select **Preview and Print** from the checklist, then click the **Next** button.

Click **Next** and you will go to the "Congratulations" screen. This screen provides information on next steps and how to finalize your document. To learn more about working with your completed document, see Part 4.

Reviewing, Changing and Printing Your Documents

After you've completed your document interview, Quicken WillMaker Plus uses your answers to create a finished document. The "Print Preview" screen, which appears at the end of each interview, lets you look at the document and make any necessary changes before you print it out.

This part of the Users' Manual explains how to change, export or print your document from the "Print Preview" screen.

Reviewing Your Document in Print Preview

We recommend that you use "Print Preview" to carefully review your finished document. If you want to change any of your answers, you can do so before you print your document.

 BEHIND THE SCENES
Those "/////" marks on your document are there for a reason.
Quicken WillMaker Plus uses "/////"—also known as "hash marks"—as a precaution and a legal necessity. They prevent someone from inserting additional language into blank spaces in the document after you have signed it.

Revising Your Document

As you are reading your document, if you find information that you want to change, return to the document interview and provide new answers. How you do this depends on whether the document uses a checklist. (To find out how to change the *appearance* of your document—fonts, page margins and so on—see "Changing How Your Document Looks," below.)

Revising a Document That Uses a Checklist

If you want to revise an estate planning document that uses a checklist, use the checklist to go directly to the part of the document interview containing the information you need to change. (To find out more about checklists, see "Using Checklists for Interview Management" in Part 3.)

To return to the appropriate part of your document interview and make changes:

1. Go to the checklist screen by clicking **Change Answers** in "Print Preview."

2. Click the name of the interview part you need to revise.

3. Click through the screens in that part of the interview to review the information you previously entered, making changes as needed. When you've made it through all the screens, you'll return to the checklist.

4. Repeat Steps 2 and 3 for any other interview parts you need to revise.

5. Click **Preview and Print** on the checklist to return to the "Print Preview" screen.

After you've made your changes, review your document once again in "Print Preview" before you print it.

Revising a Document That Doesn't Use a Checklist

If the document you want to revise doesn't use a checklist, in order to make changes, you need to return to the first interview screen for the document and step through the interview screen by screen.

To reopen your document interview and make changes:

1. From the "Print Preview" screen, click **Change Answers** to go to the first interview screen for your document.

2. Click through the screens in the interview and review the information you entered previously, making changes as needed. When you've made it through all the screens, you'll return to the "Print Preview" screen.

After you've made your changes, review your document once again in "Print Preview" before you print it.

Changing How Your Document Looks

Most of the time, you won't need to change the default formatting for your documents. However, if you do need to make formatting changes—changes to fonts, margins, spacing and so on—you can do so.

There are two places in Quicken WillMaker Plus where you can reformat documents:

- The Print Options dialog box lets you change fonts and adjust page margins, line spacing and footer format. You will find this by selecting **File** > **Print Options**.
- The Print dialog box lets you add a watermark ("Draft" or "Duplicate") to the document you are printing. Find the Print dialog box from the "Print Preview" screen, after completing your document. Either click the **Print** button or go to **File** > **Print**.

Both of these dialog boxes also let you specify basic printer setup options, including some that affect the look of your document: page orientation (portrait or landscape) and image quality.

Printing Your Document

To print your completed document:

- Go to the "Print Preview" screen.
- Click **Print** (or choose **File** > **Print**) to open the Print dialog box.

If the document is a will, durable power of attorney for finances or health care directive, you'll see a dialog box asking which specific documents in the document set you would like to display. If you don't want to print all of them, uncheck the ones you don't want before clicking **OK** (but be sure to include all of them when you print out the version you intend to sign and make legal).

CAUTION

Page range counts may include instructions. When you print your document, signing instructions are included unless you click **No** under **Print signing instructions** (found in the bottom right-hand corner of the **Print** dialog box). When included, these instructions print before the document.

If you enter page numbers in the **From** and **To** boxes of the **Print range** section of the **Print** dialog box without turning off the option to print signing instructions, keep in mind that Quicken WillMaker Plus counts from the first page actually printed, which is the first instruction page (some documents have more than one instruction page). Be sure to factor these extra pages in when you are specifying the range of pages you want to print.

If you're curious about slight differences between the printed version and the version you saw in "Print Preview"—or if you'd like to learn more about the hash marks ("/////") that print at the end of some pages—see "Reviewing Your Document in Print Preview," above.

Exporting Your Document to a PDF File

To export your document as a PDF:

1. From the "Print Preview" screen, click the **Save PDF** button.

2. In the window that opens, navigate to the place where you want to save your document and click **Save**.

3. You'll then see a dialog box asking whether you'd like to view the exported file. If you click **No**, you can later use My Computer or Windows Explorer to locate your exported file so you can open it.

Note: You will need Adobe *Reader* installed on your computer. Download it free from www.adobe.com.

Managing Your Documents in WillMaker Files

n Quicken WillMaker Plus, a "WillMaker File" is where your documents and contacts are saved. This "one file" approach offers important advantages:
- You can easily share contact information (and changes in that information) among documents.
- It helps prevent confusion that might arise from keeping your documents in multiple places.

This part of the Users' Manual describes how to create and save WillMaker Files, password protect them and back them up.

Creating a WillMaker File

Quicken WillMaker Plus uses the name you enter in the introduction to create a WillMaker File for you.

We recommend that each person who uses Quicken WillMaker Plus create a separate WillMaker File, to avoid confusion about whose documents are in what file. (To find out how to share contact information among users, see Part 6.)

If you decide to create additional WillMaker Files, you can return to the "Enter Your Name" screen. To do this:

1. Go to the Enter Your Name screen by choosing **File > New WillMaker File**.

2. Type your name (or, if the file is for someone else, his or her name) in the text entry box.

3. Click **Next**.

4. When you next see the **Save File** dialog box (either now or later, depending on your saving preferences), check that the default file name and save location are what you want, then click **Save**. For more information about saving WillMaker Files, see "Saving Your WillMaker File," below.

Unless you specify otherwise, the program names the file "WillMaker File of *[name you entered]*.pfl" and saves it to your **My Documents** (Windows *XP*) or **Documents** (Windows *Vista* and *7*) folder. It also creates an identical backup file to use if a problem occurs with the original file. (To find out more about backup files, see "Opening a Backup WillMaker File," below.)

Opening a WillMaker File

Each time you start Quicken WillMaker Plus, the program opens the WillMaker File that was open the last time the program was used. You can't have more than one WillMaker File open at a time so, if you open another file, the program closes the one that was open.

How you open a WillMaker File depends on whether you've used it recently or not.

Opening a WillMaker File You've Used Recently

To open a WillMaker File you used recently:

1. Choose **File > Recent Files** to see a submenu of recently used WillMaker Files.

2. Click the name of the WillMaker File you want to use.

The program opens the WillMaker File you selected.

Opening a WillMaker File You Haven't Used Recently

To open a WillMaker File that hasn't been recently used:

1. Choose **File > Open WillMaker File** to bring up the standard **Open** dialog box used for opening files in Windows.

2. Locate the file you want to open. In most cases, it will be in your **My Documents** (Windows *XP*) or **Documents** (Windows *7* or *Vista*) folder. If you can't find it, use the Windows Search feature (**Start > Search**) to search for all files on your computer with a ".pfl" file extension.

3. Click **Open**.

If you open a file created with a pre-2012 version of the program for the first time, you'll see a message about file conversion (confirming that you converted an older file into the current format). Also, you will confirm or change your name.

> CAUTION
>
> **Some documents from older versions of the program can't be converted**. If you've opened a WillMaker File created with a pre-2012 version of Quicken WillMaker Plus, it's possible that some of your old documents won't appear in My Documents. This happens only if we've made such substantial revisions to a document that we can no longer support earlier versions—or if the document template in question is no longer available in the program. In addition, you may be required to review some document interviews completed in your pre-2012 version of Quicken WillMaker Plus before you can print them out in the 2012 edition.

Saving Your WillMaker File

If the **Automatically save changes** feature is turned on in the program preferences, the program automatically saves data to the currently open WillMaker File as you move from one interview screen to the next. If this feature is turned off, you'll need to save data manually.

To find out how to save data manually and how to change your program preferences, see "Saving Your Data" in Part 3.

Protecting Your WillMaker File With a Password

If your computer has multiple users, you may want to ensure the privacy of your Quicken WillMaker Plus documents by assigning your WillMaker File a password. Once you've done so, no one can unlock your WillMaker File without knowing the password.

This section of the manual describes how to lock and unlock a WillMaker File, as well as how to change a WillMaker File's password.

Locking a WillMaker File

To lock the currently open WillMaker File:

1. Choose **File > Lock WillMaker File** to open the **New Password** dialog box.

2. Enter the password (the program asks you to do this twice to double-check), along with a hint to help you remember. *Note that your password is case sensitive.*

3. Click **OK** for this dialog box and the subsequent one, which tells you your WillMaker File is locked.

The next time you open the WillMaker File, you'll see a **WillMaker File Locked** dialog box before it opens. You'll need to enter the password and click **OK** to open the file.

TIP

When you choose your password, make your hint as useful as possible. For example, instead of "name of favorite horse" for your hint, say "name of favorite horse (no caps or abbreviations)" to help you remember you spelled it "mistered" instead of, say, "MrEd." Once your WillMaker File is locked, you open it by entering the correct password first. While you can unlock a WillMaker File and change its password (see below), you can only do so when the WillMaker File is open.

Unlocking a WillMaker File

To unlock an open WillMaker File:

- Choose **File > Unlock WillMaker File**.

A dialog box will confirm that your WillMaker File is now unlocked.

Changing a WillMaker File's Password

To change the password assigned to an open WillMaker File:

1. Choose **File > Change WillMaker File Password** to open the **New Password** dialog box.

2. Enter a new password, along with a hint to help you remember it.

3. Click **OK** for this dialog box and the next, which confirms that your WillMaker File is locked.

Opening a Backup WillMaker File

Whenever Quicken WillMaker Plus creates a WillMaker File, it also creates an identical backup copy of it. Each time the program saves data to your WillMaker File, it also saves the same data to your backup WillMaker File. This backup can come in handy if a problem ever occurs with your original file.

Unless you specify otherwise, Quicken WillMaker Plus stores backup WillMaker Files in the **Nolo Documents Backup** subfolder of your **My Documents** (Windows *XP*) or **Documents** (Windows *Vista* and *7*) folder.

You will be unable to open a WillMaker File stored in the **Nolo Documents Backup** folder. This prevents accidentally overwriting your backup WillMaker Files. If you encounter a problem with a WillMaker File and need to open its backup, you will first copy the backup and paste it into another location.

To open a backup WillMaker File:

1. In Windows, locate the **Nolo Documents Backup** folder. If it isn't in your **My Documents** (Windows *XP*) or **Documents** (Windows *Vista* and *7*) folder, use the Windows search feature to find it.

2. Open the **Nolo Documents Backup.**

3. Locate the backup WillMaker File you want to open.

4. Copy the backup WillMaker File and paste it into a different folder or onto the desktop.

5. In Quicken WillMaker Plus, choose **File > Open WillMaker File.**

6. Locate and open the copied WillMaker File, as described in "Opening a WillMaker File You Haven't Used Recently," above.

Managing Your Contact Information

When you enter information about people and organizations in document interviews, Quicken WillMaker Plus adds it to My Contacts. This saves you from having to reenter it in other documents. My Contacts is stored in your WillMaker File with the documents you create.

While the program creates and maintains My Contacts in the background, you can also work directly with it. For example, changing a name in My Contacts changes that name in all the documents that contain it.

This part of the Users' Manual discusses how to:

- revise contact information you've already entered
- delete names from My Contacts, and
- import contacts from another WillMaker File.

Revising Contact Information

To revise a contact:

1. From My Contacts, select and click the contact from the list on the left side of the screen.

2. Type your changes.

3. Click the **Save** button.

Deleting Names From My Contacts

If a name is not used in any of your Quicken WillMaker Plus documents, you can delete it from My Contacts as follows:

1. From My Contacts, select the contact from the list on the left side of the screen.

2. Mouse over the name you want to delete.

3. Click the **X** to the right of the name.

4. Click **OK**.

TIP

You can't delete a name that's in use. If you try to delete a name that is used in one of your documents, a dialog box will pop up that tells you that you can't delete it from My Contacts. You can revise the documents to remove the name. Then, when the name is no longer in use, you'll be able to delete it. (For information about revising documents, see "Revising Your Document" in Part 4.)

Importing Contacts From Other Contact Lists

You can share contact information between WillMaker Files by importing the data.

To import contact information:

1. Click **File** > **Import Contacts**.

2. Select the WillMaker File from which you want to import contact information. (If you're having trouble finding it, use the Windows Search feature (**Start** > **Search**) to search for all files on your computer with a ".pfl" file extension.)

3. Click **Open**.

4. A dialog box will pop up to confirm how many names you've imported.

5. Click **OK**.

When you import names, only those names not already in your WillMaker File are added.

Troubleshooting

Any time you have a question about using Quicken WillMaker Plus, help is close at hand. The key to answering your question is knowing which help resource to consult. The table below shows which help resource to use for the type of help you need.

What You Need	Help Resource to Consult
Help understanding how to complete the current interview question or screen	Helpful Information (right-hand side of screen)
In-depth legal information to help you decide how to answer an interview question	The Legal Manual
Definitions of legal terms	The Glossary or Nolo's online glossary
Help locating a lawyer	Nolo's online Lawyer Directory
Practical advice about how to use the program	The Users' Manual
Help fixing a problem you're having with the program	The Users' Manual or FAQ
Additional assistance for a problem you haven't been able to solve using the other help resources	Nolo Technical Support

Dealing With Problems

If you encounter a technical difficulty while running the program, this manual is your first resource to consult. Which section you read depends on the type of problem you're experiencing:

- If you're having trouble installing Quicken WillMaker Plus because the setup program doesn't launch, see "Jump-Starting the Setup Program," below.

- If you're having trouble printing from the program, see "Correcting Printing Problems," below.
- If you're having trouble with the program's Web Update feature (discussed in "Updating Your Version of the Program," in Part 2), see "Handling Web Update Problems," below.
- If you're encountering an error message, consult the table in Appendix C. This table explains the meaning of each error message and describes what to do if you encounter it.

If none of the above situations apply and you can't find a section of this manual that helps with your problem, look in the **FAQ** file in your **Quicken WillMaker Plus 2012** program folder; you may find advice relevant to your problem.

If none of the above suggestions help, contact Nolo Technical Support. (See "Contacting Nolo Technical Support and Customer Service," below.)

Jump-Starting the Setup Program

When you insert the Quicken WillMaker Plus Installation CD into your CD-ROM drive, setup should launch automatically. If it doesn't, here's what to do:

1. Choose **Start > Run...** (Windows *XP*) or **Start > All Programs > Accessories > Run...** (Windows *Vista* and *7*).

2. Type **D:\AUTORUN** (you may have to substitute the letter of your CD-ROM drive for "D").

3. Click **OK**.

Correcting Printing Problems

If you're having a printing problem in Quicken WillMaker Plus, try the following remedies:

- If you are having trouble getting your document to print, go to the **Print Setup** dialog box (**File > Print Setup**) and make sure the settings for your printer are correct; then, click **OK** and try to print again.

- If you are not satisfied with the formatting of a printed document, go to the **Print Options** dialog box (**File > Print Options**) to make adjustments. For example, if you're getting a page with very little text and lots of hash marks ("/////"), try making the bottom margin larger (changing it from 0.45 inch to 0.6 inch will usually correct the problem). (For information about why hash marks are legally necessary, see "Reviewing Your Document in Print Preview" in Part 4.)

If neither of the above suggestions helps, you can export your document as a PDF and print it using Adobe *Reader*. You can download Adobe *Reader* for free from www.adobe.com. Please contact Nolo Technical Support to report the problem, so we can investigate and fix it, if necessary. (See "Contacting Nolo Technical Support and Customer Service," below.)

Handling Web Update Problems

If you encounter a problem with the program's Web Update feature (see "Updating Your Version of the Program" in Part 2), check the table below. If any of the situations listed there apply to you, try the suggested remedy for your problem.

> **CAUTION**
>
> **Web Update isn't designed to work with proxy servers and other corporate VPN configurations**. If you are trying to update the program behind a corporate proxy server and getting various error messages, you won't be able to use Web Update. Web Update is designed for the home user with a basic firewall. Unfortunately, we can't support proxy servers and other corporate VPN (virtual private network) security configurations.

If you are:	Try this remedy for your problem:
A Windows *XP* user getting an error message because you don't have the administrator privileges required for installing program files …	Switch to a user with administrator privileges or have your system's security settings changed. If necessary, contact your network administrator or read Windows documentation on changing security settings.
A Windows *Vista* user encountering a "User Access Control" dialog box when the update finishes …	Click **Continue** in the dialog box or enter an administrator password as prompted.
Using a firewall or security application (see below for the case of Windows *XP* Service Pack 2) and receiving warnings …	Add "f1.nolo.com" to the "trusted site" list. If you still can't complete the update after making this addition, you may need to turn off your firewall program while retrieving the update, then turn it back on.
A Windows *XP* Service Pack 2 user getting a Windows Security Alert asking whether you want to keep blocking or to unblock your Quicken WillMaker Plus's Internet connection …	Select **Unblock**. Once you have unblocked Quicken WillMaker Plus, you should be able to download future Web Updates.

If none of the above suggestions help, and you can't find relevant advice in the **FAQ** file, contact Nolo Technical Support (see below).

When contacting Nolo Technical Support about a Web Update problem, include the following details in addition to those normally required for other types of problems:

- the type of Internet connection you have (modem dial-up, DSL, or other), and
- the name of your Internet service provider.

Contacting Nolo Technical Support and Customer Service

If you're encountering a problem that isn't addressed in this section of the manual, you may find an answer in the Quicken WillMaker Plus FAQs, which contain answers to common user questions and problems.

To find the FAQ page for this program, go to **Start > Programs** (*XP*)/ **All Programs** (*7* and *Vista*) **> Quicken Willmaker Plus 2012 > FAQ** or Nolo's Technical Support page at: www.nolo.com/technical-support/quicken-willmaker-2012.html.

If you can't find a solution on the FAQ page, contact Nolo Technical Support directly.

Email address: support@nolo.com
Phone number: 510-549-4660
Phone hours: 9:00 a.m. to 5:00 p.m. Pacific time, Monday through Friday

When you call, it's helpful to be in front of the computer with which you are having the problem. Also, whether you are emailing or calling, be sure to have the information noted below on hand.

Information to Have on Hand

When you contact Nolo Technical Support about a problem, please include the following information in your email (or have it ready before you call):

- the version of Quicken WillMaker Plus you're running (which should be 11.0 or higher), located at **Help > About Quicken WillMaker Plus 2012**
- the point in the program where the problem occurred
- whether you can duplicate the problem
- the brand and model of computer you are using
- the brand and model of printer (if you are having trouble printing)

- the name of your Internet service provider and the type of Internet connection you have (if you are having a problem that involves connecting to the Internet)
- which version of which operating system your computer is running (for example, *XP* Home Service Pack 2), and
- the amount of RAM on your computer.

If you're not sure which model of computer you have, how much RAM it has or which version of the operating system it's running, see below.

Finding Information About Your Computer System

How you find information about your computer system depends on which operating system it's running.

Windows *Vista* and *7*:

- Choose **Start > Computer > System Properties**.

Windows *XP*:

1. Right click the **My Computer** icon on your desktop.

2. Select **Properties**.

3. Choose the tab that contains the information you need.

Menu Options

This section lists the commands available in each of the program's menus and describes what they do. To access any menu option:

1. Click the menu in the Quicken WillMaker Plus menu bar.

2. Select the command.

If you prefer not using your mouse, just type the first letter in the menu name while pressing the ALT key, then type the letter underlined in the option name.

File Menu

New WillMaker File

Use this command to create a new Quicken WillMaker Plus WillMaker File.

Open WillMaker File...

Use this command to open WillMaker Files made with Quicken WillMaker Plus 2012.

Save

Use this command to manually save your currently open WillMaker File. You do not need to use this command if **Automatically save changes** is on.

Save As...

Use this command to rename your WillMaker File and/or save it to another location on your computer.

Import Contacts...

Use this command to retrieve contact information from another WillMaker file.

Lock/Unlock WillMaker File

Use this command to lock your WillMaker File and give it a password. If your WillMaker File is locked, no one can open it without first entering the password. If you want to unlock a WillMaker File you've locked, you'll first need to enter the password you assigned to it.

Change WillMaker File Password

Use this command to change your password. This command is available only if you have previously locked your WillMaker File.

Print Options...

Use this command to change the formatting for your documents, including page margins, line spacing, font type and font size. We recommend keeping the default settings.

Print Setup...

Use this command to open the standard **Print Setup** dialog box for the currently chosen printer.

Print...

Use this command to print the current document.

Export Document...

Use this command to save your displayed document as a text file that you can view, edit or print with a word processor.

Export Document as PDF...

Use this command to save your displayed document as a PDF that you can view with Adobe *Reader*.

Recent Files

Use this command to open a recently used WillMaker File (.pfl). This submenu lists up to five files.

Exit

Use this command to quit the Quicken WillMaker Plus program.

Edit Menu

Undo

Use this command to undo the last typing or editing action you performed, provided you haven't left the screen on which the changes were made.

Cut

Use this command to remove selected text and add it to the Clipboard.

Copy

Use this command to copy selected text to the Clipboard, without removing it.

Paste

Use this command to insert text that you have previously cut or copied at the blinking cursor, or to replace selected text with text that you have previously cut or copied.

Delete

Use this command to delete selected text without adding it to the Clipboard. The selected text will not be saved.

Select All

Use this command to select all the text in the currently active text field.

Check Spelling

Use this command to check the spelling of text you typed in answering an interview question. Make sure your cursor is inside the text box where you typed your answer before choosing **Edit > Check Spelling**.

Preferences...

Use this command to customize your version of Quicken WillMaker Plus. You can use the **Preferences** command to specify the following:

- whether your data will be saved automatically or manually
- whether you want the program to fill in names automatically as you type them, based on entries in My Contacts
- whether you want the program to fill in related fields automatically after you enter a name
- whether you want the program to check for Web Updates automatically when you start it up
- whether you want your entries automatically checked for spelling
- the font size of the Helpful Information text, and
- the folder where your backup WillMaker Files are stored.

Navigate Menu

Back
Use this command to go back to the previous screen.

Next
Use this command to move ahead to the next screen.

My Documents
Use this command to go to the screen that lists the five Essential Documents and the documents you have worked on.

My Contacts
Use this command to go to the My Contacts screen.

All Documents
Use this command to go to the screen that lists all the documents you can create with Quicken WillMaker Plus.

Online Menu

Web Update
Use this command to update your copy of Quicken WillMaker Plus by downloading the latest updated files from the Web. Before you use this command, you must have a live Internet connection.

Online Registration
Use this command to register your copy of Quicken WillMaker Plus. You'll need a Web browser and an Internet connection to use this command.

Nolo on the Web
Use this command to access Nolo's website at www.nolo.com. You'll need a Web browser and an Internet connection to use this command.

Find a Lawyer
Use this command to access Nolo's online Lawyer Directory.

Help Menu

Quicken WillMaker Users' Manual
Use this command to display an electronic version of this manual.

Quicken WillMaker Legal Manual
Use this command to display an electronic version of the Legal Manual.

Quicken WillMaker Glossary
Use this command to display the Glossary.

Quicken WillMaker Tutorial
Use this command to display the tutorial video.

FAQ and Support
Use this command if you need help with the program.

Keyboard Shortcuts

Use this command to see how to operate the program using a keyboard rather than a mouse.

About Quicken WillMaker Plus 2012

Use this command to see information about which version of the program you're running, plus detailed information about all the program files you've installed.

Keyboard Shortcuts

T his section lists keyboard shortcuts for performing the following types of actions:

- choosing options and exiting the program
- opening and saving WillMaker Files
- navigating within and among screens, and
- navigating in a text entry box.

To see this information when you're running the program, choose **Help > Keyboard Shortcuts**.

Choosing Options and Exiting the Program

Press ...	To ...
ENTER	Trigger the default button (as indicated by a thicker outline) or the selected button (if there is no default)—unless you are in a text entry box that allows multiple entries, in which case pressing ENTER will start a new line of text.
ESC	Trigger the **Cancel, Close** or **No** button in a pop-up dialog box.
ALT+F4	Exit the program.

Opening and Saving WillMaker Files

Press ...	To ...
CTRL+O	Open an existing WillMaker File.
CTRL+S	Save the current WillMaker File when the **Automatically save changes** function is turned off.

Navigating in a Text Entry Box

Press ...	To ...
ENTER	Start a new line, if the box allows entry of multiple items.
LEFT ARROW	Move one character to left.
RIGHT ARROW	Move one character to right.
UP ARROW	Move one line up.
DOWN ARROW	Move one line down.
HOME	Move to the beginning of the line.
END	Move to the end of the line.
CTRL+HOME	Move to the beginning of the text entry box.
CTRL+END	Move to the end of the entered text.
CTRL+LEFT ARROW	Move one word to left.
CTRL+RIGHT ARROW	Move one word to right.
CTRL+Z	Undo the most recent text editing action you have taken on the current screen, if the change has not yet been saved.
CTRL+X	Cut the selected text to the Clipboard.
CTRL+C	Copy the selected text to the Clipboard.
CTRL+V	Paste the contents of the Clipboard.
DELETE	Delete the selected text.
CTRL+A	Select all text in the current text entry box.
CTRL+SHIFT+S	Check spelling of text in current text entry box.

Navigating Within and Among Screens

Press ...	To ...
TAB	Move to the next part of the screen (such as a text box, list, button or group of option buttons).
SHIFT+TAB	Move to the previous part of the screen (such as a text box, list, button or group of option buttons).
DOWN ARROW	Highlight the next option button (in a group when one option button is selected) or the next item (in a selected list).
UP ARROW	Highlight the previous option button (in a group when one option button is selected) or the previous item (in a selected list).
ALT+RIGHT ARROW	Go to the next interview screen.
ALT+LEFT ARROW	Go back to the previous interview screen.

Error Messages

The table below describes what each error message means and what you should do if you encounter it. If the table entry for your error message suggests that you contact Nolo Technical Support, see "Contacting Nolo Technical Support and Customer Service" in Part 7 for contact information.

Error	What It Means	What You Should Do
[CD-ROM drive] is not accessible. The device is not ready if in the real Error Message	The CD you inserted is not being read.	Reinsert the CD. Wait ten seconds and double-click the CD-ROM drive icon. If that doesn't solve the problem, contact Nolo Technical Support.
[Name you're trying to edit information about]'s [name or gender] can't be changed.	Editing this information could affect the legality of another document you've made.	Think about whether this change really needs to be made. If so, check other documents to see whether they require the same revision. If they do, you can make the revisions by creating new versions of the documents in question. Please read the appropriate sections of the Legal Manual before you start creating new document versions in this manner.
A check on your interview answers revealed that some of your data is out of date or missing. Please review your answers by clicking "Change Answers" and reviewing the entire interview.	The program has determined that some of your data is out of date or missing.	Review all interview screens and make the necessary entries and revisions. If this problem continues, contact Nolo Technical Support.

Error	What It Means	What You Should Do
An error exists in this Help file. Contact your application vendor for an updated Help file.	There's a problem opening the topic you selected in the program's Help system.	First, close the windows for any open Help files (including those from other programs), keeping Quicken WillMaker Plus open. Then, repeat what you did that caused the error message. If the problem persists, contact Nolo Technical Support.
An error occurred: couldn't find the requested path name.	Quicken WillMaker Plus couldn't find the path for a file it is trying to open.	Contact Nolo Technical Support.
An error occurred while assembling the document.	The resource files of the program might be damaged.	Reinstall the program and try again. If that doesn't work, contact Nolo Technical Support.
Internal error: attempt to overwrite existing file.	Quicken WillMaker Plus is attempting to overwrite an existing file without permission.	Try to remember the steps you performed before the error appeared, then contact Nolo Technical Support.
Please select a part or option.	You clicked **Next** (or pressed ENTER) before you made a checklist selection.	Make a selection before clicking **Next** (or pressing ENTER).
Quicken WillMaker Plus cannot open that file (because it is read-only).	Quicken WillMaker Plus was not allowed to open a file, either because it is in use or because it is read-only.	Make sure the file is located on your computer's hard drive in the **My Documents** folder, and check that neither the file nor the disk is locked.

Error	What It Means	What You Should Do
Quicken WillMaker Plus was not shut down properly the last time it was run. Please run Web Update to make sure your copy of the program is up to date. If this problem continues, contact Nolo Technical Support.	Either (1) a bug in Quicken WillMaker Plus caused the program to crash the last time you used it, or (2) you turned off your computer while Quicken WillMaker Plus was still running.	Run Web Update. If the problem was Quicken WillMaker Plus, an update to fix the problem may be available. Also, make sure that you exit Quicken WillMaker Plus before shutting down your computer. If this problem continues, contact Nolo Technical Support.
Sorry, a needed resource cannot be found.	The resource files of the program might be damaged.	Reinstall the program and try again. If that doesn't work, contact Nolo Technical Support.
Sorry, an internal data-module error occurred.	Something serious is wrong with the program's internal data structures.	Contact Nolo Technical Support.
Sorry, an internal error occurred.	Something serious is wrong with the program because of a disk error, a memory error or a bug.	Quit, restart the program and attempt to repeat what you did. The problem may clear up on its own. If not, try reinstalling Quicken WillMaker Plus. If that doesn't work, contact Nolo Technical Support.
Sorry, but this version of Quicken WillMaker Plus requires *Internet Explorer* version 6.0 or greater. Please install *Internet Explorer* 6.0 or later on your machine. Quicken WillMaker Plus will now exit.	Your system does not meet the minimum requirements to run Quicken WillMaker Plus.	If you don't run *Internet Explorer*, install it. If you run an old version, upgrade. You can download *Internet Explorer* free from Microsoft. com's Download Center.
Sorry, Quicken WillMaker Plus can open only one WillMaker File at a time.	You attempted to open more than one WillMaker File.	Open only one WillMaker File at a time.

Error	What It Means	What You Should Do
Sorry, this file cannot be read by Quicken WillMaker Plus.	You are trying to open a file that Quicken WillMaker Plus doesn't recognize.	If you are sure the file you are attempting to use is a WillMaker File (that is, it has the extension ".pfl"), try a backup copy (see "Opening a Backup WillMaker File" in Part 5). If that doesn't work, contact Nolo Technical Support.
Sorry, this file has been corrupted and cannot be read.	Your WillMaker File has been seriously corrupted and cannot be read.	Use the backup WillMaker File with the same name.
Your document is not yet complete. Please complete the interview before printing your document.	The program has determined that it does not have all the information it needs to print your document.	Review all interview screens and enter any missing information. If you still can't print, contact Nolo Technical Support.

Index

A

AB living trusts, 210–211
  See also Revocable living trusts
Adoption decisions, power of attorney and, 226
Advance health care directive. *See* Health care directives
Affidavit of Domicile (Residence), 9–10
Age
  child's age limit in UTMA states, 131
  for making a will, 18
Agent. *See* Health care agent
Aging with Dignity, 298
"Aka" (name), in will, 56
Alabama
  health care agent, restrictions on, 312
  health care directive
    name for, 295
    pregnancy and, 353
    witnessing and notarization, 362
  out-of-state executors, 149
Alaska
  health care agent, restrictions on, 312
  health care directive
    name for, 295
    pregnancy and, 353
    witnessing and notarization, 362
  joint tenancy restrictions, 205
Alternate attorney-in-fact
  choosing, 239–240
  defined, 218
  delegation of powers to, 260–261
  different powers for, 263
  See also Attorney-in-fact

Alternate beneficiaries
  failure to name, 103, 107, 111, 115
  for married couples with children, 99–103
  for married couples without children, 105–107
  naming overview, 28–29
  for residuary beneficiaries, 124–125
  for single people with children, 109–111
  for single people without children, 112–115
  specific property bequests, 121–122
  See also Beneficiaries
Alternate executors, 153
Annuity policy proceeds, 81
Annuity transactions, attorney-in-fact powers, 246–247
Antibiotics, health care directive, 335
Arizona
  health care agent, restrictions on, 312
  health care directive
    name for, 295
    pregnancy and, 353
    witnessing and notarization, 362–363
  witness rules for POA, 269
Arkansas
  health care agent, restrictions on, 312
  health care directive
    name for, 295
    pregnancy and, 353
    witnessing and notarization, 363
  out-of-state executors, 149
Artificial respiration, 322, 335
Attorney-in-fact
  alternates for, 239–240
  choosing, 233–240

NOLO *Keep Up to Date*

1 Go to Nolo.com/newsletters to sign up for free newsletters and discounts on Nolo products.

- **Nolo's Special Offer.** A monthly newsletter with the biggest Nolo discounts around.

- **Landlord's Quarterly.** Deals and free tips for landlords and property managers.

2 Don't forget to check for updates. Find this book at **Nolo.com** and click "Legal Updates."

Let Us Hear From You

3 Register your Nolo product and give us your feedback at Nolo.com/book-registration.

- Once you've registered, you qualify for technical support if you have any trouble with a download or CD (though most folks don't).

- We'll send you a coupon for 15% off your next Nolo.com order!

QWMB12

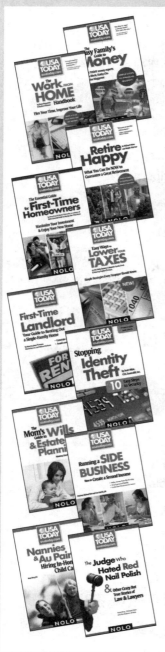

⚖ NOLO *Online Legal Forms*

Nolo offers a large library of legal solutions and forms, created by Nolo's in-house legal staff. These reliable documents can be prepared in minutes.

Create a Document

- **Incorporation.** Incorporate your business in any state.
- **LLC Formations.** Gain asset protection and pass-through tax status in any state.
- **Wills.** Nolo has helped people make over 2 million wills. Is it time to make or revise yours?
- **Living Trust (avoid probate).** Plan now to save your family the cost, delays, and hassle of probate.
- **Trademark.** Protect the name of your business or product.
- **Provisional Patent.** Preserve your rights under patent law and claim "patent pending" status.

Download a Legal Form

Nolo.com has hundreds of top quality legal forms available for download—bills of sale, promissory notes, nondisclosure agreements, LLC operating agreements, corporate minutes, commercial lease and sublease, motor vehicle bill of sale, consignment agreements and many more.

Review Your Documents

Many lawyers in Nolo's consumer-friendly lawyer directory will review Nolo documents for a very reasonable fee. Check their detailed profiles at **Nolo.com/lawyers**.

⚖ NOLO *Lawyer Directory*

Find an Estate Planning Attorney

- *Qualified lawyers*
- *In-depth profiles*
- *A pledge of respectful service*

When you want help with estate planning, you don't want just any lawyer—you want an expert in the field, who can give you and your family up-to-the-minute advice. You need a lawyer who has the experience and knowledge to answer your questions about living trusts, wills, powers of attorney, estate taxes, probate, executors, life insurance and more.

Nolo's Lawyer Directory is unique because it provides an extensive profile of every lawyer. You'll learn about not only each lawyer's education, professional history, legal specialties, credentials and fees, but also about their philosophy of practicing law and how they like to work with clients.

All lawyers listed in Nolo's directory are in good standing with their state bar association. Many will review Nolo documents, such as a will or living trust, for a fixed fee. They all pledge to work diligently and respectfully with clients—communicating regularly, providing a written agreement about how legal matters will be handled, sending clear and detailed bills and more.

www.nolo.com

The photos above are illustrative only. Any resemblance to an actual attorney is purely coincidental.